GW01458827

Publisher: Military History Group, London, United Kingdom.

E-Mail: militaryhistoryvisualized@gmail.com

Print: Lulu Press, Inc., Lulu Press, Inc. 627 Davis Drive Suite 300 Morrisville, NC 27560, USA. Massachusetts, US; Wisconsin, US; Ontario, Canada; Île-de-France, France; Wielkopolska, Poland; Cambridgeshire, United Kingdom; Victoria, Australia.

Cover image BArch, RH 11-I/14: Entwurf zur Heeresdienstvorschrift 240/2, Bild 46, modified by Bernhard Kast.

ISBN 978-1-915453-03-7

Table of Contents

Introduction - Read First

In order to publish an authentic representation of the included German documents, this translation remains as close to the original text as possible. This presents certain challenges, because composite words and phrases in "military German" from the 1940s often cannot be translated word-for-word into English. The translation of historical documents is not an exact discipline, as such we cannot rule out misleading or unclear phrases in this translation. Therefore, it is possible that the English translation leaves some room for interpretation that is not given in the original document. To clarify certain passages for the reader, we provided footnotes when needed. Following is a short overview of important aspects that need to be considered when reading and using the original and translated texts.

In this translation, the original document format was recreated as close as possible. Due to this, some empty space or even empty pages can occasionally be found. Additionally, word splits with hyphens were only kept in those cases where a page break happens so that formatting errors could be avoided. For improved formatting we added some word splits of our own a few times, yet these changes are mostly limited to tables. The only exception to this rule is found in the Glossary, where quotes usually do not conform to their original formatting. Except for *H.Dv.*[1] *130/2a*, the original writing was in "Latin text" and not in Fraktur. Germany switched from Fraktur to a regular Latin alphabet in 1940/41 and even outright banning Fraktur. Naturally, this process took some time to be completed. Words that use a hyphen in German, like "Grenadier-Kompanie" were written with a hyphen in English: "Grenadier-Company". Yet, for translations of composite words like "Sturmzug" meaning "Assault Platoon" we do not use any hyphens. Titles of books are written in *italics*. In both the German and English version, we added various footnotes to clarify certain aspects or terminology. The English version contains more notes to explain the different meanings of certain German words and phrases.

This book is best read from cover to cover but you should also be able to just pick one document at a time. As such, our doctrine is that it is better to have one footnote too much then having one missing. As such, similar footnotes

---

[1] "H.Dv." is short for "Heeresdruckvorschrift" for this period. The literal translation of a Heeresdruckvorschrift would be "Army Print Regulation". Be aware that after the Second World War the term "Heeresdienstvorschrift" literally "Army Service Regulation" was introduced. It is important to point out that Wehrmacht and Bundeswehr terminology sometimes differ.

repeatedly appear throughout the book and not just the first time a specific term or phrase is mentioned.

The page numbering system follows the content layout of the German text. Every English page retains the page number as the corresponding German page albeit with a different letter, so page 5 is DE-5 for German and EN-5 English. These are at the bottom of the page. For the documents that we translated in their entirety, a "second" page number can sometimes be found at the top or bottom of the page if these where printed in the original document. Be aware that, like in the original, these numbers usually only start after several pages. Additionally, for documents were only an excerpt is provided we did not add the original page number, yet they are indicated in the preliminary notes. The numbering of figures remains as in the original. For the captions of supplementary images in the Glossary we use "Abbildung" and "Illustration" instead of "Bild" and "Figure" as in the documents. This was done to make a clear distinction between the document and glossary images. In our German text, referrals to paragraph numbers are declared as "Nummern" not "Ziffern". However, based on *H.Dv. 30: Schrift- und Geschäftsverkehr*[2] *der Wehrmacht (Correspondence and Office Management of the Wehrmacht)* it should be "Ziffern". In the *H.Dv. 130/2a* this was not followed, whereas in the *H.Dv. 240/2* it was. In both cases we translated it to "Numbers". Spelling, grammar, and other mistakes in the original are marked with [sic!]. In a few cases we also use these brackets to add context, words, symbols, or complete abbreviations.

In the original documents various abbreviations and shortcuts were used for weapons and other terminology, e.g., "MP" for "Maschinenpistole" or "H.Dv."[3] for "Heeresdruckvorschrift". These were written inconsistently with or without dots, so "MP" versus "M.P.", or with or without spaces, so "H. Dv." and "H.Dv.". Generally, in the translation and our own texts we went with the "dotless" and "spaceless" version like "MP", "MG", "H.Dv." etc. The word "Sturmgewehr 44" has not been translated to "Assault Rifle 44" but was left in original German. Likewise, other technical designations like "Kurzpatrone" were not translated in the text, but a footnote with a translation and description was added.

---

[2] The term "Geschäftsverkehr" has a different meaning nowadays, today it is about private business and trading, yet looking at the *H.Dv. 30* it becomes apparent that this is about "Aktenverwaltung" (file management) and similar aspects.

[3] "H.Dv." is short for "Heeresdruckvorschrift" for this period. The literal translation of a Heeresdruckvorschrift would be "Army Print Regulation". Be aware that after the Second World War the term "Heeresdienstvorschrift" literally "Army Service Regulation" was introduced. It is important to point out that Wehrmacht and Bundeswehr terminology sometimes differ.

In the German text, a soldier is often referred to as "Schütze", which we translated as "rifleman". In cases where the German text then refers to "MP-Schütze", the translation reads "SMG-rifleman". This seems contradictory at first glance, yet we chose this for two reasons: First, for consistency of the translation of "Schütze" and second, technically the MP 43/1 is an assault rifle by modern understanding. For further information on the naming of the Sturmgewehr 44 see Supplement 9.

Finally, we must address the figures included in this book. It was our aim to recreate these visuals as close to the original as possible. Certain inaccuracies in the thickness of the lines and various other dimensions of the symbols might of course occur. Another issue is that some visuals contained what we consider aesthetic errors. Since some of them appear to be inconsistent and could be assumed to be reproduction errors, we think we should shortly address them here. As you can see in Illustration I, there is one large arrow pointing downwards (South), splitting up into three arrows of which two are shown in full. When crossing a trench, the arrow on the right covers the "trench lines" while this is not the case with the arrow to the left. Such aesthetic errors are to be found in the original figures. Nevertheless, any inconsistencies in our figures in comparison to the originals are of course our fault.

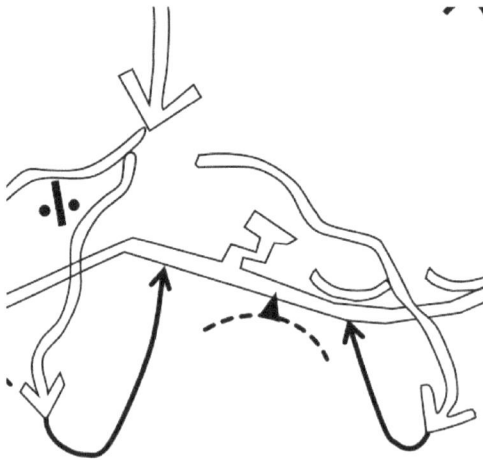

Illustration I: Visual Errors

The Assault Platoon

of the

Grenadier-Company[2]

from 15. Nov. 1944

---

[2] This and the following pages up to Supplement 1 are the transcription of the document: BArch, RH 11-I/84: *Merkblatt 25a/15: Der Sturmzug der Grenadier-Kompanie, 15.11.1944.*

Oberkommando des Heeres
Generalstab des Heeres
<u>Gen. d. Inf. b. Chef Gen.St. d. H.[4]</u>
Ia/II – Nr. 3322/44

H.Qu. O.K.H.[3],
den 15. Nov. 1944.

Mit Einverständnis des Chefs des Generalstabes des Heeres genehmige ich das Merkblatt 25a/16 „Der Sturmzug der Grenadier-Kompanie".

Mit Ausgabe dieses Merkblattes treten außer Kraft:

a) Das vorläufige Merkblatt Nr. 25a/16

„Der M.P.[5]-Zug der Grenadier-Kompanie"

vom 1. 2. 1944.

b) Entgegenstehende Bestimmungen der H.Dv. 130/2a.[6]

Jaschke[7]

General der Infanterie

---

[3] Hauptquartier, Oberkommando des Heeres.

[4] General der Infanterie beim Chef Generalstab des Heeres. Siehe Glossar: General der Infanterie.

[5] M.P. bedeutet Maschinenpistole. Technisch gesehen handelte es sich aber nicht um eine Maschinenpistole, allerdings wurde die Bezeichnung Maschinenkarabiner aufgehoben und die Bezeichnung Sturmgewehr kam erst Ende 1944 auf. Bezüglich der Namensgebung und generellen Entwicklung siehe Ergänzung 9.

[6] Die Heeresdruckvorschrift Serie 130 war die zentrale Vorschriftenreihe zur Infanterie, Heft 2a hatte den Titel *Die Schützenkompanie*.

[7] Erich Jaschke, ab 1. Mai 1943 Rang General der Infanterie, ab 16. Oktober 1943 Dienststellung General der Infanterie beim Oberbefehlshaber des Heeres. Siehe Glossar: General der Infanterie. Literatur: Keilig, Wolf: *Das Deutsche Heer 1939–1945. Gliederung – Einsatz – Stellenbesetzung.* Verlag Hans-Henning Podzun: Bad Nauheim, 1956ff, 211 - 152-.

Army High Command
General Staff of the Army
Gen. d. Inf. b. Chef Gen.St. d. H.[9]
Ia/II – No. 3322/44

H.Qu. O.K.H.[8],
the 15. Nov. 1944.

With the consent of the Chief of the General Staff of the Army, I approve pamphlet 25a/16 "The Assault Platoon of the Grenadier-Company".

With the issue of this pamphlet become invalid:

a) The preliminary Pamphlet Nr. 25a/16

"The SMG[10]-Platoon of the Grenadier-Company"

from 1. 2. 1944.[11]

b) Contradicting terms of the H.Dv. 130/2a.[12]

Jaschke[13]

General of the Infantry

---

[8] Headquarters, Army High Command.

[9] General of the Infantry at the Chief of the General Staff of the Army. See Glossary: General of the Infantry (General der Infanterie).

[10] SMG means submachine gun. Technically, this was not a submachine gun, but the designation machine carbine was abolished, and the designation assault rifle was only introduced at the end of 1944. Regarding the naming and general development see Supplement 9.

[11] Date format is Day. Month. Year.

[12] The Army Regulation Serie 130 was the key regulation-series for the infantry, issue 2a had the title „The Riflemen Company".

[13] Erich Jaschke, since 1st May 1943 rank General of the Infantry, since 16th October 1943 in the administrative position General of the Infantry at the Commander-in-Chief of the Army. See Glossary: General of the Infantry (General der Infanterie). Source: Keilig, Wolf: Das Deutsche Heer 1939–1945. Gliederung – Einsatz – Stellenbesetzung. Verlag Hans-Henning Podzun: Bad Nauheim, 1956ff, 211 -152-.

Inhaltsverzeichnis

---

[14] Ein Gegenstoß ist ein Angriff, der sofort nach Eindringen des Feindes in die eigene Stellungen durchgeführt wird, hierbei werden örtliche Reserven genutzt. Im Gegensatz zum Gegenangriff der planmäßig erfolgt und auch weiter zurückliegende Reserven nutzt. Siehe Glossar: Gegenangriff, Gegenstoß.

Table of Contents

---

[15] "Kampfweise" can also be translated with combat / battle / fighting style.

[16] This should be "Hasty Counterattack", since the Germans distinguished between a hasty counterattack ("Gegenstoß") and regular counterattack ("Gegenangriff"). We used the short version here for formatting reasons. See Glossary: Hasty Counterattack (Gegenstoß).

[17] There are various possible ways to translate "Hemmung" (singular) we looked at several, we chose stoppage since it seems the most fitting. Additionally, the *TM 30-506: German Military Dictionary* also used it.

[Leere Seite wie im Original Merkblatt.]

[Intentionally left blank like in the original pamphlet.]

I. Allgemeines.

1. Angriff und Abwehr erfordern auf Grund der Kriegserfahrungen eine neue Gliederung und Bewaffnung der Grenadier[18]-Kompanien.

Die Einteilung der Grenadier-Kompanie in Sturmzüge ermöglicht eine einheitliche und wendige Führung.

2. Der **Sturmzug** mit seinen beiden Sturmgruppen und einer Feuergruppe erhält durch die neue Gliederung und Bewaffnung eine **klar bestimmte Aufgabe.**

3. Die einheitliche Waffenausstattung der Gruppen **vereinfacht die Gruppenführung,** so daß auch noch nicht voll ausgebildete und junge, unerfahrene Gruppenführer die Gruppen im Gefecht leichter führen können. Die Bewaffnung der Sturmgruppen mit dem Sturmgewehr 44 steigert die Feuerkraft und erhöht die Beweglichkeit der Gruppen.

4. Das Herausziehen der Granatschützen[19] und Scharfschützen aus den Gruppen entlastet diese von Spezialisten. Es ermöglicht einen schwerpunktmäßigen Einsatz der Granatschützen im Zuge und der Scharfschützen in der Kompanie.

II. Die Gliederung des Sturmzuges.

5. Der Sturmzug[20] besteht aus:
     dem Zugführer,
     dem Zugtrupp mit dem Granattrupp[21],
     zwei „Sturmgruppen" (je 1-7),[22]
     einer „Feuergruppe" (1-7),

---

[18] Siehe Glossar: Grenadier.
[19] Siehe Glossar: Granatschütze.
[20] Siehe Glossar: Zug / Schützenzug bezüglich des normalen Schützenzuges im Verlauf des Krieges.
[21] Siehe Glossar: Granattrupp.
[22] Siehe Glossar: Gruppe bezüglich der Änderungen der Gruppegröße im Verlauf des Krieges.

I. General Information.

1. Due to experiences gained in the field, attack and defense require new organization and weaponry of the grenadier[23]-companies.

The subdivision of the grenadier-company into assault platoons enables a unified and agile command.

2. The **assault platoon** with its two assault squads and one fire squad is given a **clearly defined task** by the new organization and weaponry.

3. The uniform armament of the squads **simplifies the command of the squad**, so that not yet fully trained and young, inexperienced squad leaders can more readily lead the squads in combat. Arming the assault squads with the Sturmgewehr 44 improves the firepower and increases the mobility of the squads.

4. The removal of the rifle-grenade riflemen[24] and snipers from the squads relieves them of the burden of specialists. It enables a focused employment[25] of the rifle-grenade equipped riflemen in the platoon and the snipers in the company.

II. The Organization of the Assault Squad.

5. The Assault Platoon[26] consists of:
        the platoon leader,
        the platoon headquarters with the rifle-grenade section[27],
        two "assault squads" (je 1-7),[28]
        one "fire squad" (1-7),

---

[23] See Glossary: Grenadier (Grenadier).

[24] Usually "Granatschütze" would be translated with "Grenadier", the problem is that most German riflemen at that point were called "Grenadiere" (Grenadiers) as such the term is simply too ambiguous. See Glossary: Rifle-Grenade Rifleman (Granatschütze).

[25] About "Schwerpunkt" see the Glossary: Weight of Effort (Schwerpunkt).

[26] See Glossary: Rifle Platoon (Schützenzug) about the regular rifle platoon.

[27] "Granattrupp" literally means "Grenade Troop", yet for clarity we chose rifle-grenade section here, also a "Trupp" is usually about the size of a section. See Glossary: Rifle-Grenade Section (Granattrupp).

[28] See Glossary: Squad (Schützengruppe) about changes in squad size during the war.

Gliederung des Sturmzuges[29]

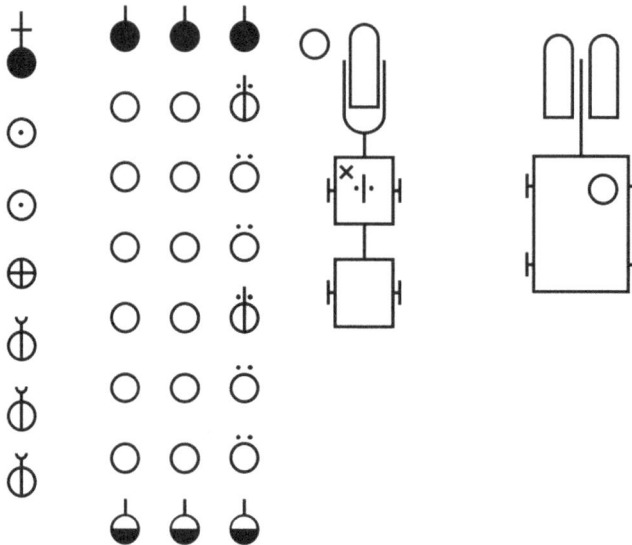

Bild 1.

2 Infanteriekarren (If. 8[30]), gekoppelt, mit einem Pferd und einem Pferdeführer,
1 Ersatzfeldwagen oder Panjewagen[31], 2spännig[sic!], dazu 1 Fahrer.

6. Der Zugtrupp besteht aus:
2 Meldern,
1 Krankenträger,
1 Granattrupp (3 Granatschützen).
Ein Granatschütze ist Truppführer.

Das Zusammenfassen der Granatschützen in der Hand des Zugführers steigert ihre Feuerwirkung und ermöglicht schwerpunktmäßigen Einsatz.

---

[29] Diese Überschrift war handschriftlich in Blockbuchstaben geschrieben und scheint Teil von Bild 1 gewesen zu sein.
[30] „If." war die Kurzform für „Infanteriefahrzeug". Beim If. 8 handelte es sich um den Infanteriekarren. Siehe Fleischer, Wolfgang: *Deutsche Infanteriekarren, Heeresfeldwagen und Heeresschlitten 1900-1945.* Podzun-Pallas-Verlag: Wölfersheim, Germany, 1995, S. 19.
[31] Siehe Glossar: Panjewagen.

Organization of the Assault Platoon[32]

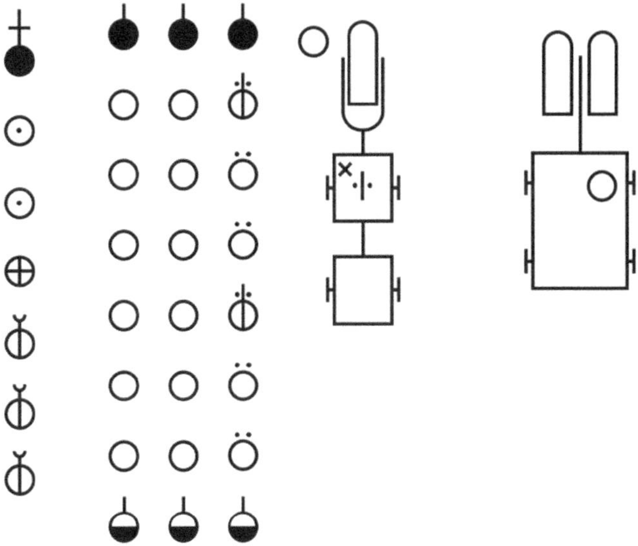

Figure 1.

2 infantry carriages (If. 8[33]), coupled, with one horse and one horse guide,
1 spare field wagon or panje carriage[34], two-horse carriage, plus 1 driver.

6. The platoon headquarters consists of:
2 messenger,
1 stretcher-bearer,
1 rifle-grenade section (3 rifle-grenade riflemen).
One rifle-grenade rifleman is section leader.

Allocating the rifle-grenade riflemen in the hand of the platoon leader increases their fire effectiveness and enables a focused employment.

---

[32] This headline was handwritten in block letters and seems to have been part of Figure 1.
[33] "If." was the short from for "infantry vehicle". The If. 8 was the infantry cart. See Fleischer, Wolfgang: *Deutsche Infanteriekarren, Heeresfeldwagen und Heeresschlitten 1900-1945*. Podzun-Pallas-Verlag: Wölfersheim, Germany, 1995, S. 19.
[34] See Glossary: Panje Carriage (Panjewagen).

7. Die „Sturmgruppe" besteht aus dem Gruppenführer und 7 Schützen.

Die Schützen der Sturmgruppe führen den Feuerkampf mit dem Sturmgewehr 44. Sie sind Nahkämpfer und reichlich mit Munition und Handgranaten auszustatten. Ein Schütze der Sturmgruppe ist stellvertretender Gruppenführer.

8. Die **„Feuergruppe"** (1-7) besteht aus 2 le.M.G.[35]-Trupps. Der Gruppenführer führt die ganze Gruppe und zugleich ein le.M.G.

Der stellv. Gruppenführer führt das 2. le.M.G. Jedes le.M.G. hat einen Schützen 1 [MG Schütze] und zwei Munitionsschützen.

Die erste Munitionsausstattung[36] beträgt je Sturmgewehr 44 720 Schuß. Beim Mann befinden sich 6 Magazine mit insgesamt 180 Schuß (je Magazin 30 Schuß).

III. Die Kampfweise des Sturmzuges.

Allgemeine Grundsätze für Führung und Verwendung.

9. Der Sturmzug hat die Aufgabe, **im Angriff den letzten Widerstand** und in der **Verteidigung den letzten Ansturm** des Feindes zu **brechen**.

10. Der Sturmzug kann jede Aufgabe im Angriff und in der Verteidigung erfüllen.

11. Der Sturmzug ist für folgende Aufgaben besonders geeignet:

a)   Für Stoß- und Spähtruppunternehmen, für Kampf im unübersichtlichen Gelände, bei Nacht und Nebel.

---

[35] Leichtes Maschinengewehr.
[36] Die erste Munitionsausstattung war jene Menge an Munition, die die kämpfende Truppe in ihren eigenen Gefechts- und Nachschubfahrzeugen mitführen konnte. Siehe: Donat, Gerhard: *Beispiele für den Munitionsverbrauch der deutschen Wehrmacht im zweiten Weltkrieg.* In: Allgemeine schweizerische Militärzeitschrift, Band 129, Jahr 1963, Heft 2, S. 76. (Online Version)

7. The "assault squad" consists of the squad leader and 7 riflemen.

The riflemen of the assault squad fight with the Sturmgewehr 44. They are close-combat fighters and are generously equipped with ammunition and hand grenades. One rifleman of the assault squad is the deputy squad leader.

8. The **"fire squad"** (1-7) consists of 2 light MG[37]-sections. The squad leader commands the whole squad and additionally one light MG.

The deputy squad leader commands the 2nd light MG. Each light MG has one rifleman 1 [MG gunner] and two ammunition bearers[38].

The first ammunition complement[39] for every Sturmgewehr 44 is 720 rounds. Each man carries 6 magazines with a total of 180 rounds (30 rounds per magazine).

III. The Combat Method of the Assault Platoon.[40]

General Principles for Command and Employment.

9. The assault platoon is tasked to **break the last resistance in the attack** and the enemies **last onslaught in the defense.**

10. The assault platoon can perform any task in the attack and in the defense.

11. The assault platoon is particularly suited for the following tasks:

a)   For raids and reconnaissance missions, for combat in complex terrain, at night and in fog.

---

[37] Light machine gun.

[38] "Munitionsschütze" literally means "munition rifleman".

[39] The first ammunition complement was the amount of ammunition that the fighting troops could carry in their own combat supply and supply vehicles. See: Donat, Gerhard: *Beispiele für den Munitionsverbrauch der deutschen Wehrmacht im zweiten Weltkrieg.* In: Allgemeine schweizerische Militärzeitschrift, Band 129, Jahr 1963, Heft 2, S. 76. (Online Version)

[40] "Kampfweise" can also be translated with combat / battle / fighting style.

b) In der Verteidigung als bewegliche Reserve für den Gegenstoß[41] und zum Schutz offener Flanken.

c) Für die Verfolgung und für Vorausabteilungen durch Vorwerfen auf Sturmgeschützen, Kfz. oder Panzern.

d) Bei Absetzbewegungen als Nachtruppe oder zum Kampf im Zwischenfeld[42].

e) Als Jagdzug einer Skitruppe oder als skibeweglicher Teil einer winterbeweglichen Truppe.

12. Der Sturmzug ist die kleinste taktische Kampfeinheit der Grenadier-Kompanie. Der Einsatz einzelner Strumgruppen [sic!] oder der Feuergruppe ist die Ausnahme.

Angriff.

13. In allen Gefechtslagen bildet die **völlig verborgene jägermäßige Annäherung** in Flanke und Rücken des Feindes und die Eröffnung starken überraschenden Feuers auf kurze Entfernungen die Grundlage jedes Erfolges.

14. Bei der **Annäherung** führt der Zugführer seinen Sturmzug **unter Vermeidung des Feuerkampfes** dicht an den Feind.

15. Eine eingehende Geländebeurteilung **vor** dem Ansatz des Zuges ist notwendig. Jede Art der Tarnung ist auszunutzen. Es kommt **weniger** darauf an, die Sturmausgangsstellung **rasch, sondern unbemerkt** vom Feind und ohne Verluste zu erreichen.

16. Der Sturmzug eröffnet das Feuer so spät wie möglich und nutzt noch mehr als bisher die Feuerunterstützung der schweren Waffen aus. Es ist **nicht** seine Aufgabe, sich auf weite oder mittlere Entfernung an die feindliche Stellung heranzuschießen.

---

[41] Ein Gegenstoß ist ein Angriff, der sofort nach Eindringen des Feindes in die eigene Stellungen durchgeführt wird, hierbei werden örtliche Reserven genutzt. Im Gegensatz zum Gegenangriff der planmäßig erfolgt und auch weiter zurückliegende Reserven nutzt. Siehe Glossar: Gegenangriff, Gegenstoß.

[42] Beim hinhaltenden Widerstand wurde das Gelände zwischen den Widerstandslinien als Zwischenfeld bezeichnet. Siehe Glossar: Zwischenfeld.

b) In the defense as mobile reserve for the hasty counterattack[43] and to protect open flanks.

c) For the pursuit and for advance detachments by moving forward quickly[44] on assault guns, cars or tanks.

d) During withdrawal as the rear party or for combat in the intermediate area[45].

e) As a hunting platoon of a ski unit or as ski-mobile element of a winter-mobile unit.

12. The assault platoon is the smallest tactical combat unit of the grenadier company. The use of individual assault squads or the fire squad is the exception.

Attack.

13. In all combat situations the **entirely hidden hunter-like approach** to the flank and back of the enemy and the use of strong surprising fire at short distances forms the basis of every success.

14. When **approaching**, the platoon leader leads his assault platoon close to the enemy, **while avoiding a firefight**.

15. A thorough terrain assessment is necessary before the platoon is committed. Any kind of camouflage is exploited. It is **less important** to reach the assault jump-off position **quickly, but rather to go unnoticed** by the enemy and arrive without losses.

16. The assault platoon opens fire as late as possible and uses the fire support of the heavy weapons even more than before. Therefore, it is **not** the task of the assault platoon to advance by firing[46] to the enemy position at long or medium range.

---

[43] The Germans distinguished between a hasty counterattack ("Gegenstoß") and regular counterattack ("Gegenangriff"). The hasty counterattack is an attack that is carried out immediately with local reserves after the enemy has broken into the friendly positions. In contrast to the counterattack, which is carried out according to plan and also makes use of more distant reserves. See Glossary: Counterattack (Gegenangriff).

[44] "Vorwerfen" literally translated means "throwing forward".

[45] In the delaying action, the area between the lines of resistance were called intermediate area. See Glossary: Intermediate Area (Zwischenfeld).

[46] "Heranzuschießen" literally "to close-in firing".

Durch Umgehen der feindlichen Feuerräume, durch Ausnutzen der kleinsten Deckungen und durch **Vortröpfeln**[47] **über eingesehenes Gelände** gewinnt der Sturmzug Raum nach vorwärts. Schmale tiefe Formen und starke Auflockerung verhindern Ausfälle.

Jede Form der Annäherung ist richtig, die dem Feind kein lohnendes Ziel bietet.

18. Zum **Vortröpfeln** über eingesehenes Gelände sind große Abstände von ½ bis 5 Minuten von Mann zu Mann oder von Paar zu Paar zu befehlen. Das Ziel des Vortröpfelns ist anzugeben. Ein energischer Gruppenführer ist als Schließender zu bestimmen. Er regelt das Ablaufen und sorgt dafür, daß dies von verschiedenen Geländepunkten aus und in unregelmäßigen Abständen durchgeführt wird (Übungsbeispiel Anlage 3).

19. Unterbrechen der Vorwärtsbewegung, um sich selbst **heranzuschießen**, ist nur gerechtfertigt, wenn alle anderen Mittel (Unterstützung schwerer Waffen, Gelände, Nebel, Dunkelheit) nicht zum Erfolge führen. Dann setzt der Gruppenführer zunächst seine Feuergruppe ein, um der Masse des Zuges vorzuhelfen.

20. Das zusammengefaßte Feuer **aller** unterstützenden Waffen ist von den Sturmgruppen zu einem schneller geschlossenen Vorwärtsstürmen auszunützen.

21. Beim Einbruch[48] des **ganzen** Sturmzuges sind eine oder die beiden Sturmgruppen nach vorn zu nehmen. Die Feuergruppe und der Granattrupp folgen dichtauf. Sie geben überall dort Feuerunterstützung, wo der Feind noch Widerstand leistet.

Sturmgruppen rollen stoßtruppartig die feindlichen Gräben auf.

---

[47] Bewegung einzeln oder paarweise: Siehe Glossar: Vortröpfeln.
[48] Der Einbruch ist das Ergebnis eines gelungenen Angriffs, der in die vorderste Stellung des Feindes eingedrungen ist. Siehe Glossar für visuelles Beispiel.

17. By bypassing enemy areas of fire, by taking advantage of the smallest cover and by **infiltrating**[49] **into surveilled terrain** the assault platoon gains space towards its front. Narrow deep formations and strong dispersal prevent losses.

Any form of approach is correct that does not offer the enemy a worthwhile target.

18. To infiltrate into surveilled terrain large intervals from ½ to 5 minutes from man to man or pair to pair are to be ordered. The goal of the infiltration is to be specified. An energetic squad leader is to be determined as the formation closer. He will control the proceeding and will ensure that this is done from different points of the terrain and at irregular intervals (training example Appendix 3).

19. Interrupting the advance to **advance by firing**[50] is only justified if all other means (support of heavy weapons, terrain, fog, darkness) do not lead to success. Then the squad leader first uses his fire squad to help the mass of the platoon.

20. The combined fire of **all** supporting weapons shall be used by the assault squads for a faster, forward assault of the whole platoon.[51]

21. During break-in[52] of the whole assault platoon one or both assault squads are to be taken forward. The fire squad and the rifle-grenade section follow close behind. They provide fire support, where the enemy still offers resistance.

Assault squads roll up the enemy trenches like shock troops.

---

[49] "Vortröpfeln" literally means "dripping forward". It means that movement should happen in pairs or alone. See Glossary: Infiltrating (Vortröpfeln).

[50] "Heranzuschießen" literally "to close-in firing".

[51] There is no English equivalent for "geschlossener Einsatz" or "geschlossen", see the Glossary Employment of the Whole Unit (Einsatz, geschlossen) for a discussion.

[52] There is no English equivalent for the military term "Einbruch". The break-in is the result of a successful attack that breached into the enemy's foremost lines. It precedes the penetration. See the Glossary for a visual example.

Einzelheiten über dieses Grabenaufrollen enthält Merkblatt 25/3 „Anleitung für den Nahkampf und die Handgranatenausbildung" Nr. 73-86.

22. Ist die Feuerunterstützung der Kompanie oder des Bataillons für den Einbruch des Sturmzuges unzureichend, so ist der Zugführer gezwungen, seine Feuergruppe und den Granattrupp zur Unterstützung oder als Feuerschutz einzusetzen.

23. Der Zugführer macht sich einen **Kampfplan** für den Ansatz seiner Gruppen (H.Dv. 130/2a Nr. 458 bis 463.[53])

24. Der **Kampfplan** des Zugführers eines Sturmzuges beruht auf folgenden Überlegungen:

„**Wo** soll ich hin?"

„**Wer** hindert mich daran?"

„**Wie** setze ich den Stoß der Sturmgruppen an?"

„Von **wo** und **wann** unterstützt die Feuergruppe den Stoß?"

25. Im Sinne dieses Kampfplanes sind die **Kampfaufträge** in Einzelbefehlen zu geben:

a) **Für die Feuergruppe:**

Wo Feuerstellung? – Wo Ziel? – Wie Feuerunterstützung? (Feuerbeginn – Feuerdauer.) – Wann und wohin nachfolgen?

b) **Für die Sturmgruppen:**

Wo Angriffsziel? – Wo Weg? – Welche Art des Vorgehens? – Welche Gliederung zum Sturm?

c) **Für den Granattrupp:**

Wo folgen? (Vorgehen mit den Sturmgruppen oder Einsatz bei der Feuergruppe?) – Wo Stellung? – Wo Ziel? – Wie Munitionseinsatz?

---

[53] Siehe Ergänzung 3.

Details about rolling up of trenches can be found in pamphlet 25/3 "Instructions for Close Combat and Hand Grenade Training" No. 73-86.

22. If the fire support of the company or battalion is insufficient for the break-in[54] of the assault platoon, the platoon leader is forced to use his fire squad and the rifle-grenade section for support or fire protection.

23. The platoon leader makes a **battle plan** for the commitment of his squads (H.Dv. 130/2a Nr. 458 to 463.[55])

24. The **battle plan** of the platoon leader of an assault platoon is based on the following considerations:

"**Where** should I go?"

"**Who** prevents me from doing so?"

"**How** do I commit the thrust of the assault squads?"

"From **where** and **when** will the fire squad support the thrust?"

25. In the sense of this battle plan **combat missions** are given in individual orders:

a) **For the fire squad:**

Where fire position?[56] – Where Target? – How fire support? (Start of fire – duration of fire.) – When and where to follow?

b) **For the assault squads:**

Where attack objective? – Where path? – What kind of advance? – What formation for the assault?

c) **For the rifle-grenade section:**

Where to follow? (Proceed with the assault squads or employment with the fire squad?) – Where position? – Where target? – How to use ammunition?

---

[54] There is no English equivalent for "Einbruch". See Glossary: Break-In (Einbruch).
[55] See Supplement 3.
[56] We went with the more literal translation of orders. As in the original, these do not feature grammatically correct sentences. Meant here of course is "Where is the fire position?" In German that would mean "Wo ist die Feuerstellung?".

26. Der **Sturmzug** ist zum Angriff folgendermaßen **anzusetzen**:

a) Beim zangenförmigen Angriff sind die Feuergruppe und beide Sturmgruppen so einzusetzen, daß die Verbindung nicht verlorengeht.

b) Der Granattrupp folgt den Sturmgruppen, um sie beim Angriff und beim Sturm gegen überraschend auftauchende Ziele zu unterstützen.

c) Das Unterstellen des Granattrupps unter die Feuergruppe bleibt Ausnahme und hängt vom Gelände und von der Schußentfernung ab.

d) Zurückhalten einer einzelnen Sturmgruppe als Reserve oder als Flankenschutz sowie Einsatz einer Sturmgruppe, um das Unterstützungsfeuer zu ergänzen, ist Ausnahme.

27. Sturm- und Feuergruppen ergänzen sich fortlaufend, auch dann, wenn eine Regelung durch Befehl nicht vorliegt.

Bei überschlagenden Stellungswechsel ergänzen sich fortlaufend, auch dann, wenn eine Regelung durch Befehl nicht vorliegt.

Die Gruppen des Sturmzuges handeln auf Zeichen oder Zuruf.

28. Der Zugführer regelt die Vorbereitungen zum Sturm. Er stürmt allen voran, reißt seine Mannschaft vor und bricht mit den Sturmgruppen ein.

Der Sturm erfolgt unter lebhaftem Feuer aller Waffen des Zuges und lauten anhaltenden Hurra-Rufen. Mit Sturmgewehren 44 ist während der Bewegung zu schießen und der Feind mit Feuer zu überschütten. Es sind schnell aufeinanderfolgende gezielte Einzelschüsse beim Sturm und Feuerstöße (2-3 Schuß) während des Einbrechens abzugeben.

26. The **assault platoon** is to be **committed** to attack as follows:

    a)   In case of a pincer attack, the fire squad and both assault squads are to be employed in such a way that their communication[57] is not lost.

    b)   The rifle-grenade section follows the assault squads in order to support them during the assault against unexpectedly appearing targets.

    c)   Subordinating the rifle-grenade section under the fire squad is the exception and is dependent on the terrain and the firing distance.

    d)   Holding back of a single assault squad as reserve or as flank protection as well as employment of an assault squad, to supplement the supporting fire, is the exception.

27. Assault and fire squads complement[58] each other continuously, even if there is no regulation by command.

In the event of a shift in overlapping positions, they will complement each other continuously, even if control by command is not available.

The squads of the assault platoon act on sign or call.

28. The platoon leader supervises the preparations for the assault. He charges ahead of everyone, pulls his men forward and breaks-in with the assault squads.

The assault takes place under lively fire of all the weapons of the platoon and with loud, sustained hurray-calls. Sturmgewehr 44 assault rifles are to be fired during the movement and the enemy is to be showered with fire. Quick successive targeted single shots are to be fired during the assault and fire bursts (2-3 shots) are to be fired during the break-in[59].

---

[57] Note the direct translation of "Verbindung" would be "connection", but communication is the more correct translation here.

[58] In German there was a difference between "unterstützen" (support) and "ergänzen" (complement). "Unterstützen" was generally used for artillery or other indirect fire units like the rifle-grenade section. Whereas "ergänzen" was used in more direct way, hence probably the best translation for ergänzen would be "supporting closely/directly".

[59] There is no English equivalent for the military term "Einbruch". See Glossary: Break-In (Einbruch).

29. Die hohe moralische Wirkung der Sturmgewehre 44 ist zu einem **schnellen Sturmlauf** bis in die feindliche Stellung auszunutzen.

Hinwerfen und Handgranatenwurf dicht vor dem Einbruchsziel führt zu unnötigen Verlusten und stellt den Erfolg in Frage.

30. Nach gelungenen Einbruch folgen Feuergruppe und Granattrupp **ohne Befehl** ihren Sturmgruppen.

31. Der Zugführer gliedert nach erfolgtem Einbruch seinen Zug für den weiteren Angriff. **Jeder Erfolg ist nach vorwärts auszunutzen,** dem Feind ist keine Zeit zu lassen, sich erneut festzusetzen.[60]

32. Beim **Angriff mit begrenztem Ziel** setzt der Zugführer **nach** Erreichen des Angriffszieles die beiden le.M.G. der Feuergruppe und den Granattrupp zum Besetzen und Halten der Stellung ein. Sie sorgen auch **ohne Befehl** dafür, daß durch feindliche Gegenstöße die Sturmgruppen nicht wieder geworfen werden.

33. Für den Nachtangriff ist das Sturmgewehr 44 infolge der schnellen Feuerbereitschaft und der hohen Feuerkraft besonders geeignet. Sturmzüge sind daher in vorderer Linie einzusetzen. Mondhelle Nächte und Schnee begünstigen den Nachtangriff.

34. Die **Durchführung** des Nachtangriffes erfordert den bis ins einzelne vorher festgelegten Angriffs- und Feuerplan. Der Kampf läuft nach einem starren Plan ab. In eine neue Richtung kann der angelaufene Angriff nicht abgedreht werden.

35. Der Nachtangriff erfolgt nur mit begrenztem Ziel. Im überraschenden Ansprung in breiter Front brechen die Sturmgruppen unter anhaltenden Feuer aller Schützen in die feindliche Stellung ein. Die Feuergruppe folgt dichtauf.

---

[60] Dies steht im Kontrast zur *H.Dv. 130/2a*, Nummer 309, S. 127. Hier wird angeführt, dass nachdem Einbruch ein Augenblick der Schwäche ist und es notwendig ist zuerst das Gewonnene zu behaupten. Und dann je nach Lage entweder weiter anzugreifen, fliehenden Feind zu vernichten oder aber zu verteidigen.

29. The high morale effect of the Sturmgewehr 44 is to be used for a **fast assault run** up to the enemy position.

Hitting the dirt[61] and throwing hand grenades close to the break-in[62] objective leads to unnecessary losses and puts success into question.

30. After a successful break-in, the fire squad and rifle-grenade section follow their assault squads **without orders.**

31. After the break-in, the platoon leader organizes his platoon for the further attack. **Every success is to be exploited towards the front**, the enemy is not to be given time to entrench[63] himself again.[64]

32. In the case of an **attack with limited objective**, the platoon leader, **after** reaching the attack objective, uses the two light MGs of the fire squad and the rifle-grenade section to occupy and hold the position. Even **without orders**, they ensure that assault squads are not pushed back[65] by enemy counterattacks.

33. The Sturmgewehr 44 is particularly suitable for night attacks due to its readiness to fire and high firepower. Assault platoons are therefore to be used on the front line. Moonlit nights and snow favor the night attack.

34. The **execution** of the night attack requires an attack and fire plan which has been predetermined in detail. The combat proceeds according to a rigid plan. The attack cannot be turned into a new direction.

35. The night attack is carried out only with limited objective. With a surprising broad frontal assault, the assault squads break into the enemy position under sustained fire from all riflemen. The fire squad follows close behind.

---

[61] "Hinwerfen" literally means "throwing", yet in this context it means to "throw oneself at the ground".

[62] There is no English equivalent for the military term "Einbruch". See Glossary: Break-In (Einbruch).

[63] "Sich erneut festzusetzen" literally means "to re-establish itself".

[64] This contrasts with *H.Dv. 130/2a*, Number 309, S. 127, where it is stated that after a break-in there is a moment of weakness and that it is necessary to first affirm what has been won. And then, depending on the situation, either continue to attack, destroy fleeing enemies or defend.

[65] "Nicht wieder geworfen" literally means "not thrown again". However, the "wieder" in this context, does not translate to "again".

Verteidigung.

a) Der Sturmzug in der Hauptkampflinie.

36. Ist der Sturmzug in der Verteidigung in **vorderer Linie** eingesetzt, so ist jede Gliederung richtig, die für das Halten der Stellung erforderlich ist.

37. Beim Abwehrkampf auf breiter Front ist das le.M.G. der **Gerätereserve** des Zugs einzusetzen. Als Schützen an diesem le.M.G. sind die Mun.-Schützen der Feuergruppe einzuteilen.

Der Zugführer teilt die Feuergruppe auf und verteilt sie nesterweise[66] im Zugabschnitt oder bildet dem Gelände entsprechende le.M.G.- und Sturmgewehrschwerpunkte.

Alle M.G.-Stellungen sind als Kampfnester auszubauen und mit Panzervernichtungsmitteln auszustatt. [sic!] Weitere Panzervernichtungsmittel sind für jeden Mann greifbar in der Stellung zu verteilen (Panzerfaust, Blendkörper, Minen, Brandflaschen).

38. Der **Granattrupp** wirkt in Geländefalten, die mit dem Feuer der le.M.G. und Sturmgewehre 44 nicht zu fassen sind. Er ergänzt die Wirkung der Handgranaten gegen tote Winkel vor der Stellung.

Granattrupps sind **beweglich** einzusetzen.

39. Die **Gegenstoßreserve**[67] des Zugführers besteht aus einer Sturmgruppe. Bei großen Abschnittsbreiten bildet der Zugführer mit nur einigen Schützen und dem Zugtrupp die Stoßreserve. Gegenstoßrichtungen sind festzulegen und einzuüben.

40. In der Verteidigung ist zwischen einer **Tag- und Nachtaufstellung** zu unterscheiden (Regelung des Postendienstes, Organisation der Ruhe, Ausnutzen in der Nähe befindlicher B.-Stellen[68]).

---

[66] Ein Nest sind mehrere Schützenlöcher, die mit Gräben verbunden sind. Siehe Glossar: Nest.

[67] Ein Gegenstoß ist ein Angriff, der sofort nach Eindringen des Feindes in die eigene Stellungen durchgeführt wird, hierbei werden örtliche Reserven genutzt. Im Gegensatz zum Gegenangriff der planmäßig erfolgt und auch weiter zurückliegende Reserven nutzt. Siehe Glossar: Gegenangriff, Gegenstoß.

[68] Beobachtungsstelle.

Defense.

a) The Assault Platoon in the Main Line of Resistance.

36. If the assault platoon is deployed in the **foremost line** of the defense, any organization required to hold the position is correct.

37. In the case of a broad defense, the light MG of the platoon's reserve equipment must be used. The riflemen on this light MG are the ammunition bearers[69] of the fire squad.

The platoon leader divides the fire squad and disperses them nest by nest[70] in the platoon sector or forms terrain appropriate light MG and assault rifle appropriate weight of efforts[71].

All MG positions are to be developed as combat nests and equipped with infantry anti-tank weapons[72]. Further infantry anti-tank weapons are to be distributed in the position within reach of every man (Panzerfaust, smoke grenade[73], mines, incendiary bottles).

38. The **rifle-grenade section** acts in terrain folds, which cannot be caught by the fire of the light MG and Sturmgewehr 44. It complements the action of the hand grenades against blind spots in front of the position.

Rifle-grenade sections are to be used in a **mobile way**.

39. The **hasty counterattack[74] reserve** of the platoon leader consists of an assault squad. In the case of large sector widths, the platoon leader forms the reserve with only a few riflemen and the platoon headquarters. Hasty counterattack directions must be determined and practiced.

40. In the defense, a distinction must be made between **day and night deployment** (regulation of guard duty, organization of rest, use of nearby observation posts).

---

[69] "Munitionsschütze" literally means "munition rifleman".
[70] "Nesterweise" is derived from "Nest", which is a collection of foxholes that are connected by trenches. See Glossary: Nest (Nest).
[71] See Glossary: Weight of Effort (Schwerpunkt).
[72] "Panzervernichtungsmittel" literally means "tank destruction means", this refers to anti-tank weapons for the infantry.
[73] "Blendkörper" literally means "dazzle/blind body", the TM 30-506 translates "Blendkörper" with "frangible glass smoke grenade".
[74] Hasty counterattack ("Gegenstoß") is different from a counterattack ("Gegenangriff").

– 14 –

b) Der Sturmzug als Gegenstoßreserve[75].

41. Die beim Bataillon und Regiment ausgeschiedene **Gegenstoßreserve** bilden normalerweise die Sturmzüge (Feuerwehr![76]).

42. In der Tiefe des Hauptkampffeldes[77] eingesetzte Sturmzüge sind so zu gliedern, daß ihre Feuergruppen eingebrochenen[78] Feind vernichten und später Sturmgruppen beim Gegenstoß unterstützen.

43. Beim Gegenstoß des ganzen Sturmzuges ist die Feuergruppe die Feuerreserve des Zugführers in der zurückgewonnenen Stellung.

44. Gegenstöße sind in die Flanke des Feindes zu führen und bringen entlang der H.K.L.[79] durchschlagenden Erfolg. **Je schneller** der Gegenstoß durch die Sturmgruppen erfolgt, **um so sicherer ist der Erfolg** auch gegenüber überlegenem Feind.

Der Entschluß zum Gegenstoß ist daher vom Führer des Sturmzuges selbstständig zu fassen.

45. Der eingebrochene Feind ist durch das Feuer aller Waffen und unter Verwendung aller Kampfmittel zu vernichten und im raschen Gegenstoß zu überrennen.

Der Gegenstoß ist mit viel Feuer und unter rücksichtslosem persönlichen Einsatz sowie unter anhaltendem Hurrarufen durchzuführen.

Absetzen.

46. Das **Absetzen** aus der Stellung erfolgt, wenn nicht zeitlich befohlen, kämpfend vor überlegenem Feind.

Der Zugführer wählt seine Stellungen in der H.K.L.

---

[75] Ein Gegenstoß ist ein Angriff, der sofort nach Eindringen des Feindes in die eigene Stellungen durchgeführt wird, hierbei werden örtliche Reserven genutzt. Im Gegensatz zum Gegenangriff der planmäßig erfolgt und auch weiter zurückliegende Reserven nutzt. Siehe Glossar: Gegenangriff, Gegenstoß.
[76] „Feuerwehr!" verweist hier darauf, dass solche Einheiten in Notfällen zur Hilfe kamen.
[77] Siehe Glossar: Hauptkampffeld.
[78] Siehe Glossar: Einbruch.
[79] Hauptkampflinie. Siehe Glossar: Hauptkampflinie.

DE-14

b) The Assault Squad as a Hasty Counterattack[80] Reserve.

41. The **hasty counterattack reserve**, which is withdrawn from the battalion and regiment, is normally the assault platoons (fire fighters![81]).

42. Assault platoons deployed in depth in the main defensive area[82] are to be organized in such a way that their fire squads destroy broken-in[83] enemies and later support assault squads in their hasty counterattack.

43. During the hasty counterattack of the whole assault platoon, the fire squad is the fire reserve of the platoon leader in the regained position.

44. Hasty counterattacks are to be led into the flank of the enemy and bring resounding success along the main line of resistance[84]. **The faster** the hasty counterattack by the assault squads, **the surer is the success** even against superior enemies.

The decision for the hasty counterattack must therefore be taken independently by the leader of the assault platoon.

45. The broken-in enemy is to be destroyed by the fire of all weapons and with the use of all ordnance and to be overrun in a rapid hasty counterattack.

The hasty counterattack is to be carried out with a lot of fire and under ruthless personal effort as well as under continuous hurray calls.

Withdrawal.

46. The withdrawal from the position takes place, if not ordered at the time, under continuous fighting with the superior enemy.

The platoon leader chooses his positions in the main line of resistance

---

[80] The Germans distinguished between a hasty counterattack ("Gegenstoß") and regular counterattack ("Gegenangriff"). See Glossary: Hasty Counterattack (Gegenstoß) and Counterattack (Gegenangriff).

[81] "Feuerwehr" (fire fighters / brigade) refers here to the fact that such units came to the rescue in emergencies.

[82] See Glossary: Main Defensive Area (Hauptkampffeld).

[83] See Glossary: Break in (Einbruch).

[84] See Glossary: Main Line of Resistance (Hauptkampflinie).

vor dem Absetzen so, daß er sich mit seinen Gruppen unbemerkt vom Gegner absetzen kann.

Den Weg für das Absetzen und den Sammelpunkt des Zuges läßt er frühzeitig erkunden. Er befiehlt rechtzeitig den Abschub von Gerät und Munition.

47. Beim Absetzen bei Nacht löst sich der Zug vom Feind und sammelt auf dem befohlenen Sammelpunkt. Gleichzeitiges Räumen und größte Lautlosigkeit sind notwendig.

Der Zugführer bleibt bei den Teilen, die sich dem Feind am nächsten befinden.

48. Die als Nachtruppe eingesetzten Sturmzüge verschleiern das Loslösen vom Feind. Sie täuschen die alte Besetzung unter Aufrechterhaltung der bisherigen Feuertätigkeit vor.

49. Je nach Lage und Befehl geht der Sturmzug unmittelbar oder abschnittsweise sich verteidigend auf die Aufnahmestellung zurück. Er darf beim Zurückgehen das Feuer der Waffen aus den rückwärtigen Stellungen nicht behindern.

Beim abschnittsweisen Zurückgehen wird unter Ausnutzen günstiger Geländepunkt wieder Front gemacht und der nachdrängende Feind mit Feuer überfallen. Durch überschlagenden Einsatz wird das Zurückgehen erleichtert.

50. Die Sturmgruppen bleiben mit dem Granattrupp am längsten am Feind, während die Feuergruppe das Absetzen deckt.

51. Im deckungsarmen Gelände nimmt der Zugführer seine Schützen einzeln zurück. Gleichzeitiges Verlassen der Stellung ist am Tage nur bei wirksamer Feuerunterstützung möglich.

in such a way before the withdrawal, that he can withdraw with his squads from the enemy without being noticed.

The route for the withdrawal and the meeting point of the platoon is scouted at an early stage. He orders the evacuation of equipment and ammunition in time.

47. When withdrawing at night the platoon separates from the enemy and meets at the ordered rally point. Simultaneous evacuation and maximum silence are necessary.

The platoon leader stays with the elements closest to the enemy.

48. The assault platoons used as the rear party conceal the disengagement from the enemy. They simulate occupancy of the former positions by maintaining the previous fire activity.

49. Depending on the situation and order, the assault platoon returns directly or sector by sector to the covering position while defending itself. It may not hinder the fire of the weapons from the rear positions when returning.

When going back in sector by sector, the front is established again by exploiting favorable terrain and surprising the advancing enemy with fire. By overlapping employment, walking back is made easier.

50. The assault squads with the rifle-grenade section keep engaging the enemy until the last moment[85], while the fire squad covers the withdrawal.

51. In terrain with little cover the platoon leader takes back his riflemen one by one. Simultaneously evacuating the position during the day is only possible with effective fire support.

---

[85] The literal translation of "am längsten am Feind bleiben" would be to "stay longest with the enemy".

IV. Der Feuerkampf des Sturmzuges.

52. Der Feuerkampf wird im Rahmen der Gruppe geführt.

Der Führer der Feuergruppe leitet das Feuer eines le.M.G. oder beider le.M.G.

53. Die **Feuergruppe** unterstützt im Kampf die Sturmgruppen durch ihr Feuer. **Schlagartige Feuereröffnung, straffe Feuerleitung und Zusammenfassen des Feuers** der le.M.G. auf die gefährlichsten Ziele und rascher Zielwechsel gestalten ihren Einsatz besonders wirkungsvoll. Die Feuerstellungen sind häufig zu wechseln.

54. Der **Granattrupp** bekämpft lästige Feindnester und Ziele hinter Deckungen selbständig oder im Zusammenwirken mit der Feuergruppe nach Weisung des Zugführers (Koppeln von Flach- und Steilfeuer).

Im Feuerbefehl ist die Gesamtzahl der zu verschießenden Granaten zu befehlen (siehe Ziff. 60c).

55. Sturmgewehre 44 sind am wirksamsten auf kurze Entfernung. **Gleichzeitiger und überraschender Einsatz** aller Schützen zum Feuerkampf steigert die hohe Feuerkraft der Sturmgruppe (Feuerüberfall[86]).

56. Als Form des Feuerkampfes der Feuergruppe und des Granattrupps ist stets der **Feuerüberfall** zu wählen.

57. Die Feuergeschwindigkeit der Sturmgewehre 44 verlangt **straffe Feuerzucht**[87] von jedem einzelnen Schützen.

Der Schütze ist so auszubilden, daß er

a) Einzelfeuer, d. h. den sorgfältig gezielten Einzelschuß abgibt,
b) zur zum Bekämpfen lohnender Augenblicksziele auf Befehl des Gruppenführers auf allen Ent-

---

[86] Siehe Glossar: Feuerüberfall.
[87] Auch Feuerdisziplin.

IV. The Firefight of the Assault Platoon.

52. The firefight is conducted as part of the squad.

The leader of the fire squad directs the fire of one light MG or of both.

53. The **fire squad** supports the assault squads in combat with its fire. **Sudden opening of fire, tight fire control and concentration of fire** by the light MG on the most dangerous targets and rapid target change make their employment particularly effective. The firing positions must be changed frequently.

54. The **rifle-grenade section** fights irritating enemy nests and targets behind cover independently or in cooperation with the fire squad according to the instructions of the platoon leader (coupling of direct and indirect fire[88]).

In the fire order the total number of grenades to be fired must be ordered (see No. 60c).

55. Sturmgewehr 44 are most effective at short range. **Simultaneous and surprising employment** of all riflemen for the firefight increases the high firepower of the assault squad (surprise fire[89]).

56. As the default form of the firefight for the fire squad and the rifle-grenade section **surprise fire** is always to be chosen.

57. The fire rate[90] of the Sturmgewehr 44 requires **tight fire discipline** from each individual rifleman.

The rifleman is trained in such a way, that he

a) uses semi-automatic fire[91], this means firing carefully aimed single shots,
b) only to combat worthwhile targets of opportunity on order of the squad leader at all ran-

---

[88] The literal translation of "Flachfeuer" would be "flat-trajectory fire". The literal translation of "Steilfeuer" would be "steep fire". Meant are direct and indirect fire.
[89] The literal translation of the German word "Feuerüberfall" would be "firing raid", although in this case "Überfall" refers to the surprise effect. See Glossary: Surprise fire (Feuerüberfall).
[90] "Feuergeschwindigkeit" literally means "speed of fire".
[91] Note the term "semi-automatic fire" is correct, yet since the common weapon was still the bolt-action rifle this terminology at least in German at the time was not used. "Einzelfeuer" literally means "single fire".

fernungen **sowie in der Entscheidung**, z. B. im Angriff beim Einbruch in die feindliche Stellung oder in der **Verteidigung** bei Abwehr des feindlichen Angriffs, auf nahe und nächste Entfernung sein Feuer zu **Feuerstößen von 2 bis 3 Schuß steigert**,

c) niemals Dauerfeuer schießt.

58. Unter günstigen Umständen, z. B. wenn der Feuerkampf aus einer Deckung oder aus einer versteckten Stellung geführt werden kann, **leitet der Gruppenführer das Feuer** der ganzen Sturmgruppe. Sonst führen die Schützen den Feuerkampf selbstständig im Rahmen des Kampfauftrages.

59. Die **Feuereröffnung** behält sich der Gruppenführer vor. Er befiehlt die Feuerart durch das Kommando „Einzelfeuer!" oder „Feuerstöße!"[.]

Die Anzahl der Einzelschüsse und der Feuerstöße ist zu befehlen (Beispiele 1 und 2).

60. Schulbeispiele für die Feuereröffnung:

a) **Feuereröffnung der Sturmgruppe:**

Beispiel 1:
Lage: „Gruppe im Angriff auf 300 m an feindliche Stellung herangekommen, vom halbrechts Gewehrfeuer."
Feuerbefehl: „Halbrechts im Acker Schützen! – Visier 300! – 5 Schuß Einzelfeuer! – Stellung! – Feuer frei!"

Beispiel 2:
Lage: „Gruppe in der Verteidigung, halbrechts greift Feind in dichten Trupps an."
Feuerbefehl: „Neuer Feind halbrechts! – Visier 200! – 3 Feuerstöße! – Stellung! – Feuer frei!"

Beispiel 3:
Lage: „Gruppe in versteckter Stellung – erkennt

ges **as well as in the decisive moment**[92], e.g., in the attack in the case of a break-in[93] into the enemy position or in the **defense** against the enemy attack, to **increase** his fire to **fire bursts of 2 to 3 shots** at close and immediate[94] ranges,

c)   never fires full-automatic fire.

58. Under favorable circumstances, e.g., if the firefight can be conducted from a cover or from a hidden position, the **squad leader directs the fire** of the whole assault squad. Otherwise, the riflemen conduct the firefight independently within the scope of the combat mission.

59. The **opening of fire** is reserved to the squad leader. He orders the type of fire by the command "semi-automatic fire!" or "burst-fire!".

The number of single shots and fire bursts must be ordered (examples 1 and 2)

60. Textbook examples for opening of fire:[95]

a)   **Opening of fire of the assault squad:**

Example 1:
Situation: "Squad in the attack advanced up to 300 m to enemy position, from half-right rifle fire"
Fire order: "Half-right in the field riflemen! – Sight 300! – 5 shots semi-automatic fire! – Position! – Fire!"

Example 2:
Situation: "Squad in the defense, half-right enemy attacks in tight sections."
Fire order: "New enemy half-right! – Sight 200! – 3 fire bursts! – Position! – Fire!"

Example 3:
Situation: "Squad in concealed position – detects

---

[92] Note the literal translation of "Entscheidung" would be "decision", but in this case it refers to the "Entscheidung" in the sense of decisive outcome, like it is used in "Entscheidungsschlacht" which is translated and well-known as "decisive battle".

[93] There is no English equivalent for the military term "Einbruch". See Glossary: Break-In (Einbruch).

[94] "Nahe" and "nächste Entfernung" refer to different distances. We translated "nahe Entfernung" to "close range" and "nächste Entfernung" to "immediate ranges".

[95] Like Number 25, due to the literal translation, articles and verbs are missing in some of these commands just as in the German original.

in 400 m Entfernung das Instellunggehen einiger Schützen und 1 M.G."
Feuerbefehl: „Geradeaus M.G.! – Feuerüberfall[96] auf Pfiff! – Visier
400! – Einzelfeuer! – Stellung!" – Pfiff!

b) **Feuereröffnung der Feuergruppe:**
   (1) **Feuerbefehl für ein le.M.G.:**
       „M.G. X[97]! – Geradeaus! – 600! – Einzelne Kusseln[98] auf der Höhe!
       – Links davon am Feldweg Schützen! – Visier 600! – Stellung! –
       Feuer frei!"
   (2) **Feuerbefehl für zwei le.M.G.:**
       „Durchrufen! – Beide M.G.! – Halblinks am Dorfrand feindliche
       Schützen! – Beide M.G.! – Visier 500! – Stellung! – Feuer frei!"
   (3) **Feuerbefehl für zwei le.M.G. und die Munitionsschützen:**
       „Beide M.G.! – Halbrechts! Einzelstehende Kiefer! – 300! – Links
       davon im Acker Schützen! – Stellung! Feuer frei!"
       Einsatz der Munitionsschützen ist erforderlich:
       „Sturmgewehre! – Visier 300! – Dasselbe Ziel! – Stellung! Marsch!
       Marsch! – Einzelfeuer! – Feuer frei!"
   (4) **Beschleunigte Feuereröffnung der ganzen Feuergruppe:**
       „Ganze Feuergruppe! – Visier 300! – Stellung! Marsch! Marsch! –
       Feuer frei!"

c) **Feuereröffnung des Granattrupps:**
   „Granattrupp! – Halbrechts Hohlweg[99]! – Daumenbreite links davon
   hinter Erdaufwurf feindliche Schützen! – 6 Sprenggranaten! – Stellung! –
   Feuer frei!"

---

[96] Siehe Glossar: Feuerüberfall.
[97] Die Feuergruppe hatte 2 Maschinengewehre.
[98] Eine Kussel ist ein junger verkümmerter Baum.
[99] Ein Weg der sich durch jahrhundertelange Nutzung als auch durch Regenwasser in
das Gelände eingeschnitten hat.

in 400 m distance the moving into position of several riflemen and 1 MG"
Fire order: "Straight ahead MG! – Surprise fire[100] on whistle! – Sight
400! – Semi-automatic fire! – Position!" – Whistle!
b) **Opening of fire of the fire squad:**
  (1) **Fire order for one light MG:**
    "MG X[101]! – Straight ahead! – 600! – Individual withered trees[102]
    on the height! – Left of them on the dirt track riflemen! – Sight 600!
    – Position! – Fire!"
  (2) **Fire order for two MG:**
    "Call! – Both MGs! – Half-left at the edge of the village enemy
    riflemen! – Both MGs! – Sight 500! – Position! – Fire!"
  (3) **Fire order for two light MG and the ammunition bearers[103]:**
    "Both MGs! – Half-right! Single standing pine! – 300! – Left of it in
    the field riflemen! – Position! Fire!"
    Employment of the ammunition bearers is required:
    "Assault rifles! – Sight 300! – Same target! – Position! Double time,
    march! – Semi-automatic fire[104]! – Fire!"
  (4) **Accelerated opening of fire of the whole fire squad:**
    "Whole fire squad! – Sight 300! – Position! Double time, march! –
    Fire!"
c) **Opening of fire of the rifle-grenade section:**
  "Rifle-grenade section! – Half-right sunken road[105]! – Thumb width left of
  it behind earth upheaval enemy riflemen! – 6 high-explosive grenades! –
  Position! – Fire!"

---

[100] See Glossary: Surprise Fire (Feuerüberfall).
[101] The fire squad had 2 machine guns.
[102] A "Kussel" is a young, withered tree.
[103] "Munitionsschütze" literally means "munition rifleman".
[104] Note the term "semi-automatic fire" is correct, yet since the common weapon was
still the bolt-action rifle this terminology at least in German at the time was not used.
"Einzelfeuer" literally means "single fire".
[105] A path that has cut into the terrain through centuries of use as well as through
rainwater.

Anlagen.

Anhalt für eine kurzfristige Ausbildung.

1. Während einer kurzfristigen Ausbildung im Feldheer oder Ersatzheer[106], umfaßt die Ausbildung vordringlich folgende Gebiete:

a) **Handhabung der Waffe** (vgl. Anlage 2).

b) **Erschießen des Haltepunktes.**

Der Waffe sind keine Trefferbilder beigegeben. Die Visiermarken lassen sich um jeweils 100 m verstellen, so daß das **Erschießen des Haltepunktes** (Ermittlung der Treffpunktlage) **die wichtigste Voraussetzung für ein gutes Schießen ist.**

Das Erschießen des Haltepunktes erfolgt auf den Entfernungen 100, 200 und 300 m.

c) **Schießübungen** (Durchführung der einzelnen Übungen siehe H.Dv. 240/2).

Im einzelnen sind zu üben:

(1) Einzelfeuer (schnell aufeinanderfolgende, gut gezielte Schüsse).

(2) Feuerstöße auf nächste Entfernung (nicht mehr als 2-3 Schuß).

(3) Feuerüberfall[107] durch Einzelfeuer (je Schütze 3-5 Schuß).

(4) Einzelfeuer in der Bewegung (Einbruch, Gegenstoß[108], Grabenkampf).

---

[106] Siehe Glossar: Ersatzheer.

[107] Siehe Glossar: Feuerüberfall.

[108] Ein Gegenstoß ist ein Angriff, der sofort nach Eindringen des Feindes in die eigene Stellungen durchgeführt wird, hierbei werden örtliche Reserven genutzt. Im Gegensatz zum Gegenangriff der planmäßig erfolgt und auch weiter zurückliegende Reserven nutzt. Siehe Glossar: Gegenangriff, Gegenstoß.

Appendices.

Guide for a Short-Term Training.

1. During a brief training period in the Field Army or Replacement Army[109], the training primarily covers the following areas:

a) **Handling of the Weapon** (see Appendix 2).
b) **Determine point of impact by firing.**[110]
There are no graphs coming with the weapon showing the shot grouping. The sighting marks can be adjusted by increments of 100 m, so that **determining the point of impact by firing** (determination of a grouping[111]) **is the most important prerequisite for accurate firing.**
The determining the point of impact by firing is done at distances of 100, 200 and 300 m.
c) **Firing exercises** (Execution of the individual exercises see H.Dv. 240/2).

In detail are to be practiced:
(1) Semi-automatic fire[112] (well-aimed shots in quick succession).
(2) Bursts at immediate range[113] (not more than 2-3 shots).
(3) Surprise fire[114] by semi-automatic fire (each rifleman 3-5 shots).
(4) Semi-automatic fire in movement (break-in[115], hasty counterattack, trench combat).

---

[109] See Glossary: Replacement Army (Ersatzheer).

[110] This action refers to establishing the point of impact of the weapon, so as to impart an understanding to the shooter where his shots are likely to land at the various combat ranges. A zeroing, that being the process of manually adjusting the sights after establishing a correct grouping so as to provide a more predictable impact position inline with the sight picture, is not discussed in the abstract.

[111] "Treffpunkt" is "point of impact", literally "Treffpunktlage" would be "point of impact location".

[112] Note the term "semi-automatic fire" is correct, yet since the common weapon was still the bolt-action rifle this terminology at least in German at the time was not used. "Einzelfeuer" literally means "single fire".

[113] "Nahe" and "nächste Entfernung" refer to different distances. We translated "nahe Entfernung" to "close range" and "nächste Entfernung" to "immediate ranges".

[114] The literal translation of the German word "Feuerüberfall" would be "firing raid", although in this case "Überfall" refers to the surprise effect. See Glossary: Surprise fire (Feuerüberfall).

[115] There is no English equivalent for the military term "Einbruch". See Glossary: Break-In (Einbruch).

d) **Gefechtsschießen** der Gruppe und des Zuges.
Einfache, den Fronterfahrungen und dem bevorstehenden Einsatz
entsprechende Aufgaben sind zu stellen. Als Anhalt dienen die
Übungsbeispiele der Anlage 3-5.

2. Die aufgeführten Schießübungen stellen ein Mindestmaß dar. Bei
vorhandener Munition und Zeit sind die Schießübungen der H.Dv. 240/2 zu
schießen.

**Nur im scharfen Schuß erhält die unbewaffnete Truppe einen Begriff von
dem Kampf, den sie mit der neuen Waffe führen kann.**

3. Die Einzelausbildung der Schützen ist im wesentlichen abzustellen auf:

- Kenntnis und Beherrschung der Waffe.

- Schießen.

- Richtiges Verhalten im Gelände, Tarnung, Eingraben.

d) **Live fire combat exercise** of the squad and the platoon.
Simple, the front experience and the forthcoming mission corresponding exercises are to be set. As a guide serve the exercises in Appendix 3-5.

2. The listed firing exercises set the minimum requirement. If ammunition and time are available, the firing exercises of the H.Dv. 240/2 are to be fired.

Only through live fire does the unarmed men[116] grasp of type of combat that it can now conduct with the new weapon.

3. The individual training of the rifleman is mainly directed at:

- Familiarization with, and command of the weapon.

- Firing.

- Correct behavior in the terrain, camouflage, digging in.

---

[116] "Unbewaffnete Truppe" literally means "unarmed troop". We assume this refers to soldiers who have yet to receive their weapons and could be, by extension, inexperienced and untrained. This passage might surprise the reader, as one would assume that experienced front line units were to be the first to receive the new weapon. However, one should consider that all infantry units were meant to standardize on the Sturmgewehr 44 as it should replace the Karabiner 98k in the German Army. This means that not only experienced frontline troops, but also new recruits could be equipped with the Sturmgewehr. Of course, the intention to phase out the Karabiner 98k completely was never realized. See also Supplement 9.

Anlage 2.

Waffentechnische Ausbildung am Sturmgewehr 44.[117]

1. Was muß jeder Schütze über das Sturmgewehr 44 wissen?

a) Vollautomatische Waffe.
b) Kurzpatrone 43 (Kaliber 7,9[118]), Wirkung bis 600 wie beim K. 98k.
c) **Vorteile:**

    (1) Hohe Feuergeschwindigkeit und Treffsicherheit im Einzelfeuer (22-28 Schuß in der Minute), bei Feuerstößen von 2-3 Schuß 40-50 Schuß in der Minute.
    (2) Geringes Gewicht: 4,65 kg.
    (3) Hohe Gefechtsbereitschaft.
    (4) Günstige Unterstützung der Waffe durch das Magazin.
    (5) Verringerung des Rückstoßes gegenüber dem K. 98k.
    (6) Kein Absetzen der Waffe notwendig.
    (7) Kein Durchladen und erneutes Kolbenhalsumfassen nach jedem Schuß.
    (8) Blick wird nicht durch Ladegriffe vom Ziel abgelenkt.
    (9) Schütze fällt nicht durch Ladebewegung auf.

2. Reihenfolge beim Auseinandernehmen des Sturmgewehrs 44:

a) Entladen.
b) Federbolzen[119] am Kolben bis zum Anschlag nach rechts ziehen.
c) Kolben nach hinten unter Abfangen der sich entspannenden Schließfeder[120] abziehen.
d) Schließfeder aus dem Gehäuse nehmen.

---

[117] Es sei angemerkt das unserer Meinung nach die folgenden Seiten das Auseinandernehmen des Sturmgewehrs teilweise nicht optimal beschreiben. So wird zum Beispiel unter 2. b) angemerkt, dass der Federbolzen am Kolben nach rechts zu ziehen ist. Bei der eigentlichen Benutzung wird dieser jedoch erst von links eingedrückt, und erst dann nach rechts gezogen. Dies sollte beim Lesen der folgenden Seiten berücksichtigt werden.
[118] Genau 7,92x33 mm im Gegensatz zur regulären Patrone des Karabiner 98k, MG 34 und MG 42 mit 7,92x57 mm.
[119] Hierbei handelt es sich um einen gefederten Bolzen, der das Bodenstück und dem Gehäuse zusammenhält. Siehe auch Ergänzung 10.
[120] Siehe Ergänzung 10.

DE-21

Technical[121] Weapons Training on the Sturmgewehr.[122]

1. What must every rifleman know about the Sturmgewehr 44?

a)   Fully automatic firearm.
b)   Kurzpatrone[123] 43 (caliber 7,9[124]), effect up to 600 [m] like the K. 98k.
c)   **Advantages:**
    (1)   High rate of fire and accuracy in semi-automatic fire (22-28 rounds per minute), with bursts of 2-3 rounds 40-50 rounds per minute.

    (2)   Low weight: 4.65 kg.
    (3)   High combat readiness.
    (4)   Favorable support of the weapon by the magazine.
    (5)   Reduction of recoil compared to the K. 98k.
    (6)   No need to put the weapon down.
    (7)   No reloading and re-gripping of the small of the stock after each shot.
    (8)   View is not distracted from the target by cycling the bolt.
    (9)   Rifleman does not attract attention by the cycling movement.

2. Order of disassembling the Sturmgewehr 44:

a)   Unload.
b)   Pull spring-loaded pin[125] on the butt to the right until the stop.
c)   Pull the butt backwards and intercept the releasing recoil spring[126].
d)   Remove the recoil spring from the housing.

---

[121] "Waffentechnisch" is an adjective and literally means "weapon technical", it is one of those words we have not found a proper one-to-one translation although it appears to be a rather "simple" word.

[122] This section contains, in our opinion, a description on the Sturmgewehr's disassembly that is sometimes not ideal, as the original document has its limitations. For example, taking point 2. b), the German manual indicates that the spring-loaded pin should be pulled to the right. Yet, during use, the most expedient method is to first push the pin from the left, and then pull it from the right. This should be kept in mind when reading through the following pages.

[123] "Kurzpatrone" means "short cartridge", but it is a technical designation.

[124] Exactly 7.92x33 mm in contrast the regular cartridge of the Karabiner 98k, MG 34 and MG 42 had 7.92x57 mm.

[125] This is a spring-loaded pin that holds the butt assembly and housing together. See also Supplement 10.

[126] See Supplement 10.

e) Schloßführung[127] am Griff nach hinten herausziehen und das lose Schloß auffangen.

f) Schlagbolzen[128] aus dem Schluß nehmen.

g) Auszieher, Ausziehfeder und Stift[129] ausbauen, dazu Stift mit Schlagbolzenspitze herausdrücken.

h) Handschutz nur bei stark verschmutzter Waffe mit Hilfe des Lösedorns nach unten abziehen, dazu abgesetztes Ende des Lösedorns in eines der vorderen Löcher des Handschutzes setzen; Dichtungsschraube ebenfalls mit dem Lösedorn herausschrauben.

Weiteres Auseinandernehmen der Waffe nur durch Waffenmeisterei.

3. Zum **Auseinandernehmen des Magazins** Blattfeder an der vorderen Seiten des Bodens abheben und Boden nach vorn abdrücken.

Feder mit Zubringer herausnehmen.

4. Zusammensetzen des Sturmgewehrs 44 erfolgt in umgekehrter Reihenfolge. Beim Einführen des Gaskolbens[130] mit Schloßführung und Schloß Waffe mit aufgeklapptem Griffstück nach oben, Mündung schräg abwärts halten, so daß der Schlagbolzen eingesetzt ist.

5. Füllen der Magazine beim Sturmgewehr 44:

a) Magazine vor dem Füllen auf Sauberkeit und Beschädigungen überprüfen. Magazinfüller auf die Führungsleiste des Magazins schieben.

b) Ladestreifen mit 5 Patronen in die Führungsnute des Magazinfüllers setzen.

c) Patronen mit dem Daumen der rechten Hand durch Druck gegen eine Tischplatte in das Magazin drücken.

Das Füllen ist auch einzeln von Hand möglich. Patronen müssen einwandfrei im Magazin lagern.

---

[127] Siehe Ergänzung 10.
[128] Siehe Ergänzung 10.
[129] Siehe Ergänzung 10.
[130] Siehe Ergänzung 10.

e) Pull the bolt carrier[131] by the handle on the rear and catch the loose bolt mechanism.
f) Remove the firing pin[132] from the bolt mechanism.
g) Remove extractor, extractor spring and pin[133] by pressing out the pin with the firing pin tip.
h) Remove the hand guard only when the weapon is very dirty with the help of the release pin; to do this, place the offset end of the release pin in one of the front holes of the hand guard; unscrew the gas plug also with the release pin.
Further disassembly of the weapon only by armory.

3. To **disassemble the magazine,** lift off the leaf spring at the front side of the bottom and push the bottom forward.

Remove spring with follower.

4. **Assembling** the Sturmgewehr 44 is done in reverse order. When inserting the gas piston[134] with bolt carrier and bolt mechanism [hold] weapon with the opened trigger group assembly upwards, hold the muzzle diagonally downwards, so that the firing pin is inserted.

5. **Filling the magazines of the Sturmgewehr 44:**

a) Check magazines for cleanliness and damage before filling. Push the magazine filler onto the guide rail of the magazine.
b) Place loading strip with 5 cartridges in the guide groove of the magazine filler.
c) Press cartridges into the magazine with the thumb of your right hand by pressing against a tabletop.
Loading is also possible individually by hand. Cartridges must be stored properly in the magazine.

---

[131] See Supplement 10.
[132] See Supplement 10.
[133] See Supplement 10.
[134] See Supplement 10.

Patronensäule mehrmals mit Daumen eindrücken, bis einwandfreies Gleiten der Patronen fühlbar.

d) Gefülltes Magazin bis zum hörbaren Einrasten einführen.

e) Staubschutzdeckel schließen.

6. Laden und Sichern des Sturmgewehrs 44:

a) Waffe mit der rechten Hand am Griffstück halten. Mündung schräg aufwärts.

b) Gefülltes Magazin mit linker Hand bis zum hörbaren Einrasten einführen.

c) Schloßführung am Griff in hinterste Stellung ziehen und vorschnellen lassen.

d) Staubschutzdeckel schließen.

e) **Sichern.**
   Dazu Hebel zur Sicherung mit rechtem Daumen nach **oben** stellen („S"[135] sichtbar). Zum Entsichern Hebel zur Sicherung nach **unten** stellen („F"[136] sichtbar).

f) **Das Sturmgewehr 44 ist stets als geladen zu betrachten, da man ihm äußerlich nicht ansieht, ob sich eine Patrone im Lauf befindet. Das Sturmgewehr 44 ist deshalb nur zum Schießen zu entsichern.**

7. Entladen:

a) Magazin der gesicherten Waffe durch Hineindrücken des Druckknopfes der Magazinsperre herausnehmen.

b) Patrone durch Ladebewegung entfernen, dabei die rechte Hand unter die Einführöffnung für das Magazin, den Daumen über die Auswurföffnung halten. Durch Blick in das Patronenlager feststellen, ob der Lauf frei ist.

---

[135] „S" für „sicher". In der D 1854/4: *Sturmgewehr 44. Gebrauchsanleitung.* ist nicht explizit definiert was „S" bedeutet, daher sinngemäße Interpretation laut Seite 10 der Gebrauchsanleitung.

[136] „F" für „Feuer", siehe vorherige Fußnote.

Press down the cartridges several times with your thumbs until you feel the cartridges glide smoothly.
d) Insert loaded magazine until audible click.
e) Close dust cover.

6. Loading and securing the Sturmgewehr 44:

a) Hold the weapon with your right hand on the trigger group assembly. Muzzle slanted upwards.
b) Insert loaded magazine with left hand until there is an audible click.
c) Pull the bolt carrier to its rearmost position and allow it to shoot forward.

d) Close dust cover.
e) **Secure.**
To do this, move the safety **upwards** with your right thumb ("S"[137] visible). To make ready, move the safety **down** ("F" [138] visible).
f) **The Sturmgewehr 44 has always to be considered loaded, since you cannot tell from the outside whether there is a cartridge in the chamber[139]. The Sturmgewehr 44 must therefore be made ready for firing.**

7. Unloading:

a) Remove the magazine of the secured weapon by pressing the button of the magazine lock.
b) Remove the chambered cartridge by using the loading movement while holding the right hand under the magazine well and the thumb over the ejection port. Check that the weapon is empty by looking into the chamber.

---

[137] "S" for "safe". In the D 1854/4: Sturmgewehr 44. Instruction Manual. is not explicitly defined what "S" means, therefore analogous interpretation based to entry on page 10 of the instruction manual.

[138] "F" for "fire", see previous footnote.

[139] "Lauf" literally means "barrel". This would be a confusing action for English native speakers – who are more used to checking the chamber rather than the barrel – to see if the weapon is loaded. That said, the weapon is always to be considered as loaded as indicated.

c) Staubschutzdeckel schließen.
d) Abziehen,
    Waffe ist entladen und entspannt!

8. Reinigen.

Zum Reinigen ist das Sturmgewehr auseinanderzunehmen (Nr. 2). Rückstände und Öl mit Lappen entfernen. Etwaige erhärtete Rückstände mit Holzspachtel beseitigen. Reinigen des Laufes mit dem Reinigungsgerät 34 (H.Dv. 256[140]).

Gaszylinder und Verbindungsstück mit der Reinigungsbürste für Gaszylinder, welche in der durch den Deckel verschließbaren Ausnehmung des Kolbens untergebracht ist, unter Zuhilfenahme der Reinigungskette säubern. Nach dem Reinigen Teil hauchartig einölen.

9. Zum Verhindern von **Hemmungen** ist das Sturmgewehr 44 folgendermaßen zu überprüfen:

a) Lauf und Patronenlager frei von Schmutz und Fremdkörpern?
b) Gaszylinder und Gehäuse nicht bestoßen oder verbeult?
c) Gaskolben mit Schloßführungsstück und Schloß müssen sich zwangslos im Gehäuse bzw. Gaszylinder vor- und zurückbewegen lassen. Frei von Pulverrückständen und Verkrustungen.
d) **Gaskolben hauchartig einölen** (Gaskolben sonst schwer gängig, Patronenboden wird nur angeschlagen).
e) Beim Vordrücken des Schlagbolzens im Schloß muß Schlagbolzenspitze genügend weit aus Stirnwand des Schlosses herausragen.
f) Auszieher unbeschädigt?
g) Auswerfer nicht beschädigt oder verbogen?

---

[140] Vollständiger Titel: *H.Dv. 256: Reinigungsgerät 34 und Reinigungsgerät 34 für Kal. 5,6. Beschreibung und Gebrauchsanleitung.* Berlin, Germany, 1936.

c) Close dust cover.
d) Pull the trigger,
   weapon is unloaded and uncocked!

8. Cleaning.

For cleaning, the assault rifle must be disassembled (No. 2). Remove residues and oil with rags. Remove any hardened residues with a wooden spatula. Clean the barrel with the Reinigungsgerät 34[141] (H.Dv. 256[142]).

Clean the gas tube and the gas block with the cleaning brush for gas tube, which is located in the recess that can be closed by a cover of the butt, with the aid of the cleaning chain. After cleaning, apply a thin layer of oil to the part.

9. To prevent **stoppages**[143], the Sturmgewehr 44 must be checked as follows:

a) Barrel and chamber free of dirt and foreign objects?
b) Gas tube and housing not bumped or dented?
c) Gas piston with bolt carrier piece and bolt mechanism must be able to move back and forth in the housing or gas tube without any resistance. Free from powder residues and encrustations.
d) **Oil gas piston lightly** (otherwise the gas piston operates sluggishly, and the cartridge head is only touched).
e) When pushing the firing pin forward into the bolt mechanism, the firing pin tip must protrude past the bolt face sufficiently
f) Extractor undamaged?
g) Ejector not damaged or bent?

---

[141] "Reinigungsgerät 34" means "cleaning device 34", it was a technical designation.

[142] Full title: *H.Dv. 256: Cleaning Device 34 and Cleaning Device 34 for Caliber 5,6. Description and Instruction Manual*. Berlin, Germany, 1936.

[143] There are various possible ways to translate "Hemmung" (singular) we looked at several, we chose stoppage since it seems the most fitting. Additionally, the *TM 30-506: German Military Dictionary* also used it.

Hemmungen (Merkmale, Ursache, Abhilfe).

	Merkmal		Ursache		Abhilfe
a)	Schuß geht nicht los	(1)	Gaskolben durch Verbrennungsrück- stände schwer gängig	(1)	Gaskolben reinigen, nur hauchartig einölen
		(2)	Patronenlager ver- schmutzt	(2)	Patronenlager und Schloß reinigen
		(3)	Verschluß nicht verriegelt		
b)	Patrone zwischen Schloß und Laufmundstück eingeklemmt		Klemmung im Magazin		Magazin ohne Anwendung von Öl reinigen, leichten Gang des Zubringers prüfen
c)	Patrone wird nicht zugeführt		Patronen verklemmt. Magazin verschmutzt oder verbeult, Lippen verbogen		Magazin entfernen, Schloßführung zurückziehen, neues Magazin einsetzen
d)	Hülse bleibt in Patronenlager stecken. Eine Patrone ist zwischen Lauf und Schloß eingeklemmt		Ausziehfeder lahm oder gebrochen, Ausziehkralle gebrochen		Neuen Auszieher oder Ausziehfeder einsetzen

Stoppages (Characteristics, Cause, Remedy).

Characteristics	Cause	Remedy
a) Shot does not go off	(1) Gas piston is sluggish due to fouling (2) Cartridge chamber dirty (3) Bolt[144] not locked	(1) Clean gas piston, oil only lightly (2) Clean cartridge chamber and bolt mechanism
b) Cartridge jammed between bolt mechanism and muzzle	Jamming in the magazine	Clean magazine without the use of oil, check smooth running of the follower
c) Cartridge is not fed	Cartridges jammed. Magazine dirty or dented, lips bent	Remove magazine, pull back bolt carrier, insert new magazine
d) Case remains stuck in cartridge chamber. A cartridge is jammed between chamber and bolt mechanism	Extractor spring lame or broken, extractor claw broken	Insert new extractor or extractor spring

---

[144] "Verschluß" can be translated in various ways like bolt, action, breech (mechanism).

	Merkmal	Ursache	Abhilfe
e)	Hülse wird nicht ausgeworfen (vom Verschluß gefangen). Eine scharfe Patrone ist zwischen Verschluß und Lauf eingeklemmt	Auswerfer gebrochen	Neuen[145] Auswerfer einsetzen
f)	Verschluß in vorderster Stellung, scharfe Patrone im Lauf. Beim Zurückziehen der Schloßführung wird eine scharfe Patrone ausgeworfen	Versager oder Schlagbolzenspitze gebrochen	Durchladen und Weiterschießen. Wenn Schlagbolzenspitze gebrochen, neuen Schlagbolzen einsetzen

---

[145] Korrektur: Originaltext war „NeuenAuswerfer einsetzen" ohne Leerzeichen.

Characteristics	Cause	Remedy
e) Case is not ejected (caught by the bolt). A live cartridge is jammed between bolt and chamber	Extractor broken	Insert new[146] extractor
f) Bolt in forward position, live cartridge in the chamber. When pulling back the bolt carrier, a live cartridge is ejected	Failure or firing pin tip broken	Load and continue firing. If firing pin tip is broken, insert new firing pin

---

[146] Correction: The original text was "NeuenAuswerfer einsetzen" without space.

Übungsbeispiel 1.

Vernichtung einer vorgeschobene Sicherung.

Übungszweck	Feind	Gruppen
Annäherung im Wald	Einzelne Artillerie-Einschläge	haben mit einer Sturmgruppe rechts und einer links den Wald erreicht (Bild 2). Zugführer erkennt auf Höhe 34 ein fdl. le.M.G. und mehrere Schützen.
Vernichtung einer vorgeschobenen Sicherung des Feindes		erhalten Kampfauftrag vom Zugführer (siehe Nr. 25).
Für den Feind: Verhalten als Horchposten	Einzelne Gewehrschüsse aus Richtung Höhe 34, M.G.-Feuer Einzelne Schützen bewegen sich in Gegend Jägerhaus	Feuergruppe geht am Wald links des Weges in Stellung. Feuergruppe schießt Feuerstöße auf erkannten Feind. Sturmgruppen erreichen in großen Abständen im Vortröpfeln die Kusseln ostwärts Höhe 34. Einzelne Schützen der Sturmgruppe sichern gegen Jägerhaus und nach rechts. Feuerüberfall[147] des Granattrupps auf fdl. M.G. auf Höhe 34.
	Einzelne Gewehrschüsse aus Richtung Jägerhaus	Masse der Sturmgruppen stürmt die Höhe 34 und überfällt fdl. M.G. von hinten – vernichtet Feind – besetzt Höhe 34 – Feuergruppe erreicht auf kürzestem Wege die Höhe 34. **Andere Möglichkeit:** Im Morgengrauen oder beim Abenddämmerung ohne „Hurra" einbrechen.

[Anmerkung: Im Original war dies eine ausfaltbare Doppelseite. Ein Drittel des obrigen Textes befand sich dabei, mit einer Karte (Bild 2), auf der zweiten Seite. Hier wurde der gesamte Text auf eine Seite abgedruckt und die Karte befindet sich auf der nächsten Seite.]

---

[147] Siehe Glossar: Feuerüberfall.

Training Example 1.

Annihilation of forward security.

Training Purpose	Enemy	Squads
Approach in the forest	Individual artillery impacts	have reached the forest with one assault squad on the right and one of the left (Figure 2). Platoon leader recognizes on height 34 an enemy light MG and several riflemen.
Annihilation of a forward security of the enemy		receive combat mission from platoon leader (see no. 25).
For the enemy: Behavior as listening post	Individual rifle shots from height 34, MG fire Individual riflemen	Fire squad takes position at the forest left of the path. Fire squad fires bursts at the recognized enemy.
	moving in the area of hunter's house	Assault squads reach with large spaces by infiltrating[148] the withered trees eastward of height 34. Individual riflemen of the assault squad secure against the hunter's house and to the right. Surprise fire of the rifle-grenade section against enemy MG on height 34.
	Individual rifle shots from direction hunter's house	Mass of the assault squads assaults the height 34 and attacks enemy MG from behind – annihilates enemy – occupies height 34 – fire squad reaches on the shortest way the height 34. **Another possibility:** Break-in[149] at dawn or dusk without "hurray".

[Note: In the original, this was a fold-out double page. A third of the above text was on the second page, where the corresponding map (Figure 2) was also printed. Here the whole text was printed on a single page and the map can be found on the next page.]

---

[148] "Vortröpfeln" literally means "dripping forward". It means that movement should happen in pairs or alone. See Glossary: Infiltrating (Vortröpfeln).

[149] There is no English equivalent for the military term "Einbruch". See Glossary: Break-In (Einbruch).

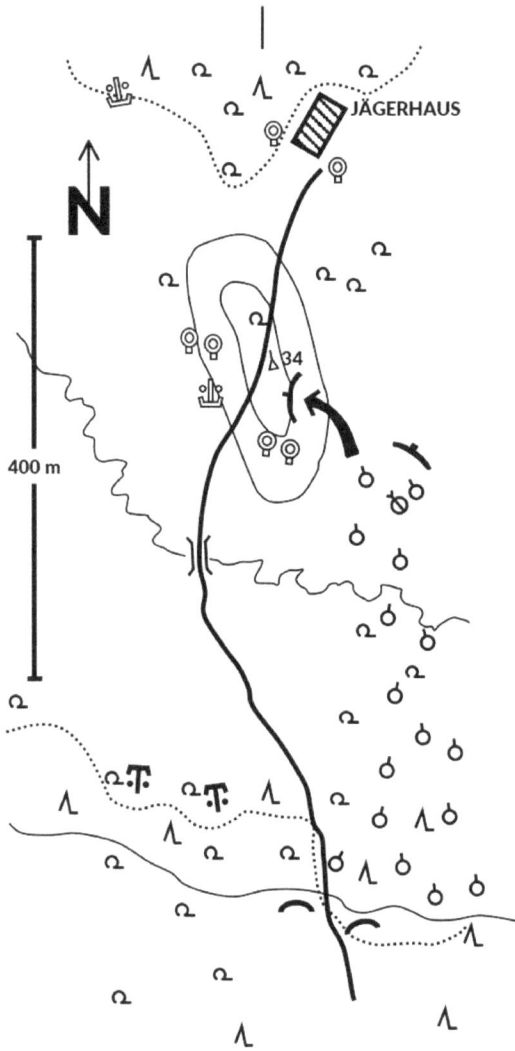

JÄGERHAUS

N

400 m

△34

Bild 2.

[Anmerkung: Diese Karte war ursprünglich auf einer ausfaltbaren Doppelseite der vorherigen Seite.]

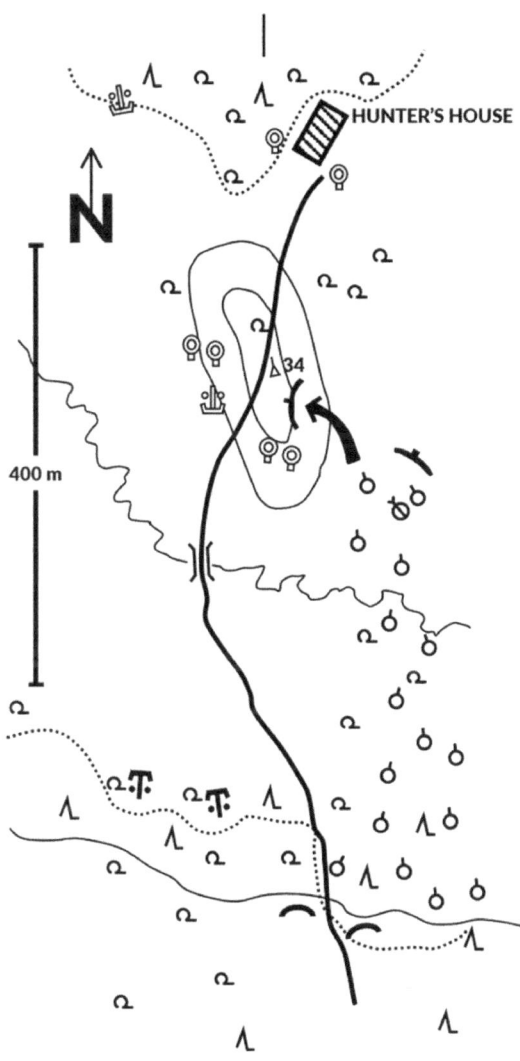

HUNTER'S HOUSE

N

400 m

34

Figure 2.

[Note: This map was originally a fold-out page on the previous page.]

Übungsbeispiel 2.

Wegnahme eines Stützpunktes.

Übungszweck	Feind	Gruppen	Eigene schwere Waffen
Gedeckte Annäherung an den Feind		erreichen mit großen Abständen und Zwischenräumen den Feldweg (Bild 3).	überwachen 300 m westl. Höhe 72 das Vorgehen mit 1 s.M.G.-Gruppe
Annäherung bis zur Sturmausgangsstellung	Posten beobachtet Artillerie-Störungsfeuer	Feuergruppe und Sturmgruppen sickern paarweise bis zur Höhe 200 m südlich Höhe 64 vor, erhalten Kampfauftrag vom Zugführer (siehe Nr. 25). Granattrupp eröffnet Feuer.	Einzelne Einschläge in Nähe A.-Dorf.
Einbruch in fdl. Stellung und Wegnahme eines Stützpunktes	Gewehr- und M.G.-Feuer von Höhe 64 Einzelne Gewehrschüsse aus Buschgruppe nordostwärts Höhe 64	Feuergruppe eröffnet das Feuer und schießt in Richtung Höhe 64. Sturmgruppen springen auf und erreichen in langem Sprung die Höhe 64 und brechen in der Bewegung schießend ein. Einbruch u. Handgranatenkampf. Ordnen sich und rollen Graben nach links und rechts auf – vernichten Gegner in Unterschlupfen.	Schießen auf Ortsausgang A.-Dorf.
Abwehr eines Gegenstoßes	Tritt aus Richtung A.-Dorf zum Gegenstoß an Schwaches M.G.-Feuer vom Nordausgang des Dorfes	Nachschwingen der Feuergruppe auf kürzestem Wege. Sturmgruppen gehen sofort in Stellung und vernichten Gegner durch Feuerstöße und Handgranaten. Verstärkung der Sturmgruppen durch die Feuergruppe.	Feuerzusammenfassung auf A.-Dorf.

[Anmerkung: Dies war eine Doppelseite, die ausfaltbar war, wie bei Übungsbeispiel 1.]

Training Example 2.

Taking a Strong Point[150].

Training Purpose	Enemy	Squads	Friendly[151] Heavy Weapons
Covered approach to the enemy		reach the field path with large spaces and distances between them (Figure 3).	monitor 300 m west of height 72 the advance with 1 heavy MG squad
Approach until assault jump-off position	Post observed Artillery harassment fire	fire squad and assault squads infiltrate in pairs up to height 200 m south of height 64, receive combat mission from platoon leader (see No. 25). Rifle-grenade section opens fire.	Individual impacts near village A.
Break-in into enemy position and taking a strong point	Rifle and MG fire from height 64 Individual rifle shots from bush group northeast height 64	fire squad opens fire and fires in the direction of height 64. Assault squads rush forward and reach height 64 in a long bounding move, breaking-in, firing while moving. Break-in and hand grenade combat. Form up and clear out trenches left and right – annihilate enemy in shelters.	Firing at village exit village A.
Defense of a hasty counterattack	Comes from direction Village A for a hasty counterattack Weak MG fire from the village's north exit.	follow up[152] of the fire squad on the shortest way. Assault squads immediately take position and annihilate enemies with burst fire and hand grenades. Reinforcement of the assault squads by the fire squad.	Fire concentration on Village A.

[Note: This map was a fold-out double page, similar to Training example 1.]

[150] "Stützpunkt" is a generic term (like bases, camps, etc.) and "strong point" is the most literal. A fitting descriptive term is "organized tactical locality", see TM 30-506, p. 182.

[151] The literal translation of "eigene" would be "own".

[152] The verb "nachschwingen" was used as a noun (Nominative) and was thus capitalized.

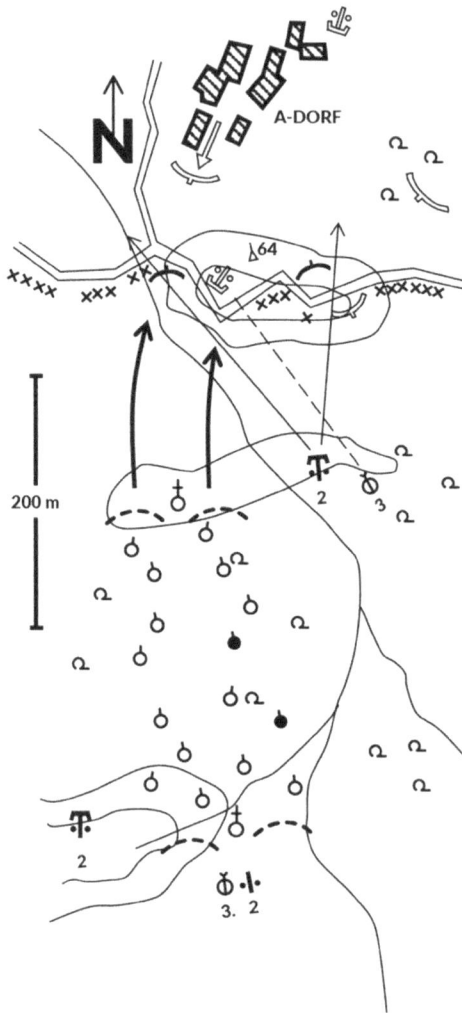

Bild 3.

[Anmerkungen: Der Eintrag „3." ist wohl falsch und sollte „3" bedeuten, also 3 Granatschützen. Die Zahl gibt die Anzahl der Waffen bzw. des Truppentyps an. Ebenso müsste bei den Symbolen des Zugführers der Kreis schwarz gefüllt sein.]

[Anmerkung: Diese Karte war ursprünglich auf einer ausfaltbaren Doppelseite der vorherigen Seite.]

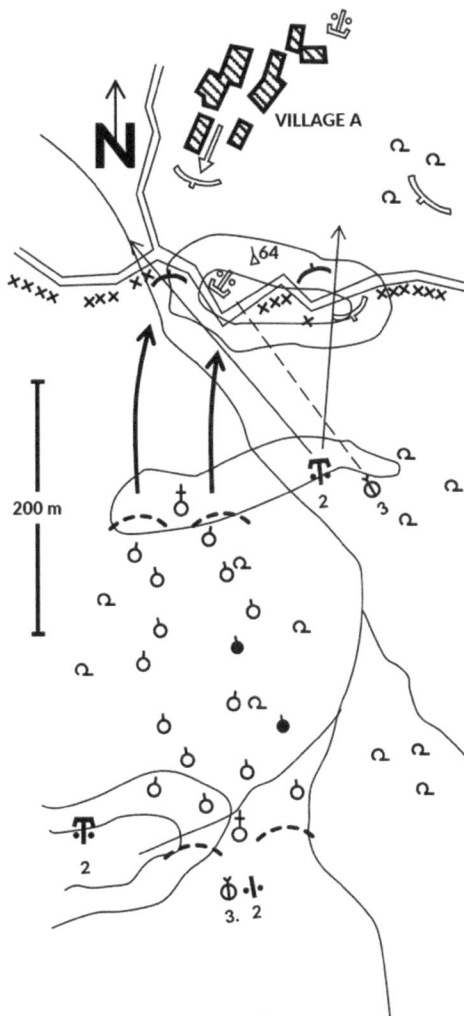

Figure 3.

[Notes: The entry "3." is likely wrong and should mean "3", hence 3 rifle-grenade riflemen. The number indicates die number of weapons respectively the troop type. Likewise, the symbols of the platoon leader the circle should have been filled in black.]

[Note: This map was originally a fold-out page on the previous page.]

Übungsbeispiel 3.

Gegenstoß einer Gruppe.

Feind	Aufgabe der Gruppe	Ausführung
greift an und bricht in Zug-stärke ein (Bild 4)	Gegenstoß aus eigenem Ent-schluß des Gruppenführers	Sturmgruppe als Stoßreserve im Unterstand besetzt sofort Annäherungsgraben und zwingt Gegner durch Feuer in den Graben. Geschlossener Gegenstoß zum vorderen Graben und Aufrollen des Grabens mit Handgranaten – Verbindungsaufnahme mit den übriggebliebenen Teilen des Zuges – besetzt wiedergewonnene Stellung[.]
greift in Blt.-Stärke [sic!][153] an und bricht in Komp.-Stärke ein (Bild 5)	Abriegeln des eingebrochenen Feindes	Schnelles Besetzen der vorbereiteten Stellung im Verbindungsgraben, Abriegeln des Grabens durch vorhandene spanische Reiter[154]; Sicherung der Sperre durch zwei Sturmgewehre. Rundumverteidigung der noch vorhandenen Schützen im vordersten Graben. Zurückwerfen des eingedrungenen Feindes aus dem 2. Graben durch Flankenstoß der Gruppe. Nahkampf mit Handgranaten, Pistolen, notfalls Einsatz der Panzerfaust. Besetzen von Wechselstellungen aller Schützen während des Feuerkampfes. Einsatz von Versprengten aus der vorderen Linie durch Gruppenführer. Munitionsergänzung. Abschieben von Verwundeten.

[Anmerkung: Dies war eine Doppelseite, die ausfaltbar war, wie bei Übungsbeispiel 1.]

[153] Die Abkürzung für „Bataillon" ist „Btl." nicht „Blt.".
[154] „Spanische Reiter" sind tragbare Konstruktionen aus spitzen Pfählen die einst der Abwehr von Reitern dienten.

Training Example 3.

Hasty Counterattack[155] of a Squad.

Enemy	Task of the Squad	Execution
attacks and breaks-in with platoon strength (Figure 4)	Hasty counterattack on initiative of the squad leader	Assault squad as reserve in the shelter immediately occupies the approach trench and forces enemies by fire into the trench. Hasty counterattack of the whole squad to the front trench and roll up the trench with hand grenades - Establishing contact with the remaining parts of the platoon - occupies regained position[.]
attacks in battalion strength and breaks-in with company strength (Figure 5)	Sealing off the broken-in enemy	Quick occupation of the prepared position in the fire trench[156], Sealing off the trench by available cheval-de-frise[157], securing the barrier with two assault rifles. All-round defense of the remaining riflemen in the front trench. Throwing back the infiltrated enemy from the 2nd trench by a flanking thrust of the squad. Close combat with hand grenades, pistols, and if necessary, use of the Panzerfaust. Occupying alternate positions for all riflemen during the firefight. Employment of stragglers from the front line by the squad leader. Ammunition replenishment. Evacuating of wounded.

[Note: This map was a fold-out double page, similar to Training example 1.]

[155] Hasty counterattack ("Gegenstoß") is different from a counterattack ("Gegenangriff").
[156] Note "Verbindungsgraben" literally means "connection trench". See Glossary.
[157] "Cheval-de-frise" are portable frames of spikes, initially developed to deter cavalry.

Bild 4.

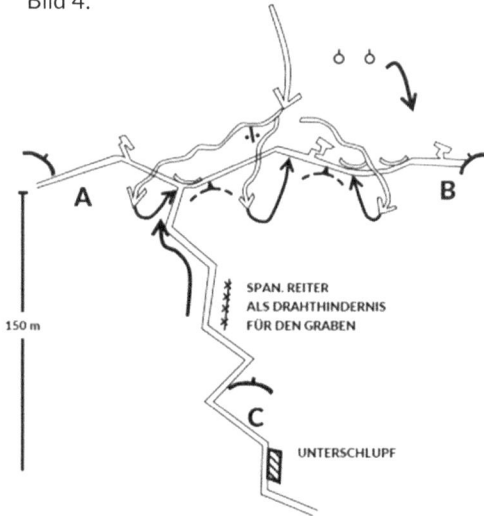

SPAN. REITER
ALS DRAHTHINDERNIS
FÜR DEN GRABEN

150 m

A

B

C

UNTERSCHLUPF

(Bild 5. [sic!]

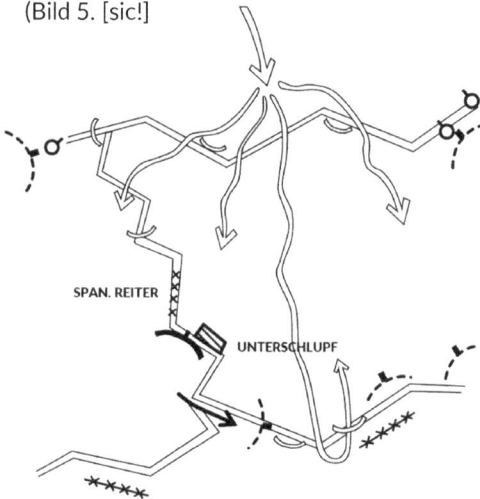

SPAN. REITER

UNTERSCHLUPF

[Anmerkung: Im Original wurden die Bildbeschriftungen zu Bild 4. und 5. wie hier dargestellt nach links oben versetzt und nicht wie bisher unten zentriert dargestellt.]

[Anmerkung: Diesen Karte waren ursprünglich auf einer ausfaltbaren Doppelseite der vorherigen Seite.]

Figure 4.

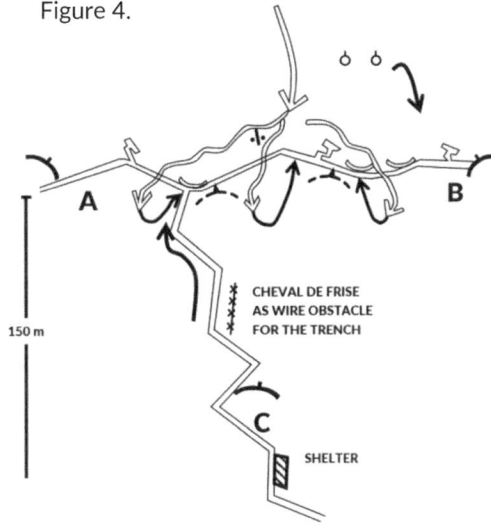

150 m

A

B

CHEVAL DE FRISE
AS WIRE OBSTACLE
FOR THE TRENCH

C

SHELTER

(Figure 5. [sic!]

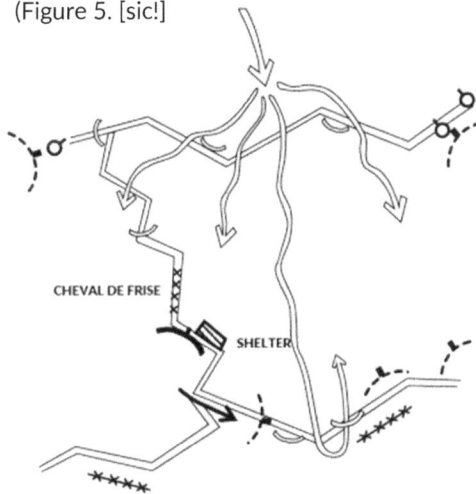

CHEVAL DE FRISE

SHELTER

[Note: In the original, the captions of Figure 4. and 5. were off-set like shown here to the top left and not positioned below the figures like in previous examples.]

[Note: This map was originally a fold-out page on the previous page.]

Der Zug in geschlossener[158] Ordnung[.][159]

Der Zug in „Linie"[160]

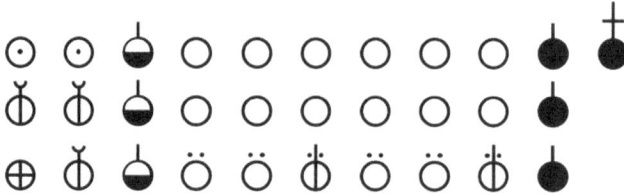

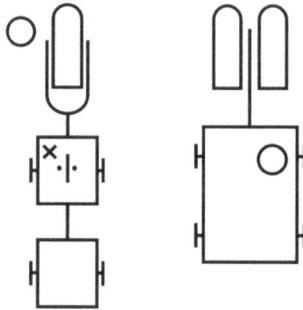

*)[161] 1 le.M.G. als Gerätreserve

Bild 6.

---

[158] Die Überschrift im Inhaltsverzeichnis gab „geschlossenen" statt, wie hier vermerkt, „geschlossener" an.

[159] Dieser Text war in Hand geschrieben, alle Buchstaben waren großgeschrieben und unterstrichen bzw. es war eine Trennlinie darunter, ebenso fehlte der Punkt am Ende. Wir haben den Text der üblichen Formatierung angepasst.

[160] Dieser Text war ebenso mit der Hand geschrieben und alle Buchstaben waren großgeschrieben, Formatierung wie im Original, allerdings wurde auf die Großschreibung verzichtet.

[161] Der „*" verweist auf das „x" in der Grafik, da sich neben dem „x" ein leichtes Maschinengewehr Symbol befindet.

The Platoon in Close[162] Order[.][163]

The Platoon in "Line"[164]

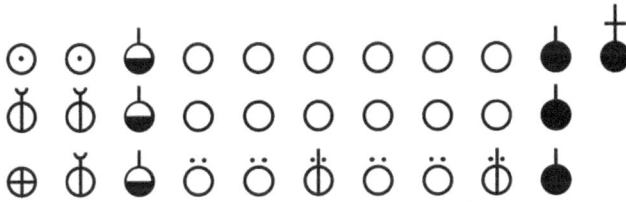

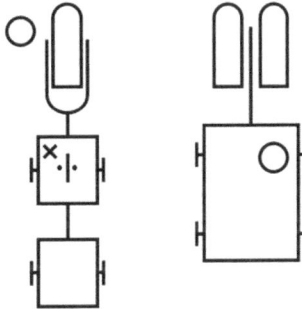

*)[165] 1 LMG as reserve equipment

Figure 6.

---

[162] The heading in the table of contents was "geschlossenen" instead of, as noted here, "geschlossener".

[163] This text was written by hand, all letters were capitalized and underlined or there was a dividing live underneath, also the period at end was missing. We have adapted the text to the usual formatting.

[164] This text was also written by hand and all letters were capitalized, formatting like the original, but without capitalization.

[165] The "*" refers to the "x" in the graphic, because next to the "x" there is a light machine gun symbol.

Der Zug in „Marschordnung"[166]

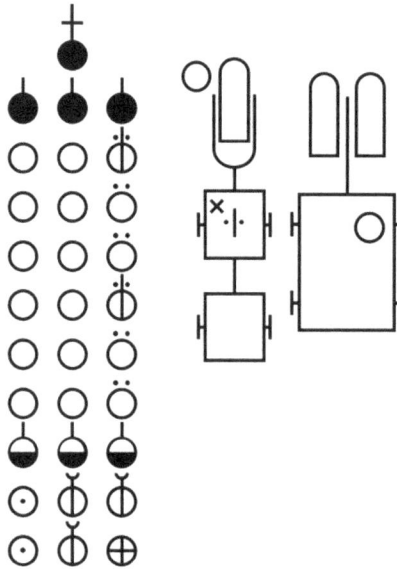

*)[167] 1 le.M.G. als Gerätreserve

Bild 7.

---

[166] Dieser Text war mit der Hand geschrieben und alle Buchstaben waren großgeschrieben, Formatierung wie im Original, allerdings wurde auf die Großschreibung verzichtet.
[167] Der „*" verweist auf das „x" in der Grafik, da neben dem „x" sich ein leichtes Maschinengewehr Symbol befindet.

The Platoon in "March Formation"[168]

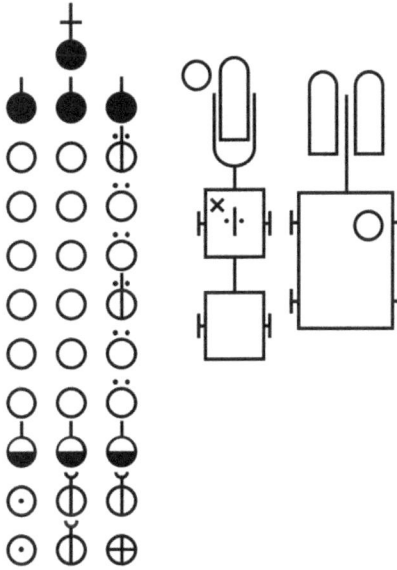

*)[169] 1 LMG as reserve equipment

Figure 7.

---

[168] This text was written by hand and all letters were capitalized, formatted like the original, but without capitalization.
[169] The "*" refers to the "x" in the graphic, because next to the "x" there is a light machine gun symbol.

EN-34

Ergänzung 1: Merkblatt 25a/16: Vorläufiges Merkblatt „Der M.P.-Zug der Grenadier-Kompanie" vom 1. 2. 1944

Supplement 1: Pamphlet 25a/16: Preliminary Pamphlet "The SMG-Platoon of the Grenadier-Company" from 1. 2. 1944[170]

Vorläufiges

Merkblatt

„Der M.P.[171]-Zug

der Grenadier-Kompanie"[172]

vom 1. 2. 1944

---

[171] M.P. bedeutet Maschinenpistole. Technisch gesehen handelte es sich aber nicht um eine Maschinenpistole, allerdings wurde die Bezeichnung Maschinenkarabiner aufgehoben und die Bezeichnung Sturmgewehr kam erst Ende 1944 auf. Bezüglich der Namensgebung und generellen Entwicklung siehe Ergänzung 9.

[172] Hierbei und den folgenden Seiten bis zur Ergänzung 2 handelt es sich um die Transkription des Dokumentes BArch, RH 11-I/83: *Merkblatt 25a/16: Vorläufiges Merkblatt „Der M.P.-Zug der Grenadier-Kompanie", 1.2.1944.*

Preliminary

Pamphlet

"The SMG[173]-Platoon

of the Grenadier-Company"[174]

from 1. 2. 1944[175]

---

[173] SMG means submachine gun. Technically, this was not a submachine gun, but the designation machine carbine was abolished, and the designation assault rifle was only introduced at the end of 1944. Regarding the naming and general development see Supplement 9.

[174] This and the following pages up to Supplement 2 are the transcription of the document: BArch, RH 11-I/83: *Merkblatt 25a/16: Vorläufiges Merkblatt "Der M.P.-Zug der Grenadier-Kompanie"*, 1.2.1944.

[175] Date format: Day. Month. Year.

[Leere Seite wie im Original Merkblatt.]

[Intentionally left blank like in the original pamphlet.]

Oberkommando des Heeres
Gen.d.Inf.b. Chef Gen.St.d.H.[177]
II – Nr. 150/44

H.Qu. O.K.H.[176],
den 1. 2. 1944.

Das vorläufige Merkblatt „Der M.P.[178]-Zug der Grenadier-Kompanie" soll als Anhalt für die Durchführung der zur Zeit laufenden Truppenversuche mit der M.P. 43/1[179] dienen.

Hierzu ist die Gliederung eines einheitlich mit M.P. 43/1 bewaffneten Zuges o h n e le.M.G. zugrunde gelegt worden.

Erfahrungen über den Einsatz von M.P.-Einheiten und Vorschläge für eine Neufassung des Merkblattes sind baldmöglichst einzureichen.

Im Auftrage

J a s c h k e[180]

---

[176] Hauptquartier, Oberkommando des Heeres.

[177] General der Infanterie beim Chef Generalstab des Heeres.

[178] M.P. bedeutet Maschinenpistole. Technisch gesehen handelte es sich aber nicht um eine Maschinenpistole, allerdings wurde die Bezeichnung Maschinenkarabiner aufgehoben und die Bezeichnung Sturmgewehr kam erst Ende 1944 auf. Bezüglich der Namensgebung und generellen Entwicklung siehe Ergänzung 9.

[179] Siehe Ergänzung 9 bezüglich der verschiedenen Namen.

[180] Erich Jaschke, ab 1. Mai 1943 Rang General der Infanterie, ab 16. Oktober 1943 Dienststellung General der Infanterie beim Oberbefehlshaber des Heeres. Siehe Glossar: General der Infanterie. Literatur: Keilig, Wolf: *Das Deutsche Heer 1939–1945. Gliederung – Einsatz – Stellenbesetzung.* Verlag Hans-Henning Podzun: Bad Nauheim, 1956ff, 211 - 152-.

The preliminary pamphlet "The SMG[184]-Platoon of the Grenadier-Company" is intended to serve as a guide for the conduct of the troop trials currently underway with the MP 43/1[185].

This is based on the organization of a platoon uniformly armed with MP 43/1 w i t h o u t light MG.

Experience with the use of SMG-units and proposals for a new version of the pamphlet should be submitted as soon as possible.

On behalf

J a s c h k e[186]

---

[181] Headquarters, Army High Command.

[182] General of the Infantry at the Chief of the General Staff of the Army.

[183] Date format: Day. Month. Year.

[184] SMG means submachine gun. Technically, this was not a submachine gun, but the designation machine carbine was abolished, and the designation assault rifle was only introduced at the end of 1944. Regarding the naming and general development see Supplement 9.

[185] See Supplement 9 about the different names.

[186] Erich Jaschke, since 1st May 1943 rank General of the Infantry, since 16th October 1943 in the administrative position General of the Infantry at the Commander-in-Chief of the Army. See Glossary: General of the Infantry (General der Infanterie). Source: Keilig, Wolf: *Das Deutsche Heer 1939–1945. Gliederung – Einsatz – Stellenbesetzung.* Verlag Hans-Henning Podzun: Bad Nauheim, 1956ff, 211 -152-.

Inhaltsverzeichnis

Table of Contents

I. Die Waffe

1.[187] Die M.P. 43/1[188] ist **eine vollautomatische Waffe**. Beschreibung, Behandlung und Bedienung enthält die D 1854/2[189].

2. Der **Wert** der Waffe liegt in der hohen Feuergeschwindigkeit und Treffsicherheit im **Einzelfeuer** (22-28 Schuß in der Minute) sowie in der Möglichkeit der Feuersteigerung zu **Feuerstößen von 2 bis 3 Schuß** (40-50 Schuß in der Minute).

3. **Vorzüge der Waffe:**

a)   Geringes Gewicht: 4,65 kg
b)   Hohe Gefechtsbereitschaft
c)   Günstige Unterstützung der Waffe durch das Magazin
d)   Verringerung des Rückstoßes gegenüber dem des Gewehres bei gleichbleibender Schußleistung
e)   Kein Absetzen der Waffe, kein Durchladen und erneutes Koblenhalsumfassen nach jedem Schuß. Daher:
    - Gute und schnelle Ausnützung günstiger Augenblicke

5

---

[187] Anders als sonst üblich sind in diesem Dokument die Nummern nicht fett gedruckt wie sonst bei Merkblättern und Heeresdruckvorschriften üblich.
[188] Siehe Ergänzung 9.
[189] D 1854/2: *Maschinenpistole 43/1. Beschreibung, Handhabung und Behandlung*, Berlin, Germany, 31. August 1943.

I. The Weapon

1.[190] The MP 43/1[191] is **a fully automatic weapon.** Description, handling and operation are included in D 1854/2[192].

2. The **value** of the weapon lies in its high rate of fire and accuracy in **semi-automatic fire** (22-28 rounds per minute) as well as in the possibility of increasing the fire rate to **bursts of 2 to 3 rounds** (40-50 rounds per minute).

3. **Advantages of the weapon:**

a) Low weight: 4.65 kg
b) High combat readiness
c) Favorable support of the weapon by the magazine
d) Reduction of recoil compared to the rifle while maintaining firing performance
e) No need to put the weapon down, no reloading and re-gripping of the small of the stock after each shot. As a result:
- Good and fast exploitation of favorable moments

5

---

[190] In contrast to usual practice, the numbers in this document are not printed in bold as is usual for pamphlets and army regulations.
[191] See Supplement 9.
[192] D 1854/2: *Maschinenpistole 43/1. Description, Handling and Treatment*, Berlin, Germany, 31. August 1943.

- Blick wird nicht durch Ladegriffe vom Ziel abgelenkt
- Schütze fällt nicht durch Ladebewegung auf
- Vereinfachung der Schießausbildung

f) Einheitliche Bewaffnung der ganzen Gruppe wird ermöglicht, dadurch Vereinfachung der Ausbildung und Führung.

4. **Funktionsstörungen** sind selten. Soweit sie auftreten, sind sie durch wenige Griffe in kurzer Zeit zu beseitigen. Einzelteile, wie Auszieher und Schlagbolzen, können schnell ausgewechselt werden (siehe D 1854/2[193]).

5. Die **Wirkung** der Pistolenmunition 43 (Kaliber 7,9) entspricht bis zu **600 m** der des Gewehrs. Der Stahlhelm wird auf diese Entfernung durchschlagen. Die Durchschlagswirkung reicht aus, lebende Ziele bis **1000 m** zu vernichten. Die Patrone wiegt 17 g.

6. Die **erste Munitionsausstattung**[194] beträgt je M.P. 720 Schuß. Beim Mann befinden sich 6 Magazine mit insgesamt 180 Schuß (je Magazin 30 Schuß).

7. Die **Weiterentwicklung** sieht die Verwendung der M.P. 43/1 auch mit Gewehrgranatgerät[195] und Zielfernrohr vierfach vor. Bis zur Zuführung dieser Waffen verbleiben in den M.P.-Gruppen die Karabiner mit Zielfernrohr und Gewehrgranatgerät (siehe „Gliederung der M.P.-Gruppe").

6

---

[193] D 1854/2: *Maschinenpistole 43/1. Beschreibung, Handhabung und Behandlung*, Berlin, Germany, 31. August 1943.
[194] Die erste Munitionsausstattung war jene Menge an Munition, die die kämpfende Truppe in ihren eigenen Gefechts- und Nachschubfahrzeugen mitführen konnte. Siehe: Donat, Gerhard: *Beispiele für den Munitionsverbrauch der deutschen Wehrmacht im zweiten Weltkrieg*. In: Allgemeine schweizerische Militärzeitschrift, Band 129, Jahr 1963, Heft 2, S. 76. (Online Version)
[195] Siehe Glossar: Gewehrgranatgerät.

- View is not distracted from the target by cycling the bolt
- Rifleman does not attract attention by cycling movement
- Simplification of the firing training

f) A uniform armament of the whole squad is made possible, thus simplifying training and leadership.

4. **Malfunctions** are rare. If they occur, they can be eliminated in a short time with just a few movements. Individual parts, such as extractor and firing pin, can be replaced quickly (see D 1854/2[196]).

5. The **effect** of the Pistolenmunition[197] 43 (caliber 7.9) is equivalent to that of the rifle up to **600 m**. The German steel helmet will be penetrated at this distance. The penetrating effect is sufficient to annihilate living targets up to **1000 m**. The cartridge weighs **17 g**.

6. The **first ammunition complement**[198] is 720 rounds for each SMG. Each man has 6 magazines with a total of 180 rounds (30 round per magazine).

7. **Future development** also foresees the use of the MP 43/1 with rifle-grenade[199] launcher[200] and a four-power rifle scope. Until these weapons are provided, the carbines with rifle scope and rifle-grenade launchers remain in the SMG-squads (see "organization of the SMG-squad").

6

---

[196] D 1854/2: *Maschinenpistole 43/1. Description, Handling and Treatment*, Berlin, Germany, 31. August 1943.

[197] Note "Pistolenmunition" literally means "pistol ammunition", yet in this case it is a technical designation.

[198] The first ammunition complement was the amount of ammunition that the fighting troops could carry in their own combat supply and supply vehicles. See: Donat, Gerhard: *Beispiele für den Munitionsverbrauch der deutschen Wehrmacht im zweiten Weltkrieg.* In: Allgemeine schweizerische Militärzeitschrift, Band 129, Jahr 1963, Heft 2, S. 76. (Online Version)

[199] See Glossary: Rifle-Grenade Launcher (Gewehrgranatgerät).

[200] The literal translation of "Gewehrgranatgerät" is "rifle-grenade device".

II. Die Gliederung des Zuges und der Gruppe

1. Der **M.P.-Zug** besteht aus:

    dem Zugtrupp

        mit dem Zugführer

        zwei Meldern

        einem Krankenträger

    drei Gruppen (1 : 8)

    den Gefechtsfahrzeugen[201]

        mit **2 Infanteriekarren** (gekoppelt), gezogen von

        einem Pferd, dazu ein Pferdeführer

        einem Panjewagen mit einem angehängten Infanteriekarren, gezogen von zwei Pferden, dazu ein Pferdeführer.

2. Die **M.P.-Gruppe** besteht aus dem Gruppenführer und 8 Mann.

Einteilung	Ausrüstung	Aufgaben	Munition
Gruppen-führer	M.P. mit 6 Magazinen, Doppelfernrohr, Drahtschere, Signalpfeife	Führer u. Vorkämpfer der Gruppe. Verantwortlich für a) Durchführung des Kampf-auftrages,	180 sS[202] kurz

7

---

[201] Hierbei handelt es sich um Fahrzeuge, die alles mitführen was die Truppe am Gefechtsfeld braucht, es handelt sich um Transport- nicht um Kampffahrzeuge. Siehe Glossar: Gefechtsfahrzeug.

[202] „sS" steht für „schweres Spitzgeschoß". Siehe Glossar: sS Munition.

II. The Organization of the Platoon and the Squad

1. The **SMG-Platoon** consists of:

the **platoon headquarters**

with the platoon leader

two messengers

one stretcher-bearer

three squads (1 : 8)

the **combat supply**[203] **vehicles**[204]

with **2 infantry carriages** (coupled), drawn by

one horse, with a horse handler

one panje carriage with an attached infantry carriage, pulled by two horses, plus a horse handler.

2. The **SMG-Squad** consists of squad leader and 8 men.

Classification	Equipment	Tasks	Ammunition
Squad leader	SMG with 6 magazines, binoculars, wire cutters, signal whistle	Leader and primary fighter[205] of the squad. Responsible for a) Execution of the combat mission,	180 sS[206] kurz

7

[203] Note that "Gefechtsfahrzeug" literally means "combat vehicle", this naming might seem counter-intuitive at first. See next footnote or Glossary for clarification.

[204] These are vehicles that carry everything the troops need in the combat zone, they are transport vehicles, not combat vehicles.

[205] Note that "Vorkämpfer" has various translations like "protagonist" or "pioneer", although literally it means "first/primary fighter", the "vor" referring to being before others.

[206] "sS" means "schweres Spitzgeschoß" which literally means "heavy pointed bullet". See Glossary: sS Ammunition (sS Munition).

Einteilung	Ausrüstung	Aufgaben	Munition
		b) Leitung des Feuers, Überwachung des Mun.-Verbrauchs, c) Einsatz des Gewehrgranat- und des Zielfernrohr-schützen sowie der Panzernah-bekämpfungsmittel, d) Kriegsbrauchbarkeit und Vollzähligkeit von Waffen, Munition und Gerät	
Schütze 1	Gewehr, Gewehrgranatgerät, Spaten	a) Beteiligt sich als Gewehrschütze am Feuerkampf der Gruppe, b) Bekämpft Ziele, die nicht mit der M.P. gefaßt werden können, mit der Gewehrsprenggranate und Panzer mit Gewehrpanzer-granate	Gewehr-munition, Kartuschen[207], Gewehrspreng- und gr. Gewehr-panzergranaten

8

---

[207] Siehe Glossar: Kartusche.

Classification	Equipment	Tasks		Ammunition
		b)	Direction of fire, monitoring of ammunition consumption,	
		c)	Employment of the rifle-grenade rifleman and the sniper as well as the close combat anti-tank weapons.	
		d)	War usability and completeness of weapons, ammunition and equipment	
Rifleman 1	rifle, rifle-grenade launcher, spade	a)	Participates as a regular rifleman[208] in the firefight of the squad	Rifle ammunition, rifle-grenade cartridge[211], Gewehr-spreng- and gr. Gewehr-panzer-granaten[212]
		b)	Engages targets that cannot be engaged by the SMG with the Gewehrspreng-granate[209] and tanks with the Gewehrpanzer-granaten[210]	

8

---

[208] Note that "Schütze" is generally translated with "rifleman", yet since "Gewehr" means "rifle" this would mean "Gewehrschütze" is "rifle rifleman", hence "regular rifleman".

[209] Technical designation, literally translated it means explosive rifle-grenade.

[210] Technical designation, literally translated it means tank rifle-grenade, so an anti-tank rifle-grenade.

[211] See Glossary: Rifle-Grenade Cartridge (Kartusche).

[212] Technical designation, literally translated it means large tank rifle-grenade, there was a regular and larger version of the anti-tank rifle-grenade.

Einteilung	Ausrüstung	Aufgaben	Munition
Schütze 2	Gewehr, Zielfernrohr, Spaten	Bekämpft schwer erkennbare Einzelziele	Gewehrmunition
Schütze 3-8	M.P. mit 6 Magazinen, Spaten	Sie führen den Feuerkampf mit der M.P. und sind Nahkämpfer. Einer von ihnen ist der stellv. Gruppenführer. Er ist verantwortlich für a) Wahrung des Zusammenhalts innerhalb der Gruppe, b) Überwachung der Ausführung der vom Gruppenführer gegebenen Befehle, c) Verbindung zum Zugführer und Nachbarn	180 sS[213] kurz, Panzernahbe-kämpfungsmittel

9

---

[213] „sS" steht für „schweres Spitzgeschoß". Siehe Glossar: sS Munition.

Classification	Equipment	Tasks	Ammunition
Rifleman 2	Rifle, rifle scope, spade	Engages single hard-to-detect targets	Rifle ammunition
Rifleman 3-8	SMG with 6 magazines, spade	They lead the firefight with the SMG and are close-combat fighters. One of them is the deputy squad leader. He is responsible for a) Maintaining cohesion within the squad, b) Monitoring the execution of the orders given by the squad leader, c) Communication to the platoon leader and neighbors[214]	180 sS[215] kurz, close combat anti-tank weapons

9

---

[214] This is referring to neighboring units.
[215] "sS" means "schweres Spitzgeschoß" which literally means "heavy pointed bullet". See Glossary: sS Ammunition (sS Munition).

III. Die Ausbildung

1. Die Bestimmungen der H.Dv. 130/2a über die geschlossene und geöffnete Ordnung sowie über die Kampfweise der Gruppe und es Zuges gelten sinngemäß.

2. Die hohe Feuergeschwindigkeit der M.P. 43/1 verlangt **straffe Feuerzucht** von jedem einzelnen M.P.-Schützen. Der Schütze muß so ausgebildet werden, daß er

a) in der Regel **Einzelfeuer**, d. h. den **sorgfältig gezielten** Einzelschuß abgibt,
b) nur zur **Bekämpfung lohnender Augenblicksziele** auf alle Entfernungen sowie **in der Entscheidung**, z. B. **im Angriff** beim Einbruch in die feindliche Stellung oder **in der Verteidigung** bei der Abwehr des feindlichen Angriffs, auf nahe und nächste Entfernungen sein Feuer zu **Feuerstößen von 2-3 Schuß** steigert,
c) **niemals Dauerfeuer** schießt.

3. Der **Schwerpunkt** der Ausbildung liegt in der Handhabung der Waffe und **im Schulgefechtsschießen**. Für Schulschießen werden nach Auswertung der Erfahrungen bestimmte Bedingungen vorgeschrieben werden.

4. Die Ausbildung umfaßt vordringlich folgende Gebiete:

10

III. The Training

1. The terms of the H.Dv. 130/2a concerning the close and extended order as well as the combat method of the squad and the platoon shall apply accordingly.

2. The high rate of fire of the MP 43/1 requires **strict fire discipline** from each individual SMG-rifleman[216]. The rifleman must be trained so that he

a) fires as a rule, **semi-automatic fire**, meaning the **carefully aimed** single shot,
b) only increase his fire to **fire bursts of 2 to 3 shots** at close and immediate ranges[217] to **fight worthwhile targets of opportunity** at all distances and, when in the decisive moment[218], e.g., in **the attack** in the case of a break-in[219] into the enemy position or **in the defense** against the enemy attack,
c) **never** fires **full-automatic fire**.

3. The **focus**[220] of the training is on the handling of the weapon and **in basic live fire combat exercise**. After evaluation of experiences, certain conditions will be specified for the practice firing.

4. The training primarily covers the following areas:

10

---

[216] Note that SMG-rifleman might be contradictory at first, yet, despite its name the MP 43/1 was an assault rifle.

[217] "Nahe" and "nächste Entfernung" refer to different distances. We translated "nahe Entfernung" to "close range" and "nächste Entfernung" to "immediate ranges".

[218] Note the literal translation of "Entscheidung" would be "decision", but in this case it refers to the "Entscheidung" in the sense of decisive outcome, like it is used in "Entscheidungsschlacht" which is translated and well-known as "decisive battle".

[219] There is no English equivalent for the military term "Einbruch". See Glossary: Break-In (Einbruch).

[220] See Glossary: Weight of Effort (Schwerpunkt).

a) **Handhabung der Waffe** (vgl. D 1854/2[221])
   (1) Auseinandernehmen und Zusammensetzen der Waffe, Auswechseln des Schlagbolzens und des Ausziehers
   (2) Füllen und Entleeren des Magazins
   (3) Ladegriffe und Anschlagübungen
   (4) Reinigen und Pflegen der Waffe
   (5) Beseitigen von Hemmungen.
b) **Anschießen der Waffe** (Ermitteln der Treffpunktlage)
   Das Anschießen erfolgt im Einzelfeuer auf 100 m.
c) **Schulschießen**
   Das Schulschießen mit der M.P. 43/1 ist auf Entfernungen von 100-300 m durchzuführen. Die Abgabe von schnell aufeinanderfolgenden, gut gezielten Einzelschüssen und von mehreren Feuerstößen ist zu üben.
d) **Schulgefechtschießen**
   Auch an der Front sind, soweit es Zeit und Umstände zulassen, Schulgefechtsschießen durchzuführen. Auf einfache, den Fronterfahrungen entsprechende Aufgaben ist Wert zu legen. Hierbei ist folgendes zu üben:
   (1) Einzelfeuer (schnell aufeinanderfolgende, gut gezielte Schüsse)
   (2) Feuerstöße (nicht mehr als 2-3 Schuß)

11

---

[221] D 1854/2: *Maschinenpistole 43/1. Beschreibung, Handhabung und Behandlung*, Berlin, Germany, 31. August 1943.

a) **Handling of the weapon** (see. D 1854/2[222])
    (1) Disassembling and assembling the weapon, replacing the firing pin and extractor
    (2) Filling and emptying the magazine
    (3) Loading movements and aiming drill[223]
    (4) Cleaning and maintaining the weapon
    (5) Removing of stoppages.
b) **Zeroing of the weapon** (determining point of impact[224])
    The harmonization is done with semi-automatic fire at 100 m.
c) **Practice firing**
    The practice firing with the M.P. 43/1 must be carried out at distances of 100-300 m. The firing of fast successive, well-aimed single shots and of several fire bursts is to be practiced.
d) **Basic live fire combat exercise**
    Basic live fire combat exercise is also to be carried out at the front, as far as time and circumstances permit. Emphasis should be placed on simple tasks corresponding to the experience at the front. The following is to be practiced:
    (1) Semi-automatic fire (well-aimed shots in quick succession)
    (2) Bursts (not more than 2-3 shots)

11

---

[222] D 1854/2: *Maschinenpistole 43/1. Description, Handling and Treatment*, Berlin, Germany, 31. August 1943.

[223] Note that "Anschlag" has different meanings in German, one is attack, e.g., a "terrorist attack" – "Terroranschlag". Yet, in this case it refers to aiming / firing positions.

[224] "Treffpunkt" is "point of impact", literally "Treffpunktlage" would be "point of impact location".

(3)   Feuerüberfall[225] durch Einzelfeuer (je Schütze 3-5 Schuß)

(4)   Einzelfeuer und Feuerstöße in der Bewegung (Einbruch, Gegenstoß[226], Grabenkampf).

Das Schulgefechtsschießen ist baldmöglichst im Rahmen der Gruppe durchzuführen.

IV. Der Feuerkampf

1. Die M.P.-Gruppe führt in der Regel keine langen Feuerkämpfe. Es muß ihr Bestreben sein, das Feuer so spät wie möglich zu eröffnen und noch mehr als bisher die Feuerunterstützung der schweren Waffen auszunutzen.

2. Auf Entfernungen über 600 m ist der Feuerkampf mit M.G. und Steilfeuerwaffen zu führen.

Auch unter 600 m nehmen die M.P.-Schützen erst am Feuerkampf teil, wenn die Lage dazu zwingt.

3. Der Feuerkampf wird im Rahmen der Gruppe geführt.

4. Gleichzeitiger Einsatz a l l e r Schützen zum Feuerkampf bringt die hohe Feuerkraft der M.P.-Gruppe am besten zur Wirkung.

5. Als Form des Feuerkampfes ist stets der **Feuerüberfall** anzustreben.

12

---

[225] Siehe Glossar: Feuerüberfall.

[226] Ein Gegenstoß ist ein Angriff, der sofort nach Eindringen des Feindes in die eigene Stellungen durchgeführt wird, hierbei werden örtliche Reserven genutzt. Im Gegensatz zum Gegenangriff der planmäßig erfolgt und auch weiter zurückliegende Reserven nutzt. Siehe Glossar: Gegenangriff, Gegenstoß.

(3) Surprise fire[227] with semi-automatic fire (each rifleman 3-5 shots)

(4) Semi-automatic fire and bursts during movement (break-in[228], hasty counterattack[229], trench combat).

The basic live fire combat exercise should be carried out as soon as possible within the squad.

IV. The Firefight

1. The SMG-squad usually does not conduct long firefights. It must strive to open fire as late as possible and to use the fire support of the heavy weapons even more than before.

2. At distances over 600 m the firefight is to be conducted with MG and indirect fire weapons[230].

Even below 600 m the SMG-rifleman[231] do not take part in the firefight until the situation forces them to.

3. The firefight is conducted as part of the squad.

4. Simultaneous employment of a l l riflemen for the firefight brings the large firepower of the SMG-squad to the best effect.

5. The method of the firefight shall always be the **surprise fire**.

12

---

[227] The literal translation of the German word "Feuerüberfall" would be "firing raid", although in this case "Überfall" refers to the surprise effect. See Glossary: Surprise fire (Feuerüberfall).

[228] There is no English equivalent for the military term "Einbruch". See Glossary: Break-In (Einbruch).

[229] The Germans distinguished between a hasty counterattack ("Gegenstoß") and regular counterattack ("Gegenangriff"). See Glossary: Hasty Counterattack (Gegenstoß) and Counterattack (Gegenangriff).

[230] The literal translation of "Steilfeuerwaffen" would be "high-angle fire weapons" or "steep fire weapons". The complementary word was "Flachfeuerwaffen" meaning "flat-trajectory fire weapons" so direct fire weapons, the Germans stressed the that the combination of direct and indirect fire is crucial.

[231] Note that SMG-rifleman might be contradictory at first, yet, despite its name the MP 43/1 was an assault rifle.

6. Gegen **Einzelziele** ist es oft zweckmäßig, lediglich den Zielfernrohrschützen einzusetzen.

7. **Sparsamer Munitionsverbrauch** ist wichtig! Er muß vom Gruppenführer überwacht werden.

Durch **straffe Feuerzucht** jedes einzelnen Schützen wird der Munitionsverbrauch in den erforderlichen Grenzen gehalten und doch eine wirksame Bekämpfung des Zieles erreicht.

Der Gruppenführer muß immer den Munitionsbestand seiner Gruppe kennen und wissen, wann er mit Munitionsergänzung rechnen kann.

8. Unter günstigen Umständen, z. B. wenn der Feuerkampf aus einer Deckung oder in einer versteckten Stellung geführt werden kann, **leitet der Gruppenführer das Feuer** der ganzen Gruppe. Sonst führen die Schützen den Feuerkampf selbstständig im Rahmen des Kampfauftrages.

9. Die **Feuereröffnung** behält sich der Gruppenführer in der Regel vor. Hierbei ist die Feuerart zu befehlen:

Einzelfeuer durch das Kommando „Einzelfeuer!" (wie im Beispiel 1).

Feuerstöße durch das Kommando „Feuerstöße!" (Beispiel 2).

Oft wird es zweckmäßig sein, die Anzahl der Einzelschüsse und der Feuerstöße zu befehlen (Beispiel 1 und 2).

13

6. Against **single targets** it is often advisable to use only the sniper.

7. **Economical ammunition consumption** is important! It must be monitored by the squad leader.

Tight fire discipline of each individual rifleman keeps the ammunition consumption within the required limits and still accomplishes an effective engagement of the target.

The squad leader must always know the ammunition stock of his squad and when he can expect ammunition replenishment.

8. Under favorable circumstances, e.g., if the firefight can be conducted from cover or from a hidden position, the **squad leader directs the fire** of the whole squad. Otherwise, the riflemen conduct the firefight independently within the scope of the combat mission.

9. As a rule, the squad leader reserves the authority[232] for **opening fire**. Here is the type of fire to be ordered:

Semi-automatic fire with the command "Semi-automatic fire!" (see Example 1).

Bursts with the command "Bursts!" (Example 2).

It will often be useful to order the number of single shots and bursts (Example1 and 2).

13

---

[232] Note that "behält sich vor" translates to "reserves right / authority for", although the word "Recht" for "right" nor "Autorität" for "authority" are in the German phrase.

10. Beispiele für die Feuereröffnung der ganzen Gruppe:

Beispiel 1:

Lage: Gruppe im Angriff auf 300 m an feindliche Stellung herangekommen, von halbrechts Gewehrfeuer.

Feuerbefehl: „Halbrechts im Acker feindliche Schützen! – Ganze Gruppe! – Visier 300! – 5 Schuß Einzelfeuer! – Stellung, Feuer frei!"

Beispiel 2:

Lage: Gruppe in der Verteidigung; halbrechts greift Feind in dichten Trupps an.

Feuerbefehl: „Neuer Feind halbrechts! – Ganze Gruppe! – Visier 200! – 5 Feuerstöße! – Stellung, Feuer frei!"

Beispiel 3:

Lage: Gruppe im Angriff. Gruppenführer erkennt in 400 m Entfernung das Instellunggehen einiger Schützen und eines M.G.

Feuerbefehl: „Geradeaus M.G.! – Ganze Gruppe! – Visier 400! – Einzelfeuer! – Stellung, Feuer frei!"

11. In den Fällen, in denen der M.P.-Schütze das Feuer selbstständig eröffnet, muß er entscheiden, ob für die Bekämpfung des Zieles Einzelfeuer genügt oder Feuerstöße notwendig sind.

14

10. **Examples of opening fire by the whole squad:**

Example 1:

Situation: During the attack, the squad advanced up to 300 m from enemy position, from half-right[233] rifle fire.

Fire order: "Half-right in the field riflemen! – Squad! – Sight 300! – 5 shots semi-automatic fire! – Position! – Fire!"

Example 2:

Situation: Squad in the defense, half-right enemy attacks in tight sections.

Fire order: "New enemy half-right! – Squad! – Sight 200! –5 bursts! – Position! – Fire!"

Example 3:

Situation: Squad in the attack. Squad leader detects in several riflemen and one MG at 400 m distance moving into position.

Fire order: "Straight ahead MG! – Squad! – Sight 400! – Semi-automatic fire! – Position, fire!"

11. In cases where the SMG-rifleman[234] opens fire on his own, he must decide whether semi-automatic fire is sufficient or whether bursts are necessary to engage the target.

14

---

[233] "Half-right" means diagonally from the right side.

[234] Note that SMG-rifleman might be contradictory at first, yet, despite its name the MP 43/1 was an assault rifle.

Zum Einlegen in das Merkblatt 25a/16

Gliederung des M.P.-Zuges der Gren.-Komp.

x)
GERÄTERESERVE

Anmerkung:

Die Abschnitte II u. V des Merkblattes 25a/16 gelten nach der o.a.[235] Gliederung des Zuges nur noch sinngemäß.

Jn[236] den M.P.-Zügen der Volks-Gren.-Div. befinden sich 2 le M.G. als Gerätereserve. Die Scharfschützen sind im Komp.-Trupp zu-[sammengefasst. (siehe [unleserlich] [237])

---

[235] „o.a. " steht für „oben angegebenen".

[236] Dies ist kein Tippfehler, das „J" als erster Buchstabes eines Wortes, welches mit einem „I" (i) beginnt, wurde damals generell häufig genutzt: Infanteriegeschütz wurde meist mit „J.G." abgekürzt. Dies hat zum Teil historische und zum Teil praktische Gründe, da es in gewissen Schriftarten zu Verwechslungen zwischen dem kleinen „L" und großen „i" kommen kann.

[237] Die Zeile ist abgeschnitten und der Text in Klammer nicht wiederherstellbar. Aber in der Anlage zu OKH/Gen.St.H./Org.Abt. Nr.I/11028/44 geh. v. 27.9.44 enthält eine ähnliche Grafik ohne Scharfschützen Symbole mit folgender Anmerkung in Großbuchstaben: „Die bisher in den Gruppen enthaltenen Scharfschützen entfallen und sind dafür im Komp-Trupp zusammengefasst." (BArch, RH 11/I/54 ,Bl. 122.)

[This page was handwritten in block letters.]

To be inserted in the Pamphlet 25a/16

Organization of the SMG-Platoon of the Gren.-Comp.

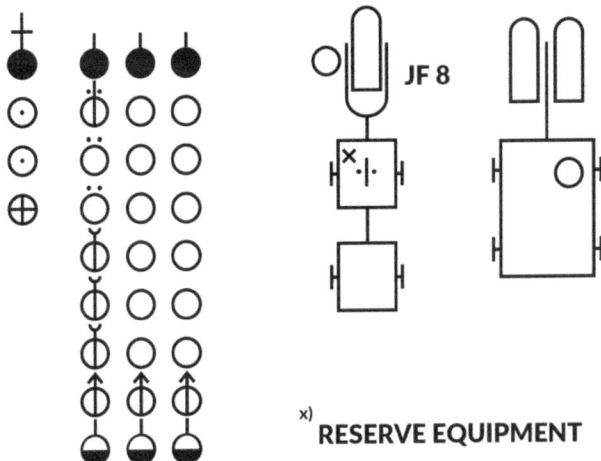

JF 8

^{x)} **RESERVE EQUIPMENT**

Note:

The Sections II and IV of the Pamphlet 25a/16 apply only in a general sense according to the above-mentioned organization of the platoon.

In[238] the SMG-Platoons of the Volks-Grenadier-Division there are 2 light MG as reserve equipment. The snipers are grouped together in the company headquarters (see [unreadable][239])

---

[238] This is not a typo, the "J" as the first letter of a word beginning with an "I" (i) was generally used in those days: "Infanteriegeschütz" (infantry support gun) was usually abbreviated with "J.G.". This has partly historical and partly practical reasons, because in certain fonts there can be confusion between the small "L" and the capital "i".

[239] The line is truncated and the text in brackets is unrecoverable. But in the appendix to OKH/Gen.St.H./Org.Abt.Nr.I/11028/44 dated 27. September 1944 a similar graphic without sniper symbols contains the following note in capitalized letters: "The snipers previously contained in the squads are no longer included and are instead combined in the company headquarters." (BArch, RH 11/I/54, Bl. 122.)

EN-50

V. Der Einsatz des Zuges

1. In der Regel ist der M.P.-Zug geschlossen einzusetzen. Der Einsatz der einzelnen M.P.-Gruppen bildet die Ausnahme.

2. Seine Beweglichkeit und seine Feuerkraft befähigen den M.P.-Zug besonders zur Lösung folgender Aufgaben:

a) Für die Durchführung von Stoß- und Spähtruppunternehmen, für den Kampf im unübersichtlichen Gelände und bei Nebel.

b) In der Verteidigung als bewegliche Reserve für den Gegenstoß[240] und zum Schutz offener Flanken.

c) Im Angriff als bewegliche Reserve zur Bildung eines neuen Schwerpunktes.

d) In der Verfolgung und bei Vorausabteilungen durch Vorwerfen auf Kfz. oder Panzern.

e) In der Absetzbewegung als bewegliche Sicherung, die durch Angriffe aus Hinterhalten und durch Flankenstöße die feindlichen Kräfte bindet und schwächt.

f) Im Winter als Jagdzug in der Skitruppe oder als skibeweglicher Teil einer winterbeweglichen Truppe.

---

[240] Ein Gegenstoß ist ein Angriff, der sofort nach Eindringen des Feindes in die eigene Stellungen durchgeführt wird, hierbei werden örtliche Reserven genutzt. Im Gegensatz zum Gegenangriff der planmäßig erfolgt und auch weiter zurückliegende Reserven nutzt. Siehe Glossar: Gegenangriff, Gegenstoß.

V. The Employment of the Platoon

1. As a rule the SMG-platoon is to employed as a whole unit[241]. The employment of individual SMG-squads is the exception.

2. Its mobility and firepower enable the SMG-platoon to be particularly suited to solving the following tasks:

a)   For the conduct of raids and reconnaissance missions, for the combat in complex terrain and in fog.

b)   In the defense as a mobile reserve for the hasty counterattack[242] and to protect open flanks.

c)   In the attack as a mobile reserve to create a weight of effort[243].

d)   In the pursuit and within advance detachments moving forward quickly[244] [mounted] on cars or tanks.

e)   During the withdrawal as a mobile security, which binds and weakens the enemy forces by attacks via ambushes and flanking thrusts.

f)   In the winter as a hunting platoon of a ski unit or as ski-mobile element of a winter-mobile unit.

---

[241] See Glossary: Employment of the Whole Unit (Einsatz, geschlossener).

[242] The Germans distinguished between a hasty counterattack ("Gegenstoß") and regular counterattack ("Gegenangriff"). See Glossary: Hasty Counterattack (Gegenstoß) and Counterattack (Gegenangriff).

[243] See Glossary: Weight of Effort (Schwerpunkt).

[244] "Vorwerfen" literally translated means "throwing forward".

Ergänzung 2: Auszug H.Dv. 130/2a:

Nummern 231-267: Geschlossene und

Geöffnete Ordnung

Vorbemerkung

Hierbei handelt es sich um die erwähnten Nummern 231 bis 267 der *H.Dv. 130/2a: Ausbildungsvorschrift für die Infanterie Heft 2 a: Die Schützenkompanie* vom 16. 3. 1941. (Entwurf) Nachdruck mit eingearbeiteten Berichtigungen gemäß H. M.[245] 41 Nr. 189 u. H. V. Bl.[246] (C) 41 Nr. 890. Gedruckt 1942. Laut unseren Recherchen ist dies die aktuellste Variante der *H.Dv. 130/2a*.[247] Obwohl sie als „Entwurf" gekennzeichnet ist, scheint sie veröffentlicht worden zu sein, zumindest liegt sie in gedruckter Form in größerer Anzahl vor.

Die Nummern befinden sich auf Seite 100-113. Dieser Text hält sich an die generelle Formatierung der Quelle, ebenso ist jede einzelne Seite der Vorschrift auf eine eigene Seite hier abgedruckt.

Text

Der folgende Text befindet sich im Abschnitt „*B. Die Gruppe*".

---

[245] Heeresmitteilungen, hierbei handelt es sich um die Allgemeinen Heeresmitteilungen.
[246] Heeresverordnungsblatt.
[247] Siehe Eintrag im Bundesarchiv: BArch, RH 1/1189: „*H.Dv. 130/2a Entwurf: Ausbildungsvorschrift für die Infanterie.- Heft 2a: Die Schützenkompanie, 16.03.1941. [...] Nachdruck mit eingearbeiteten Berichtigungen, 1942.*"

Supplement 2: Excerpt H.Dv. 130/2a:

Numbers 231-267: Close and Extended

Order

Preliminary Note

This concerns the mentioned numbers 231 to 267 of *H.Dv. 130/2a: Training Regulation for the Infantry Booklet 2 a: The Rifle Company* of 16 March 1941. (Draft) Reprint with incorporated corrections according to H. M.[248] 41 No. 189 and H. V. Bl.[249] (C) 41 No. 890. Printed 1942. According to our research, this is the most current variant of *H.Dv. 130/2a*.[250] Although it is marked as a "draft", it seems to have been published, at least it is available in printed form in larger numbers.

The numbers are on pages 100-113. This text adheres to the general formatting of the source, and every single page of the regulation is printed on a separate page here.

Text

The following text is located in the section *"B. The Squad"*.

---

[248] H. M. is short for "Heeresmitteilungen" (Army Announcements), which actually refers to the "Allgemeinen Heeresmitteilungen" literally "General Army Announcements".

[249] H. V. Bl. is short for "Heeresverordnungsblatt" which literally translated means "Army Regulation Magazine/Sheet".

[250] See entry in the Federal Archive: BArch, RH 1/1189: *"H.Dv. 130/2a Entwurf: Ausbildungsvorschrift für die Infanterie.- Heft 2a: Die Schützenkompanie, 16.03.1941. [...] Nachdruck mit eingearbeiteten Berichtigungen, 1942."*

III. Die geschlossene Ordnung

Formen

231. Die Formen der geschlossenen Ordnung sind:

(1) Die „Linie zu einem Gliede" (Bild 15)

(2) Die „Reihe" (Bild 16)

(3) Die „Marschordnung" (Bild 17).

232. Auf der Stelle werden die genannten Formen auf folgende Kommandos eingenommen: „**In Linie zu einem Gliede**" oder „**In Reihe**" oder „**In Marschordnung**" – „**Angetreten!**" („**Angetreten – Marsch! Marsch!**")

Auf „**Angetreten**" wird nach kurzem Ausrichten stillgestanden. Diese Kommandos gelten sinngemäß auch für den Schützenzug und die Schützenkompanie.

233. Beim Antreten berühren sich die Nebenleute leicht mit den Ellbogen.

Der Abstand in der Reihe und Marschordnung von Mann zu Mann beträgt 80 cm vom Rücken zur Brust. Als Anhalt für den Abstand kann gelten, daß der vorgestreckte Arm fast das Rückengepäck des Vordermannes berührt.

Die M.P. ist schon vor dem Antreten über die rechte Schulter zu hängen. Magazintaschen sind am Koppel[251] zu tragen.

234. Richtung und Fühlung sind, wenn nichts andere befohlen ist, nach rechts. Die Richtung ist gut, wenn der Mann bei tadelloser eigener Stellung durch eine Wendung des Kopfes nach dem Richtungsflügel mit dem anderen Auge die ganze Linie schimmern sieht.

235. Wird auf der Stelle „**Rührt Euch!**" kommandiert, so sind Fühlung, Vordermann und Richtung, die Stellung des Gewehrs und die Aufstellung des frei gemachten Geräts zu verbessern. (Nr. 5).

---

[251] „Koppel" ist ein Wort für Gürtel, siehe auch Glossar: Koppel.

III. The Close Order

Formations

231. The formations of the close order are:

(1) The "line in one rank" (Figure 15)

(2) The "column" (Figure 16)

(3) The "march formation" (Figure 17).

232. On the spot, the above formations are entered on the following commands: **"In line to one rank"** or **"In column"** or **"In march formation"** – **"Fall in at attention[252]"** (**"Fall in at attention– March! March!"**)

On **"Fall in at attention"** after a short alignment [everyone] stands at attention. These commands are also valid for the rifle platoon and the rifle company.

233. When falling in the men's elbows touch lightly.

The space in the column and march formation from man to man is 80 cm from the back to chest. As an indication of the space, it can be considered that the outstretched arm almost touches the backpack of the man in front.

The SMG must be hung over the right shoulder before falling in. Magazine pouches are to be carried on the belt.[253]

234. Direction and touch are to the right, unless otherwise ordered. The direction is good, when the man, after turning his head towards the dressing flank in his own impeccable position, sees the whole line in the peripheral of his other eye.

235. If the command **"At ease!"** is given on the spot, improvements are made to the touch, [the alignment to] the person in front and the direction, the position of the rifle and the placement of the cleared equipment. (No. 5)

---

[252] The *TM 30-506 German Military Dictionary* by the US War Department from 1944 translates "angetreten" with "fall in at attention". *Reibert: Dienstunterricht im Heere from 1940* for the rifleman in the rifle company notes that after the command "angetreten", the men place themselves into their correct position shortly before they are at attention on the command of "stillgestanden".

[253] "Koppel" is an old word for belt, see Glossary: Belt (Koppel).

Bild 15

Gruppe in Linie zu einem Gliede[254]

Bild 16

Gruppe in Reihe

Bild 17

Gruppe in Marschordnung

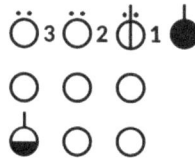

---

[254] Handschriftliche Druckschrift nicht in Fraktur, wohingegen „Bild 15" in Fraktur gedruckt ist. Die anderen Bilder sind genauso beschriftet in diesem Dokument.

Figure 15

Squad in Line to one Rank[255][256]

| | 3 | 2 | 1 | |

Figure 16

Squad in Column

Figure 17

Squad in March Formation

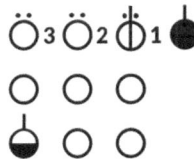

---

[255] Handwritten block letters not in Fraktur, whereas "Figure 15" is printed in Fraktur. The other pictures are labeled in the same way in this document.
[256] Note that TM 30-506 (1944) uses "line to one rank" for the command, whereas the German Squad in Combat (1943) uses "Squad line, one deep" for describing this formation. We do not know if this is a different translation or a difference between command versus formation naming. Likely the first, since German Squad in Combat (1943) translates "Marschordnung" with "march order", yet FM 22-5 (1941) uses "march formation", whereas "march order" could not be found by us.

EN-54

236. Zum Verbessern der Richtung kann außerdem ausnahmsweise „**Richt Euch!**" oder „**Nach links – Richt Euch!**" kommandiert werden.

Das Kommando „**Augen gerade-aus!**" beendet dieses Richten.

Marsch, Lauf und Schwenkungen

237. „**Abteilung (im Gleichschritt, ohne Tritt) – Marsch!**" „**Abteilung – Halt!**"

Die Richtung wird durch gleichmäßige Schrittweite und richtige Fühlung erhalten. Der Mann wirft jedoch hin und wieder eine Blick nach dem Richtungsflügel. Dem Druck von dem Richtungsflügel wird nachgegeben.

238. Beschleunigtes Antreten aus dem Liegen erfolgt auf „**Ohne Tritt – Marsch!**" Auf das Ankündigungskommando steht der Schütze kurz auf. Das Gewehr wird wie vor dem Hinlegen getragen, das abgesetzte Gerät aufgenommen.

239. Laufen in der geschlossenen Ordnung erfolgt auf „**Laufschritt – Marsch! Marsch!**" Der Zusammenhalt in der Abteilung darf nicht verlorengehen. Die Trageweise der Waffen und des Geräts ist beizubehalten. Das Laufen wird durch „**Abteilung – Halt!**" oder „**Im Schritt!**" beendet.

240. Marscherleichterungen auf „**Rührt Euch!**":

(1) Der Führer ist an keinen bestimmten Platz gebunden.

(2) Es darf, wenn nichts anderes befohlen wird, gesprochen, gesungen, gegessen, getrunken und geraucht werden.

(3) Das Gewehr wird in bequemer Lage geschultert auf der rechten oder linken Schulter, umgehängt, auf dem Rücken oder um den Hals getragen.

(4) Die M.P. wird über die rechte oder linke Schulter gehängt oder vor dem Körper getragen.

236. To improve the direction, the command **"Dress!"** or **"Left – Dress!"** can be commanded.

The command **"Ready front!"** ends this dressing.

March, Double Time and Wheeling Maneuvers

237. "[Unit],[257] (forward, route step) - March!" "Unit – Halt!"

The direction is maintained by even step size and correct touch. The man, however, casts a glance at the dressing flank every now and then. The pressure from the dressing flank is given way.

238. Accelerated falling in from a lying position is carried out on **"Route step - march!"** At the preparatory command the rifleman stands up briefly. The rifle is carried as before lying down, the set down equipment [is] picked up.

239. Double time in close order is carried out on **"Double time – March!"** The cohesion of the unit[258] must not be lost. The carrying method of the weapons and the equipment must be maintained. Double time is stopped with **"Unit – Halt!"** or **"Mark time!"**.

240. Marching conveniences at **"At ease!"**:

(1) The leader is not bound to any particular position in the formation.

(2) It is permitted to, unless otherwise ordered, speak, sing, eat, drink and smoke.

(3) The rifle is shouldered in a comfortable position on the right or left shoulder, slung over, worn on the back or around the neck.

(4) The SMG is hung over the right or left shoulder worn in front of the body.

---

[257] The "Abteilung" in this case is a generic term for the current unit and not referring to a battalion-sized unit also called "Abteilung". Since, an "Abteilung" was in the German Army of the Second World War a unit designation in some arms (like tanks, artillery, signal, etc.) with the strength of a battalion. There was also the "Bataillon" which was used by some arms. Note that "Abteilung" literally means "detachment" or "department". American commands of the time according to the TM 30-506 often did not include such a generic unit reference when performing commands, of course there were exceptions, e.g., "Detail – halt!". Note the German equivalent to "unit" would be "Einheit".
[258] See previous footnote.

(5) Die Trageweise des M.G. enthält Nr. 62 (2).

(6) Trageweise der Waffen ist innerhalb der Kompanie gleichmäßig (Nr. 642).

241. Soll die Truppe an einem Vorgesetzten im „Rührt Euch!" vorbeimarschieren, so macht der nächste Führer oder Unterführer die Truppe durch Zuruf darauf aufmerksam (z. B. „Achtung! Der Herr Divisionskommandeur rechts!") Der Zuruf ist nach rückwärts weiterzugeben. Der Vorgesetzte ist in aufrechter Haltung frei anzusehen. Die Arme werden bewegt. Trageweise der Waffen und Marscherleichterungen werden beibehalten.

Eingetretene Offiziere grüßen, der Führer der Abteilung meldet.

Sollen die Marscherleichterungen wegfallen, ist „**Marschordnung**" zu kommandieren.

242. Kommandos für Schwenkungen:

In der Bewegung:

„**Rechts (links) schwenkt-Marsch!" („Marsch! Marsch!")**

Aus dem Halten:

„**Rechts (links) schwenkt, ohne Tritt (im Gleichschritt) – Marsch!"** Auf „**Marsch!" („Marsch! Marsch!")** wird die Schwenkung sofort ausgeführt.

Die Richtung ist nach dem schwenkenden Flügel. Dort befindliche Schützen behalten die vorgeschriebene Schrittweite bei und sehen nach innen. Die anderen Schützen verkürzen den Schritt um so mehr, je näher sie sich am Drehpunkt befinden. Der Flügelmann am Drehpunkt wendet sich allmählich auf der Stelle. Steht neben ihm ein Führer, so richtet sich dieser nach dem Flügelmann. Die Fühlung ist nach dem Drehpunkt.

Die Schwenkung wird beendet durch „**Halt!"** oder „**Gerade-aus!"** Auf „**Gerade**" wird in halben Schritten in der neuen Richtung weitermarschiert. Die Richtung

(5) The carrying method of the MG contains No. 62 (2).

(6) Carrying method of the weapons is uniform within the company (No. 642).

241. If the unit[259] is to p a s s i n r e v i e w by a superior in "A t e a s e !", the next leader or subordinate leader shall call the attention to the unit[260] by shouting (e.g., "Attention! The division commander on the right!") The call must be passed on backwards. The superior is to be looked at freely in an u p r i g h t position. The arms are moved. Carrying method and marching conveniences are maintained.

Officers that enter the formation greet, the leader of the unit[261] reports.

Should the marching conveniences be discontinued, **"march formation"** is to be commanded.

242. C o m m a n d s f o r w h e e l i n g m a n e u v e r s :

I n m o v e m e n t :

"Column right (left) – March!" ("March! March!")

F r o m t h e h a l t :

"Column right (left), route step (mark time), forward – March!" On **"March!"** ("March! March!") the wheeling maneuver is executed immediately.

The direction is according to the turning flank.[262] Riflemen located there maintain the prescribed step size and look inside. The other riflemen shorten the step the closer they are to the pivot point. The pivot man at the pivot point gradually turns on the spot. If a leader stands beside him, he directs himself after the pivot man. The touch is according to the pivot point.

The wheeling maneuver is stopped with **"Halt!"** or **"Ready, front!"** On **"Ready"**[263] marching continues in half steps in the new direction. The direction

---

[259] "Die Truppe" literally means "the troops", yet it refers to the men of current unit.
[260] See previous footnote.
[261] The "Abteilung" in this case is a generic term for the current unit and not referring to a battalion-sized unit also called "Abteilung". See footnotes on p. EN-54 for more information.
[262] Note the literal translation of "Flügel" would be "wing" and on the tactical side there was a distinction between "Flügel" and "Flanke".
[263] Note we chose the first word of the command here not the translation of "Gerade".

geht nach dem Richtungsflügel. Auf „Aus!" wird mit vorgeschriebener Schrittweite weitermarschiert. Schwenkungen in der Marschordnung und Reihe führen die einzelnen Glieder nach und nach an der gleichen Stelle aus (Hakenschwenkungen). Der innere Flügel beschreibt einen kleinen Bogen. Der Abstand verringert sich am Schwenkungspunkt. Die hinteren Glieder marschieren auf Vordermann.

Formveränderungen

243. Aufmärsche und Abbrechen erfolgen ohne Tritt oder im Laufen. Nach Durchführung der Formveränderung wird ohne Tritt weitermarschiert. Abbrechen nach links, Aufmärsche nach rechts und Bewegungen im Kehrt sind nicht zu üben.

Formveränderung	Kommando	Ausführung zu a)
(1) Aus der Linie zu einem Gliede in die Reihe	Auf der Stelle: a) „**Reihe rechts, ohne Tritt – Marsch!**" b) „**Rechts – um!**" „**Ohne Tritt – Marsch!**" In der Bewegung: c) „**Reihe rechts!**" oder d) „**Rechts – um!**"	Der Gruppenführer am rechten Flügel geht geradeaus, die anderen Schützen machen rechts um und setzen sich dahinter.
(2) Aus der Linie zu einem Gliede in die Marschordnung	Auf der Stelle: a) „**Marschordnung rechts, ohne Tritt – Marsch!**"	Die ersten drei Schützen des rechten Flügels gehen geradeaus. Die übrigen Schützen setzen sich jeweils in Glieder zu dreien dahinter.

is aligned after the dressing flank. On **"Front!"** [264] marching is continued with the ordered step spacing. Wheeling maneuvers in march formation and column are carried out by the individual ranks one after the other at the same position (pivoting maneuver). The pivot flank[265] describes a small arc. The spaces decrease at the pivot. The rear ranks march behind the man in front.

Formation Changes

243. Forming up and breaking off are performed in route step and double time. After the formation has changed, marching continuous in route step. Breaking off to the left, forming up to the right and making an about face are not to be practiced.

Formation Changes	Command	Execution for a)

(1) From the line in one rank to the column	On the spot:
	a) **"Column right, route step – March!"**
	b) **"Right – Face!"**
	  "Route step – March!"
	In movement:
	c) **"Column right!"**
	  or
	d) **"Right – Face!"**
		The squad leader on the right flank goes straight ahead, the other riflemen turn right and settle behind him.

(2) From the line in one rank to the march formation	On the spot: a) **"March formation right, route step – March!"**	The first three riflemen of the right flank go straight ahead. The remaining riflemen settle ranks of three behind them.

---

[264] Note we chose the second word of the command here not the translation of "Aus!".
[265] Described here is the part of the individual ranks that are closest to the pivot point and thus cover less distance during a pivot.

Formveränderung	Kommando	Ausführung
	In der Bewegung: b) „**Marschordnung –** **rechts!**"	Der Gruppenführer bleibt am rechten Flügel.
(3) Aus der Marschordnung in die Reihe	„Reihe – rechts!"	Der Gruppenführer am rechten Flügel geht geradeaus. Die einzelnen Glieder machen rechts um und setzen sich dahinter.
(4) Aus der Reihe in die Marschordnung	„**In Marschordnung links** **marschiert auf – Marsch!** **Marsch!**" (Marsch!)	Die Gruppe marschiert gliederweise nach links auf. Der Gruppenführer tritt auf seinen Platz nach Bild 17.
(5) Aus der Reihe oder Marschordnung in die Linie zu einem Gliede	„**In Linie zu einem Gliede** **links marschiert auf –** **Marsch! Marsch!**" (Marsch!)	Der Gruppenführer bzw. das vorderste Glied geht beim Aufmarsch in der Bewegung geradeaus weiter, die übrigen Schützen marschieren links auf. Beim Aufmarsch auf der Stelle bleiben der Gruppenführer bzw. das vorderste Glied stehen.

Formation Changes	Command	Execution
	In movement: b) **"March formation – right!"**	The squad leader remains on the right flank.
(3) From the march formation to the column	**"Column - right!"**	The squad leader on the right flank walks straight ahead. The individual ranks turn right and settle behind.
(4) From the column to the march formation	**"In march formation left moves up – March! March!" (March!)**	The squad marches in ranks to the left. The squad leader steps on his place to his place according to Figure 17.
(5) From the column or the march formation to the line in one rank	**"In line to one rank left moves up – March! March!" (March!)**	The squad leader or the foremost rank move during the forming up straight ahead, the remaining riflemen march to the left. When forming up on the spot, the squad leader or the foremost rank will stop.

Hinlegen

244. In der Reihe legen sich die Schützen schräg nach rechts hin, so daß der Oberkörper neben den Beinen des Vordermannes liegt. Beim Hinlegen in der „Marschordnung" machen die rechte und mittlere Reihe halbrechts, die linke Reihe halblinks um. Die Abteilung legt sich hin, die mittlere Reihe rechts auf Lücke.

Gleichmäßigkeit beim Hinlegen ist nicht zu fordern. Nach dem Hinlegen und nach dem Aufstehen wird gerührt. Weitere Einzelheiten enthält Nr. 31 und 32.

Zusammensetzen der Gewehre

245. Das Zusammensetzen der Gewehre in der Gruppe erfolgt sinngemäß wie im Zuge (Nr. 428 bis 438).

IV. Die geöffnete Ordnung

Formen

246. Wo nach Lage, Gelände und Feindeinwirkung die geschlossene Ordnung nicht mehr aufrechterhalten werden kann, wird zur geöffneten Ordnung übergegangen (Entwicklung[266]) (Nr. 444).

247. Die Grundformen der geöffneten Ordnung der Gruppe sind:

die „Schützenreihe" (Bild 18)

die „Schützenkette" (Bild 19)

248. Falls die Lage dazu zwingt, kann jede andere Form oder ein Absetzen einzelner Teile der Gruppe befohlen werden. Der Zusammenhalt der Gruppe muß dabei gewährleistet sein.

249. Aus der Schützenreihe und Schützenkette können nach Breite und Tiefe vielfach wechselnde Formen ent=

---

[266] Siehe Glossar: Entwicklung.

Lying Down

244. In the column, the riflemen lie down diagonally to the right, so that the upper part of the body lies next to the legs of the person in front. When lying down in the "march formation", the right and middle columns turn half right, the left column half left. The unit[267] lies down, the middle column right to the gap.

Uniformity while lying down is not to be demanded. After lying down and getting up [the men are] at ease. Further details are contained in No. 31 and 32.

Assembling the Rifles

245. The assembly of the rifles in the squad is done the same way as in the platoon (No. 428 bis 438).

IV. The Extended Order

Formations

246. Where the close order can no longer be maintained due to location, terrain, and enemy action, the extended order is adopted (full deployment[268]) (No. 444).

247. The basic formations of the extended order for the squad are:

the "Column" (Figure 18)

the "Skirmishing Line" (Figure 19)

248. If the situation requires it, any other formation or a withdrawal of individual elements of the squad can be ordered. Throughout this the cohesion of the squad must be guaranteed.

249. From the column and skirmishing line multiple different formations in width and depth can e-

---

[267] "Die Truppe" literally means "the troops", yet it refers to the men of current unit.
[268] See Glossary: Full Deployment (Entwicklung).

Bild 18

Gruppe in Schützenreihe

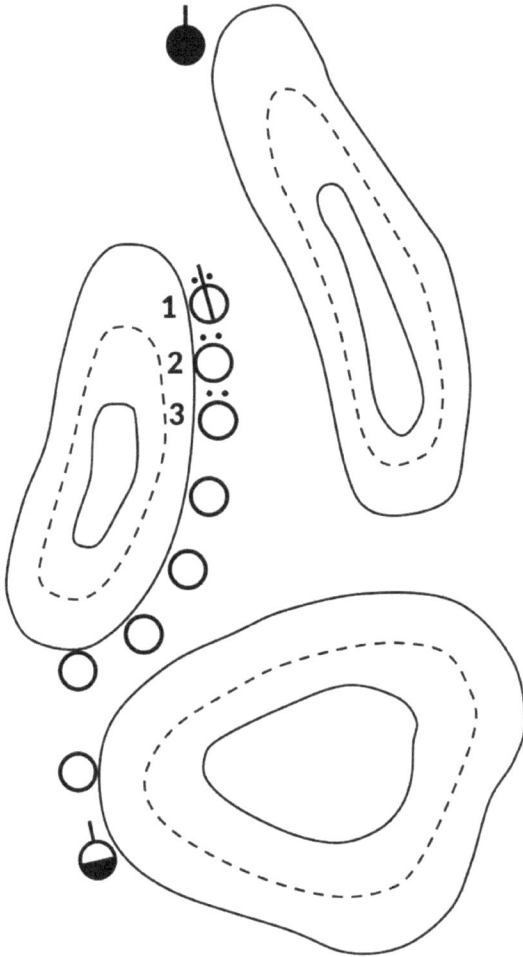

1
2
3

DE-60

Figure 18

Squad in Column

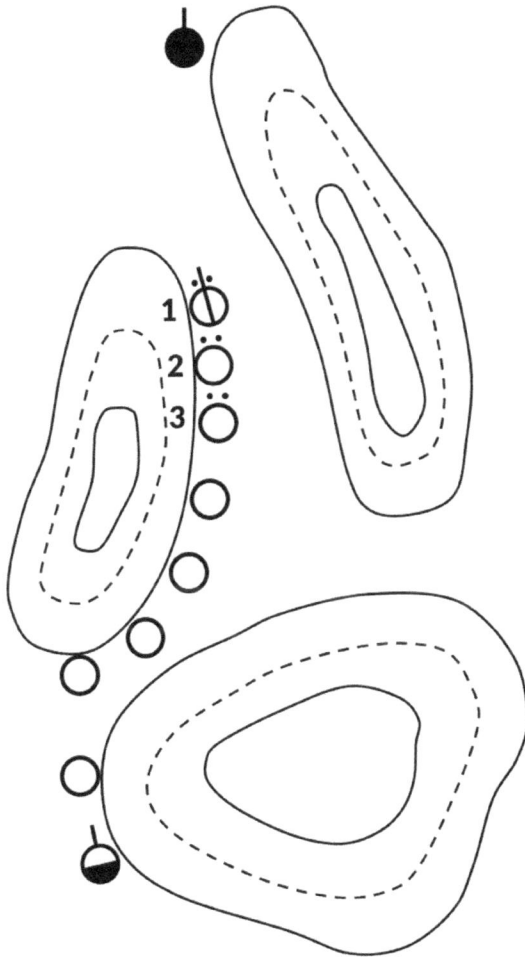

stehen. Sie ergeben sich in stark durchschnittenem Gelände, beim Überwinden und Umgehen von Hindernissen oder beim Aufschließen rückwärtiger Gruppen.

250. Die Schützenreihe ist die Form der Annäherung. Sie ermöglicht es, sich weitgehend dem Gelände anzupassen und Geländebedeckungen auszunutzen. Sie erschwert dem Feind das Beobachten und erleichtert die eigene Führung. Sie eignet sich zum Feuerkampf, wenn das l.M.G. allein feuert.

251. Die Schützenkette ist vor allem für den Feuerkampf der ganzen Gruppe anzuwenden.

Sie kann auf Kommando oder Zeichen „Ganze Gruppe – Stellung!" gebildet werden. Die Gewehrschützen gehen, dem Gelände angepaßt, beiderseits des l.M.G. in Stellung. Ein Zusammenballen um das l.M.G. ist zu vermeiden.

Vor dem Instellunggehen der ganzen Gruppe kann auch vor dem Kommando „Stellung!" zunächst "Schützenkette!" kommandiert werden.

Zum schnellen Überwinden eingesehener Geländestrecken und zum Vorbrechen aus Deckungen kann sie vorübergehend erforderlich sein. Längere Bewegungen in Schützenkette erschweren das Ausnutzen des Geländes und den Zusammenhalt der Gruppe und sind daher zu vermeiden.

252. Solange nichts anderes befohlen ist, sind bei der Schützenreihe durchschnittlich 5 Schritt Abstand, bei der Schützenkette durchschnittlich 5 Schritt Zwischenraum zu

merge. They result in deeply intersected terrain, when overcoming and avoiding obstacles or when rearward squads connect.

250. The column is the formation of the approach. It permits [the unit] to adapt to the terrain and to exploit of terrain coverage as much as possible. It makes it more difficult for the enemy to observe, while making it easier to command. It is suited for the firefight if the light MG fires alone.

251. The skirmishing line is particularly useful for the firefight of the whole squad.

It can be created by the command or by the sign **"Squad[269] – Position!"**. The riflemen move, adapting to the terrain, into position on both sides of the light MG. A bunching up around the light MG should be avoided.

Before the whole squad gets into position, before the command **"Position!"** first **"Skirmishing line!"** can be commanded.

[A skirmishing line] may be required temporarily to quickly overcome visible stretches of terrain and while breaking out of cover. Prolonged movements in a skirmishing line make it difficult to exploit the terrain and to maintain the cohesion of the squad and should therefore be avoided.

252. As long as nothing different is ordered, the average space with the column is 5 paces, with the skirmishing line 5 paces distances are to be

---

[269] The literal translation of "Ganze Gruppe" would be "Whole squad".

nehmen. Lage, Gelände, Dunkelheit oder Nebel machen oft andere Abstände oder Zwischenräume erforderlich. Um die feindliche Feuerwirkung abzuschwächen, sind lockere Formen bei der Annäherung anzustreben. Je schwieriger aber die Lage, z.B. beim Einbruch[270], je unübersichtlicher das Gefechtsfeld, je unerfahrener die Gruppe im Kampf ist, desto mehr halten die Gruppenführer ihre Schützen zusammen.

Bild 19

Gruppe in Schützenkette

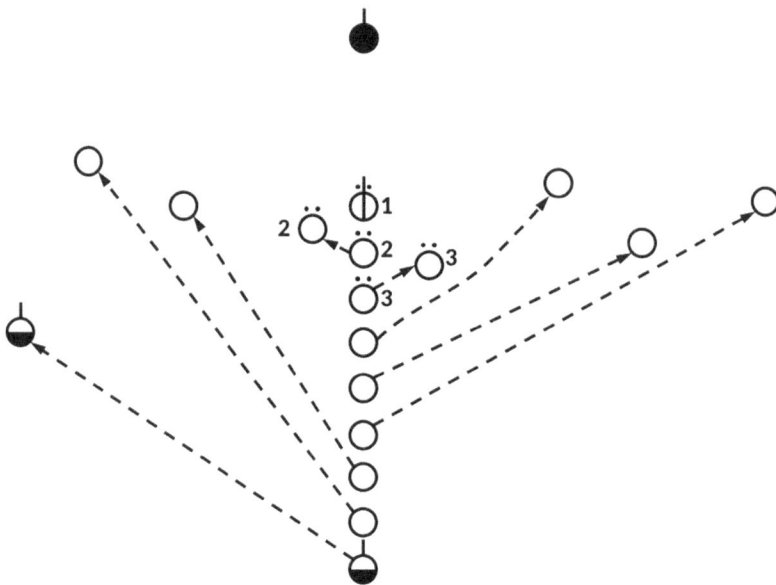

253. Die Entwicklung[271] der Gruppe erfolgt auf den Schützen 1 als Anschlußmann[272]. Auf ihn werden Abstände und Zwischenräume genommen. Ist kein Weg, Ziel oder Richtungspunkt angegeben, folgt der Anschlußmann dem voreilenden Gruppenführer.

---

[270] Siehe Glossar: Einbruch.
[271] Siehe Glossar: Entwicklung.
[272] Siehe Glossar: Anschlußmann.

taken. Situation, terrain, darkness or fog often make other spaces or distances necessary. To weaken the effect of hostile fire, l o o s e   f o r m a t i o n s   a r e   t o b e   d e s i r e d   d u r i n g   t h e   a p p r o a c h . The more difficult the situation, e.g., break-in[273], the more confusing the combat zone, the less experienced the squad is in combat, the more the squad leaders hold their riflemen together.

Figure 19

Squad in Skirmishing Line

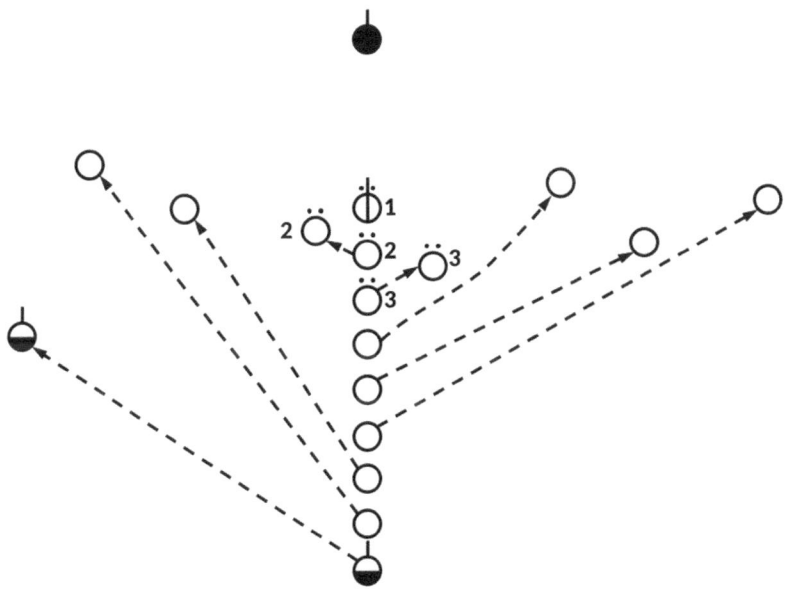

253. The full deployment[274] of the squad takes place on the rifleman 1 [machine gunner] as a connecting file[275]. On him spaces and distances are taken. If no route, target or direction point is given, the connecting file follows the leading squad leader.

---

[273] There is no English equivalent for "Einbruch". See Glossary: Break-In (Einbruch).
[274] See Glossary: Full Deployment (Entwicklung).
[275] See Glossary: Connecting File (Anschlußmann).

254. Bei der Entwicklung zur Schützenreihe in der Bewegung verhalten die letzten Schützen (Bild 18).

Zum Bilden der Schützenkette entwickelt[276] sich aus der Reihe die vordere Hälfte der Gewehrschützen rechts, die hintere Hälfte links vom Schützen 1 [MG Schütze] (Bild 19).

Die Entwicklung nach einer Seite ist ausdrücklich zu befehlen.

Bei der Entwicklung aus der Marschordnung nehmen die Schützen die gleichen Plätze wie im Bild 18 und 19 ein.

255. Beispiele für Befehle und Kommandos zur Entwicklung.

a) In der Vorwärtsbewegung:
    (1) „Richtung Waldecke! – Schützenreihe!"
    (2) „Richtung Kirchturm! 10 Schritt Zwischenraum! – Schützenkette! Marsch! Marsch!"
b) Aus dem Halten in die Bewegung:
    (1) „Entlang der Buschreihe mit 2 Schritt Abstand folgen!"
    (2) „Zum Besetzen der Höhe dort vor uns! Ganze Gruppe! – Stellung!"
c) Auf der Stelle:
    (1) „Front wie ich stehe! 10 Schritt Abstand! – Schützenreihe!"
    (2) „Hinter dieser Hecke! – Schützenkette!"

256. Der Gruppenführer ist an keinen bestimmten Platz gebunden. In der Regel befindet er sich vor seiner Gruppe. Zum Beobachten des Gegners, zum Erkunden

---

[276] Siehe Glossar: Entwicklung.

254. During the full deployment to the column during movement the last riflemen remain at their position (Figure 18).

To form the skirmishing line the column fully deploys[277], the front half of the riflemen to the right, the rear half to the left of rifleman 1 [MG gunner] (Figure 19).

The full deployment to one side must be ordered explicitly.

During the full deployment from the march formation, the riflemen occupy the same positions as in Figure 18 and Figure 19.

255. Examples for orders and commands for full deployment.

a)　In the forward movement:
　　(1)　"Direction forest corner! – Column!"
　　(2)　"Direction church tower! 10 paces distance! – Skirmishing line! March! March!"
b)　From the halt to the movement:
　　(1)　"Follow along the row of bushes with 2 paces distance!"
　　(2)　"To occupy the height there before us! Squad! – Position!"
c)　On the spot:
　　(1)　"Front as I stand! 10 paces distance! – Skirmishing line!"
　　(2)　"Behind this hedge! – Skirmishing line!"

256. The squad leader is not tied to specific position in the formation. Usually he is in front of the squad. To observe the enemy, to scout

---

[277] See Glossary: Full Deployment (Entwicklung).

des Geländes und zum Verbindunghalten entfernt er sich oft vorübergehend von seiner Gruppe. Bei wirksamen feindlichen Feuer befindet er sich inmitten seiner Schützen.

257. Am Schluß der Schützenreihe befindet sich der stellvertretende Gruppenführer. Er sorgt dafür, daß niemand zurückbleibt.

258. Jeder Schütze darf seine Waffen in der geöffneten Ordnung so tragen, wie es ihm am handlichsten ist. L.M.G.[278] und Gewehre sind nicht geschultert zu tragen. In Feindnähe muß schneller Gebrauch der Waffen gewährleistet sein.

Gleichmäßigkeit ist nicht zu fordern.

Der Gewehrriemen wird stets lang gemacht.

259. In der geöffneten Ordnung darf gesprochen werden, wenn es zum Austausch von Beobachtungen über Feind, Nachbarn[279] und Gelände erforderlich ist. Im übrigen hat – besonders bei Nacht, Nebel und im Walde – Ruhe zu herrschen. Sie ist ein Kennzeichen für die Manneszucht[280] der Truppe.

Bewegungen

260. Jeder Schütze ist dafür verantwortlich, daß vor Beginn jeder Bewegung seine Waffen gesichert, Patronenkästen und Patronentaschen geschlossen sind.

261. Nur zum Schießen während der Bewegung darf das l.M.G. geladen und gesichert sein (Nr. 227).

Bei Bewegungen ist es zur schnellen Feuerbereitschaft nach Nr. 70 vorzubereiten (d.h. Schloß entspannt, Gurttrommel angehängt, Gurt eingelegt, l.M.G. entsichert).

---

[278] Kurzform für leichtes Maschinengewehr.
[279] Hierbei sind benachbarte Einheiten gemeint.
[280] Manneszucht ist ein altes Wort für Disziplin bzw. militärische Disziplin.

out the terrain and to keep in touch, he often distances himself from his squad. During effective enemy fire, he is in the midst of his riflemen.

257. At the end of the column is the deputy squad leader. He makes sure that nobody is left behind.

258. In the extended order, each rifleman may carry his weapons in the way that is most convenient for him. Light MG and rifles are not to be carried shouldered. Near the enemy, quick use of the weapons must be guaranteed.

Uniformity is not to be demanded.

The rifle sling is always made long.

259. In the extended order it is permitted to speak if it is necessary to exchange observations about the enemy, neighbors[281] and terrain. In all other cases – especially at night, fog and in the forest – there has to be silence[282]. This is the characteristic of a disciplined[283] troop.

Movements

260. Each rifleman is responsible for ensuring that his weapon is secured, ammunition boxes and pouches are closed before the start of each movement.

261. The light MG may only be loaded and secured for firing during movement (No. 227).

In case of movements it must be prepared for quick readiness according to No. 70 (that means bolt uncocked, drum magazine attached, belt inserted, light MG armed).

---

[281] This is referring to neighboring units.
[282] The literal translation of "hat Ruhe zu herrschen" is "silence has to reign".
[283] "Manneszucht" is an old word for discipline respectively military discipline. Literally translated it means "Man's Discipline".

262. Antreten in der geöffneten Ordnung erfolgt auf Kommando: „**Marsch!**" („**Marsch! Marsch!**") oder auf Zeichen.

Kurze Seitenbewegungen erfolgen auf Befehl oder Zeichen.

Rückwärtsbewegungen werden auf „**Kehrt Marsch!**" ausgeführt und auf „**H-a-l-t! Kehrt!**" unterbrochen. Alle Führer bleiben auf der Feindseite.

263. Vorwärtsbewegungen in der geöffneten Ordnung werden auf „**H-a-l-t!**" oder „**Hinlegen!**" oder „**Volle Deckung!**" oder „**Stellung!**" unterbrochen.

Auf:

(1)   „**H-a-l-t!**" bleiben die Schützen stehen, das Gewehr wird in die Stellung „Gewehr ab" gebracht. Das Gerät wird abgesetzt.

(2)   „**Hinlegen!**" legt sich der Schütze an Ort und Stelle hin.

(3)   „**Volle Deckung!**" sucht sich der Schütze schnell einen geeigneten Platz in seiner Nähe und legt sich hin. Deckung gegen feindliche Feuerwirkung, Erd- und Luftbeobachtung sind anzustreben. Verbindung zum Führer, die Beobachtung des Gefechtsfeldes und der Zusammenhang der Gruppe darf nicht verlorengehen. Eingraben kann notwendig werden.

Sammeln

264. Die Gruppe sammelt in Reihe und nimmt dabei selbstständig die ursprüngliche Gliederung ein.

Vor dem Sammeln im Zuge oder in der Kompanie ist Marschordnung zu bilden (Nr. 447).

265. Beim Sammeln auf der Stelle gehen die Schützen auf dem kürzesten Wege auf den befohlenen Platz. In der Bewegung sammeln sie strahlenförmig hinter dem vorangehenden Gruppenführer.

262. Falling in in extended order occurs on the command: **"March!"** (**"March! March!"**) or on signal.

Short lateral movements are made on order or signal.

Backward movements are executed on **"About face March!"** and on **"H-a-l-t! About face!"** interrupted. All leaders stay on the enemy side.

263. Forward movements in the extended order are interrupted on **"H-a-l-t!"** or **"Lie down!"** or **"Full cover!"** or **"Position!"**.

On:

(1) **"H-a-l-t!"** the riflemen stop, the rifle is brought into the position "rifle down". The equipment is lowered.
(2) **"Lie down!"** the rifleman lies down on the spot.
(3) **"Full cover!"** the rifleman quickly finds a suitable place near him and lies down. Cover against enemy fire, ground and air observation are to be aimed for. Communication[284] with the leader, the observation of the combat zone and the cohesion of the squad are not to be lost. Digging in might be necessary.

Rallying

264. The squad rallies in a column and independently adopts into the original formation.

Before the rallying the platoon or the company the march formation has to formed (No. 447).

265. When rallying on the position, the riflemen walk by the shortest route to the ordered place. In movement, they rally radially behind the leading squad leader.

---

[284] Note the direct translation of "Verbindung" would be "connection", but communication is the more correct translation here.

266. Die Trageweise der Waffen richtet sich nach dem Gruppenführer. Das Gerät ist aufzunehmen.

267. Das Sammeln erfolgt auf das Kommando „**Sammeln!**" oder auf Zeichen (Nr. 662).

266. The carrying method is determined by the squad leader. The equipment is to be carried.

267. Rallying is performed on the command **"Rally!"** or on signal (No. 662).

Ergänzung 3: Auszug H.Dv. 130/2a:

Nummern 458-464: Kampfplan

Vorbemerkung

Hierbei handelt es sich um die erwähnten Nummern 458 bis 463 und 464 als Ergänzung der *H.Dv. 130/2a: Ausbildungsvorschrift für die Infanterie Heft 2 a: Die Schützenkompanie* vom 16. 3. 1941. (Entwurf) Nachdruck mit eingearbeiteten Berichtigungen gemäß H. M.[285] 41 Nr. 189 u. H. V. Bl.[286] (C) 41 Nr. 890. Gedruckt 1942. Laut unseren Recherchen ist dies die aktuellste Variante der *H.Dv. 130/2a* im Bundesarchiv.[287]

Die Nummern befinden sich auf Seite 180-182. Dieser Text hält sich an die generelle Formatierung der Quelle, jedoch wurde darauf verzichtet Seitenumbrüche zu übernehmen.

---

[285] Heeresmitteilungen, hierbei handelt es sich um die Allgemeinen Heeresmitteilungen.
[286] Heeresverordnungsblatt.
[287] Siehe Eintrag im Bundesarchiv: BArch, RH 1/1189: „H.Dv. 130/2a Entwurf: *Ausbildungsvorschrift für die Infanterie.- Heft 2a: Die Schützenkompanie, 16.03.1941. [...] Nachdruck mit eingearbeiteten Berichtigungen, 1942.“*

Supplement 3: Excerpt H.Dv. 130/2a:

Numbers 458-464: Battle Plan

Preliminary Note

This concerns the mentioned numbers 458 to 463 of *H.Dv. 130/2a: Training Regulation for the Infantry Booklet 2 a: The Rifle Company* from 16 March 1941. (Draft) Reprint with incorporated corrections according to H. M.[288] 41 No. 189 and H. V. Bl.[289] (C) 41 No. 890. Printed 1942. According to our research, this is the most current version of the *H.Dv. 130/2a.*[290]

The numbers are on pages 180-182. This text follows the general formatting of the source, although original page breaks have not been included.

---

[288] H. M. is short for "Heeresmitteilungen" (Army Announcements), which actually refers to the "Allgemeinen Heeresmitteilungen" literally "General Army Announcements".

[289] H. V. Bl. is short for "Heeresverordnungsblatt" which literally translated means "Army Regulation Magazine/Sheet".

[290] See entry in the Federal Archive: BArch, RH 1/1189: "*H.Dv. 130/2a Entwurf: Ausbildungsvorschrift für die Infanterie.- Heft 2a: Die Schützenkompanie, 16.03.1941. [...] Nachdruck mit eingearbeiteten Berichtigungen, 1942.*"

Text

458. Der **Kampfplan** des Zugführers für den Angriff beruht:

(1) Auf der Beurteilung des Feindes (Angriffsziel? Welche feindlichen Waffen sind außerdem auszuschalten?).

(2) Auf der Beurteilung der eigenen Lage (Welche Waffen können beim Angriff mitwirken? Welche Zeit ist verfügbar?).

(3) Auf der Beurteilung des Geländes (Wo ist die günstigste Annäherungsmöglichkeit für den Stoß? Wo sind die günstigsten Feuerstellungen für die unterstützenden Waffen?).

Im Sinne dieses Kampfplanes erfolgen die **Kampfaufträge** für den Ansatz der Gruppen.

459. Der Angriff ist möglichst unter Umfassung zu führen.

Der Zugführer muß anstreben, seine Gruppen zangenförmig aus verschiedener Richtung auf das Angriffsziel anzusetzen. Durch diese Art des Angriffs wird das feindliche Feuer zersplittert.

Lücken in der Gliederung der feindlichen Verteidigungsstellung begünstigen die örtliche Umfassung.

460. Für den Ansatz des Zuges zum Angriff ist das Gelände ausschlaggebend.

Ob die Umfassung durch Feuer oder durch Stoß[291] erreicht werden soll, richtet sich nach dem Gelände.

Dort, wo es die beste Annäherungsmöglichkeit bietet, setzt der Zugführer meist seine Gruppen zum Stoß an.

---

[291] Hier geht es um die Stoßkraft, sie wird erzielt durch den Schwung der Soldaten im Sturmangriff. Siehe Glossar: Stoßkraft und Feuerkraft.

Text

458. The **battle plan** of the platoon leader for the attack is based on:

(1) On the assessment of the enemy (Attack objective? Which enemy weapons should also be eliminated?).

(2) On the assessment of the friendly situation (Which weapons can participate in the attack? What time is available?)

(3) On the evaluation of the terrain (Where is the most favorable approach for the thrust? Where are the most favorable firing positions for the supporting weapons?).

According to this battle plan the **combat missions** for the commitment of the squads are carried out.

459. The attack is to be carried out preferably as an envelopment.

The platoon leader must strive to set his squads in a pincer-like manner from different directions towards the attack objective. This way of attacking splits the enemy fire.

Gaps in the positioning of the enemy defensive position favor the local envelopment.

460. For the commitment of the platoon for the attack the terrain is decisive.

Whether the envelopment should be achieved by fire or shock[292] depends on the terrain.

Where there is the best possibility for an approach, the platoon leader commits his squads usually for a thrust.

---

[292] This is about shock action, which is achieved by the momentum of the soldiers in the assault. See Glossary: Shock Action (Stoßkraft) and Fire Power (Feuerkraft).

Die notwendige Feuerunterstützung geben die restlichen Teile des Zuges, der leichte Granatwerfer[293] und schwere Waffen.

461. Oft läßt der Zugführer ein feindliches Widerstandsnest frontal mit Feuer bekämpfen und seine Gruppen seitlich daran vorbeistoßen. Wegnahme des feindlichen Widerstandnestes und Säubern des Geländes vom Feinde bleibt nachfolgenden Kräften überlassen.

462. Jeder Waffe, die den Angriff des Zuges unterstützt, wird befohlen wann und wohin sie das Feuer eröffnen soll.

463. Der l.Gr.W.[294] erhält das feindliche Ziel zugewiesen, welches das Heranarbeiten der vordersten Gruppen auf Einbruchsentfernung am meisten aufhält.

Oft bezeichnet der Zugführer ihm die Linie, bei deren Erreichen durch die vordersten Gruppen das Feuer des Werfers abzubrechen ist.

464. Beispiele für **Kampfaufträge:**

(1) „Gruppe X unterstützt von hier aus frontal das umfassende Vorgehen des Zuges dort rechts durch die Hecke. Feuereröffnung gegen das gezeigte Nest erst, wenn ich vom Schuppen mit dem Zug vorbreche!"

(2) „Ihre Gruppe gewinnt rechts die Windmühle und kämpft von dort aus das gezeigte Feindnest flankierend nieder, wenn ich mit der Masse des Zuges hier frontal vorstürme!"

---

[293] Der Standard leichte Granatwerfer der Wehrmacht war der Granatwerfer 36 mit Kaliber 5 cm. Es handelt sich dabei um einen Mörser, nicht um einen Granatwerfer im heutigen Sinn. Siehe Glossar: Granatwerfer, leicht.

[294] Leichter Granatwerfer.

The necessary fire support is provided by the remaining elements of the platoon, the light mortar[295] and heavy weapons.

461. Often the platoon leader lets an enemy fighting positions[296] be engaged frontally with fire and his squads bypass it on the side. Removal of the enemy resistance-nest and clearing of the terrain of the enemy is left to follow-up forces.

462. Each weapon that supports the attack of the platoon is ordered when and where to open fire.

463. The light mortar is assigned the enemy target that is most likely to slow down the advancing foremost squads towards break-in[297] distance.

Often the platoon leader indicates the line to it [light mortar], on which the fire of the mortar[298] is to be cancelled when the foremost squads reach it.

464. Examples for **combat missions**:

(1) "From here Squad X frontally supports the enveloping advance of the platoon over to the right through the hedge. Opening of fire against the indicated nest only, when I move forward[299] with the platoon from the shed!"

(2) "Your squad takes[300] the windmill on the right and from there flanking overpowers the indicated enemy nest, when I assault with the mass of the platoon!"

---

[295] The standard light mortar of the Wehrmacht was the Granatwerfer 36 with 5 cm caliber. "Granatwerfer" literally means "grenade thrower", which nowadays in German would be a grenade launcher. This was a mortar, not a grenade launcher in the modern sense. See Glossary: Mortar, light (Granatwerfer, leicht).

[296] "Widerstandsnest" literally means "resistance nest".

[297] There is no English equivalent for the military term "Einbruch". The break-in is the result of a successful attack that breached into the enemy's foremost lines. It precedes the penetration. See the Glossary for a visual example.

[298] "Werfer" literally means "thrower" referring to second word in "Granatwerfer".

[299] "Vorbrechen" literally means "break forward".

[300] "Gewinnt" literally means "wins".

(3) „S.M.G.[301] und l.Gr.W.[302] kämpfen von hier aus das gezeigte Angriffsziel frontal nieder, bis der ganze Zug aus dem Waldstück hier links herausbricht. Feuer frei!"

(4) „L.Gr.W. – Einschießen auf Angriffsziel! Wirkungsschießen erst, wenn der Zug von hier vorbricht. Beim Erreichen des grünen Saatfeldes Feuer auf Feind an der Ruine legen!"

(5) „L.Gr.W. kämpft von hier aus Feind an der Einbruchsstelle nieder. Auf grünes Leuchtzeichen vom Feldweg letzter Feuerüberfall[303] – 8 Schuß auf Einbruchsstelle! – L.Gr.W.! Feuer frei!"

---

[301] Schweres Maschinengewehr. Hierbei handelt es sich üblicherweise um das MG 34 oder MG 42 auf der Lafette 34 bzw. 42. Beide MGs mit Zweibein aber auch normalen Dreibein (für Fliegerabwehr nicht die Lafette 34 bzw. 42) waren als leichtes Maschinengewehr klassifiziert.

[302] Der leichte Granatwerfer. Der Standard leichte Granatwerfer der Wehrmacht war der Granatwerfer 36 mit Kaliber 5 cm. Es handelt sich dabei um einen Mörser, nicht um einen Granatwerfer im heutigen Sinn. Siehe Glossar: Granatwerfer, leicht.

[303] Siehe Glossar: Feuerüberfall.

(3) "Heavy machine gun[304] and light mortar[305] overpower the indicated attack objective from here, until the whole platoon breaks out of this forest area. Fire!"

(4) "Light mortar – Adjusting fire on attack objective! Fire for effect only, when the platoon pushes forward from here. When reaching the green seed field lay fire on the enemy at the ruins!"

(5) "Light mortar overpowers from here the enemy at the break-in[306] location. On green signal flare from dirt road last surprise fire[307] - 8 shots on the break-in location! – Light Mortar! Fire!"

---

[304] Heavy machine gun, usually the MG 34 or MG 42 on the Lafette 34 or 42 mount. Both MGs with bipod and normal tripod (for anti-aircraft defense not the Lafette 34 or 42 mount) were classified as light machine guns.

[305] The standard light mortar of the Wehrmacht was the Granatwerfer 36 with 5 cm caliber. "Granatwerfer" literally means "grenade thrower", which nowadays in German would be a grenade launcher. This was a mortar, not a grenade launcher in the modern sense. See Glossary: Mortar, light (Granatwerfer, leicht).

[306] There is no English equivalent for the military term "Einbruch". The break-in is the result of a successful attack that breached into the enemy's foremost lines. It precedes the penetration. See the Glossary Break-In (Einbruch) for a visual example.

[307] The literal translation of the German word "Feuerüberfall" would be "firing raid", although in this case "Überfall" refers to the surprise effect. See Glossary: Surprise Fire (Feuerüberfall).

Ergänzung 4: H.Dv. 240/2: Nr. 113-133: Schießübungen für das Sturmgewehr 44

Quellenlage, Aktualität und Formatierung

Hierbei handelt es sich um Auszüge aus einem Entwurf der *H.Dv. 240/2 Kriegsnahe Schießausbildung des Einzelschützen mit Gewehr, Sturmgewehr 44, leichtem Maschinengewehr und Pistole*. Von dieser Heeresdruckvorschrift liegen drei Entwürfe im Militärarchiv in Freiburg vor. Eine gedruckte Version ist auf den 2. November 1944 datiert, allerdings enthält dieser Entwurf kein einziges Bild.[308] Die vermutlich letzte Version wurde auf einer Schreibmaschine geschrieben und ist mit einem handschriftlichen Vermerk auf Dezember 1944 datiert.[309] Sie enthält einige handschriftliche Korrekturen und enthält die meisten darin vermerkten Bilder. Diese beiden Entwürfe sind nicht identisch. Der gedruckte Entwurf beginnt bei Nummer 100 mit der Schießausbildung für das Sturmgewehr, während dieser Abschnitt in der Schreibmaschinen-Version bei Nummer 113 anfängt. Wir haben uns entschieden die Inhalte der neueren Schreibmaschinen-Version zu übernehmen, da in dieser auch die meisten Bilder enthalten waren. Allerdings halten wir uns in Sachen Formatierung an die gedruckte Version, da sich diese, im Gegensatz zur Schreibmaschinen-Entwurf, an die übliche Formatierung von Druckvorschriften und Merkblätter hält. Zum Beispiel finden sich bei der Schreibmaschinen-Version, Unterstreichungen, Sperrungen und keine Punkte „." nach den Nummern. Wir folgen auch hier der Formatierung der Druck-Version und verzichten auf die Unterstreichungen und Sperrungen und fügten auch einen Punkt an die jeweilige Nummern hinzu.

Die Seiten dieses Dokuments enthalten zum Teil mehr Text als in den vorherigen Merkblättern. Um die beiliegenden Bilder nicht stark verkleinern zu müssen haben wir uns bei diesem Dokument dazu entschieden den Abstand zwischen den Zeilen und Absätzen auf den letzten beiden Seiten zu verkleinern. Auch können Abstände zwischen Absätzen und die Position vom Bildern stärker als üblich abweichen.

---

[308] BArch, RH 1/1463: *H.Dv. 240/2 Entwurf: Kriegsnahe Schießausbildung des Einzelschützen mit Gewehr, Sturmgewehr 44, leichtem Maschinengewehr und Pistole*. 2. November 1944.

[309] BArch, RH 11-I/14: *Entwurf zur Heeresdienstvorschrift [sic!] 240/2*. Dezember 1944.

Supplement 4: H.Dv. 240/2: No. 113-133: Firing Exercises for the Sturmgewehr 44

Source Situation, Actuality and Formatting

These are excerpts from a draft of the *H.Dv. 240/2 War Like Firing Training of the Single Rifleman with Rifle, Sturmgewehr 44, Light Machine Gun and Pistol.* Three drafts of this regulation are available in the Military Archive in Freiburg. One printed version is dated November 2, 1944, but this draft does not contain a single picture.[310] The presumably last version is written on a typewriter and is dated December 1944 with a handwritten note.[311] It contains some handwritten corrections and includes most of the referenced pictures. These two drafts are not identical. The printed draft starts at number 100 with the firing training for the assault rifle, while this section is found in the typewriter version at number 113. Since it included most of the pictures, we have decided to translate the contents of the newer typewriter version. However, in terms of formatting we stick to the printed version, as it follows the typical formatting of regulations and pamphlets whereas the typewriter did not. For example, the typewriter version included underlining, word spacings and there are no dots "." following the numbers. As such, we applied the formatting of the print version without underlining, additional spacings and have added a dot to the respective numbers.

The pages of this document sometimes contain more text than previous pamphlets. So as to not reduce the size of the pictures considerably, we decided to reduce the space between the lines and paragraphs on the last two pages of this document. Additionally, distances between paragraphs and the position of the pictures can differ more than usual.

---

[310] BArch, RH 1/1463: *H.Dv. 240/2 Entwurf: Kriegsnahe Schießausbildung des Einzelschützen mit Gewehr, Sturmgewehr 44, leichtem Maschinengewehr und Pistole. 2. November 1944.*

[311] BArch, RH 11-I/14: *Entwurf zur Heeresdienstvorschrift [sic!] 240/2. Dezember 1944.*

Da es teilweise auch Vorschriften gibt, die nicht im Militärarchiv in Freiburg vorliegen, haben wir eine Anfrage beim Militärhistorischen Museum der Bundeswehr Dresden gestellt, ob sich im Bestand noch weitere Versionen der *H.Dv. 240/2* finden bzw. eine Version aus dem Jahre 1945 vorliegt. Die Antwort war, dass es laut aktuellem Stand keine andere Version mehr gibt.[312] Ebenso führt der *Katalog der Druckvorschriften der ehemaligen deutschen Wehrmacht - Teil I Heer* von 1960 für die Vorschrift nur das Jahr 1944.[313] Basierend auf diesen Informationen, sind wir ziemlich sicher, dass es sich bei der von uns übersetzten Fassung um die aktuellste Version der *H.Dv. 240/2* handelt, die sowohl bekannt wie auch verfügbar ist.

Anmerkung zu Anmerkungen

Bei diesem Entwurf sind einige Tippfehler, Korrekturen und andere Fehler enthalten. Die meisten davon sind von uns in den Fußnoten angemerkt. Vereinzelt sind auch Buchstaben hochgestellt. Dabei dürfte es sich um Fehler handeln, die durch die mechanische Schreibmaschine bedingt sind. Diese haben wir normalerweise nicht angemerkt.

---

[312] Email Jens Wehner vom 3. August 2020, Verweis auf Auskunft durch die Bibliothek.
[313] Bundesministerium der Verteidigung: *Katalog der Druckvorschriften der ehemaligen deutschen Wehrmacht – Teil 1 Heer*. Bonn, Germany, 1960, S. 25.

Since there are some regulations which are not available at the Military Archive in Freiburg, we asked the Military History Museum of the Bundeswehr in Dresden whether another version of the *H.Dv. 240/2* exists within their records and whether a version from 1945 is available. The answer was that currently no other version exists.[314] Likewise, the *Catalog of Regulations of the former German Wehrmacht - Part I Army* from 1960 only lists the year 1944 for this regulation.[315] Based on this information, we are fairly certain that our translated document is the most recent *H.Dv. 240/2*, both known and available.

Note about the Notes

This draft includes some typos, corrections and other mistakes. Most of them are identified by us in the footnotes. Some letters were also written as superscript and are probably errors caused by the mechanical typewriter. These are not specifically mentioned by us.

---

[314] Email Jens Wehner from 3rd August 2020, reference to information from the library.
[315] Bundesministerium der Verteidigung: *Katalog der Druckvorschriften der ehemaligen deutschen Wehrmacht – Teil 1 Heer*. Bonn, Germany, 1960, S. 25.

B. Schießausbildung mit Sturmgewehr 44.[316]

I. Allgemeines

113. Die Schießausbildung mit dem Sturmgewehr 44 ist nach den gleichen Grundsätzen wie mit Gewehr zu betreiben. In den Stationen sind nur die Abweichungen enthalten, die durch die Eigenart der Waffe bedingt sind.

Ist der Schütze an Gewehr ausgebildet, so baut sich die Schießausbildung auf das bereits am Gewehr Erlernte auf.

114. Der kaum spürbare Rückstoß und die Unterstützung durch das Magazin begünstigen die Schußleistungen erheblich und heben die Nachteile der kürzeren Visierlinie auf.

115. Mit dem Sturmgewehr 44 können keine Platzpatronen verschossen werden. Es ist deshalb frühzeitig mit der Ausbildung im scharfen Schuß zu beginnen.

116. Da man es der Waffe äußerlich nicht ansehen kann, ob sich eine Patrone im Lauf befindet oder nicht, ist die Waffe stets zu sichern. Es darf nie vergessen werden, daß die Waffe **nach jedem Schuß wieder geladen und gespannt ist.**

117. Der Schütze muß so ausgebildet werden, daß er

a)   in der Regel Einzelfeuer, d.h. den sorgfältig gezielten Einzelschuß abgibt.
b)   nur zur Bekämpfung von Feindmassierungen (Pulke) beim Einbruch[317] oder in der Sturmabwehr auf nahe oder nächste Entfernungen sein Feuer zu Feuerstößen von 2 – 3 Schuß steigert.
c)   niemals Dauerfeuer schießt.

---

[316] Hierbei und den folgenden Seiten bis zur Ergänzung 5 handelt es sich um die Transkription des Dokumentes BArch, RH 11-I/14: *Entwurf zur Heeresdienstvorschrift [sic!] 240/2.* Dezember 1944.
[317] Siehe Glossar: Einbruch.

B. Firing Training with the Sturmgewehr 44.[318]

I. General Information

113. The firing training with the Sturmgewehr 44 is to be conducted according to the same principles as with the rifle. The stations contain only those deviations that are due to the characteristics of the weapon.

If the rifleman has been trained on a rifle, the firing training is based on what has already been learned on the rifle.

114. The barely noticeable recoil and the support of the magazine considerably improve the firing performance and eliminate the disadvantages of the shorter sight radius.

115. The Sturmgewehr 44 cannot fire blanks. Therefore, at an early stage start training with live[319] fire.

116. As it is not possible to tell from the outside whether a cartridge is in the chamber[320] or not, the gun must always be on safe. It should never be forgotten that **the gun is loaded and cocked after each shot.**

117. The rifleman must be trained so that

a) as a rule, semi-automatic fire, meaning carefully aimed single shots.
b) only to combat enemy masses (pulks) during the break-in[321] or in defense against assaults in close and immediate ranges[322] [he] increases his fire to bursts of 2 – 3 shots.
c) never fires full-automatic fire.

---

[318] This and the following pages up to Supplement 5 are the transcription of the document: BArch, RH 11-I/14: *Entwurf zur Heeresdienstvorschrift [sic!] 240/2.* Dezember 1944.

[319] Note that "scharfen Schuß" literally means "sharp shot".

[320] "Lauf" literally means "barrel". This would be a confusing action for English native speakers – who are more used to checking the chamber rather than the barrel – to see if the weapon is loaded. That said, the weapon is always to be considered as loaded.

[321] There is no English equivalent for the military term "Einbruch". The break-in is the result of a successful attack that breached into the enemy's foremost lines. It precedes the penetration. See the Glossary Break-In (Einbruch) for a visual example.

[322] "Nahe" and "nächste Entfernung" refer to different distances. We translated "nahe Entfernung" to "close range" and "nächste Entfernung" to "immediate ranges".

118. Die Erlernung desx [sic!] gut gezielten Einzelschusses steht deshalb im Vordergrund der Schießausbildung.

Hieran anschließend muß der Schütze lernen, sicher gezielte Einzelschüsse in rascher Folge abzugeben. Die hohe Feuergeschwindigkeit der Waffe im Einzelschuß ermöglicht es, mehrere Ziele nacheinander in kurzer Zeit im Einzelschuß zu bekämpfen (bis 30 Schuß in der Minute).

Die Feuergeschwindigkeit ist langsam zu steigern! Die Schnelligkeit der Schußabgabe darf nicht auf Kosten der Genauigkeit der Einzelschüsse gehen.

Im Einzelschuß sind mit dem Sturmgewehr 44 gute Trefferergebnisse auf Entfernungen bis 400 m, im zusammengefaßten Feuer mehrerer Schützen auf Entfernungen bis zu 600 m zu erzielen.

119. Nachdem der Schütze den wohlgezielten Einzelschuß beherrscht, erlernt er das Schießen in rasch aufeinanderfolgenden kurzen Feuerstößen von 2 – 3 Schuß auf nächste Entfernung.

120. Die hohe Feuergeschwindigkeit des Sturmgewehrs 44 macht eine straffe Feuerzucht des Schützen erforderlich. Hierauf ist der Hauptwert der Ausbildung zu legen. Zur Feuerzucht gehört insbesondere die richtige Anwendung des Einzelfeuers und des Feuerstoßes.

118. The training of well-aimed single shots are therefore in the foreground of the firing training.

Subsequent to this the rifleman must learn to fire reliably aimed single shots in rapid succession. The high rate of fire of the weapon in semi-automatic fire allows the engagement of several targets one after the other in a short time with single shots (up to 30 shots per minute).

The rate of fire must be increased slowly! The speed of firing must not be at the expense of the accuracy of single shots.

With the Sturmgewehr 44 good hits can be achieved with a single shot at distances up to 400 m, with combined fire of several riflemen at distances up to 600 m.

119. After the shooter has mastered the well-aimed single shot, he or she learns to fire in quick succession with short bursts of 2-3 shots at immediate ranges[323].

120. The high rate of fire of the Sturmgewehr 44 makes a tight fire discipline of the rifleman necessary. The main emphasis[324] of training is to be focused on this. The correct use of semi-automatic fire and bursts is particularly important for fire discipline.

---

[323] "Nahe" and "nächste Entfernung" refer to different distances. We translated "nahe Entfernung" to "close range" and "nächste Entfernung" to "immediate ranges".
[324] Note that "Hauptwert" literally translated means "main value".

Schußtafel für Sturmgewehr 44

mit Pist.Patr. 43 m.E.[325]

Entfernung in m	Abgangs – Fall - winkel						Gipfel entf. höhe in Meter		Flugzeiten in Sekund.	Endgeschwindigkeit in m/sec.
	Grad	Min	Str.	Grad	Min	Str.				
100	.	4,05	1,2	.	4,50	1,3	53	0,03	0,16	576
200	.	9.02[!]	2,8	.	11,45	3,4	106	0,15	0,35	479
300	.	16,00	4,7	.	23,00	7,0	164	0,4	0,58	398
400	.	24,80	7,4	.	39,90	11,9	224	0,9	0,85	338
500	.	35,80	10,6	1	2,80	18,5	285	1,7	1,18	292
[6]00[326]	.	49,45	14,6	1	29,10	26,5	345	2,9	1,54	274
700	1	6,10	19,6	2	1,10	36,0	403	4,8	1,93	253
800	1	26,20	25,6	2	41,60	48,0	460	7,3	2,35	234

Anfangsgeschwindigkeit: 685 m/sec.

Kaliber: 7,9 mm

Geschoßgewicht: 8,00 g.

Ladung: 1,59 g.

Gewicht der Patrone: 17 g.

---

[325] „m. E." steht für „mit Eisenkern".
[326] Hier befand sich ein Loch im Originaldokument.

Firing Table for Sturmgewehr 44

with Pist.Patr.[327] 43 m.E.[328]

Distance in m	Quadrant – Fall – angle of departure						Summit dist[ance]. height in meter		Flight time in sec.	Final velocity in m/sec..
	Degree	Min	Mil.	Degree	Min	Mil.				
100	.	4.05	1.2	.	4.50	1.3	53	0.03	0.16	576
200	.	9.02	2.8	.	11.45	3.4	106	0.15	0.35	479
300	.	16.00	4.7	.	23.00	7.0	164	0.4	0.58	398
400	.	24.80	7.4	.	39.90	11.9	224	0.9	0.85	338
500	.	35.80	10.6	1	2.80	18.5	285	1.7	1.18	292
[6]00[329]	.	49.45	14.6	1	29.10	26.5	345	2.9	1.54	274
700	1	6.10	19.6	2	1.10	36.0	403	4.8	1.93	253
800	1	26.20	25.6	2	41.60	48.0	460	7.3	2.35	234

Muzzle Velocity[330]: 685 m/sec.

Caliber: 7.9 mm

Projectile Weight: 8.00 g.

Propellant[331]: 1.59 g.

Cartridge Weight: 17 g.

---

[327] "Pist.Patr." means "Pistolen Patrone" literally "pistol cartridge", yet in this case it is a technical designation.

[328] "m. E." is short for "mit Eisenkern", which means "with iron core".

[329] Here was a hole in the original document.

[330] "Anfangsgeschwindigkeit" literally means "starting/initial velocity". The German word for "muzzle velocity" would be "Mündungsgeschwindigkeit".

[331] Note "Ladung" here is short for "Treibladung". "Ladung" alone can also mean "charge" or "payload".

1. Station:

Erlernen des Zielens.

122. Die Ziffern 31 – 52 der Schießausbildung mit Gewehr gelten ebensfal[ls][332] für das Sturmgewehr 44.

Beim Einrichten des Sturmgewehres 44 ist das Magazin zu entnehmen und als Auflage unter dem Magazinhalter einen Sandsack zu benutzen.

Merkpunkte für den Schießlehrer.

Zielfehler wie Voll-, Fein- oder geklemmtes Korn wirken sich wegen der kurzen Visierlinie und des größeren Abstandes zwischen Visierlinie und Seelenachse auf die Trefferlage ungünstiger aus als beim Gewehr.

Deshalb erfordert bereits diese Station größte Genauigkeit!

2. Station:

Zielen auf Feindziele.

Haltepunkt, „Zielaufsitzen u[n]d[333] Zielmitte", Haltepunktverlegen.

123. Die Ausbildung in dieser Station hat[334] sinngemäß wie mit dem Gewehr zu erfolgen (vergl. Ziff. 53-60).

Ziffer 59 und Bild 14 haben wegen der abweichenden Gestalt der Flugbahn[335] für das Sturmgewehr keine Gültigkeit.

Merkpunkte für Schießlehrer.

Da das Visier nur von 100 zu 100[336] gestellt werden kann, ist vermehrt das Zielen auf den Zwischenentfernungen und die Wahl des dafür in Frage kommenden Haltepunktes zu üben.

---

[332] Das Blatt ist am Außenrand frühzeitig abgeschnitten und es steht nur „ebenfal" mit einem hochgestellten aber auch abgeschnitten „s" oberhalb von „ebenfal".

[333] Statt dem „n" war ein Leerzeichen vorhanden, vermutlich hat die Schreibmaschine nicht ordentlich angeschlagen.

[334] Hier stand „beginnt" welches aber durchgestrichen ist, „hat" ist mit Schreibmaschine darüber geschrieben.

[335] Hier fehlte ein Leerzeichen, es wurde handschriftlich mit eine Schrägstrich korrigiert.

[336] Hierbei ist die Justierung in 100 m Schritten gemeint. In der D 1854/3 ist angeführt, dass auch die Entfernungen 250, 350 und 450 m einstellbar sein müssten.

1. Station:

Learning How to Aim.

122. The numbers 31 – 52 of the firing training with the rifle also[337] apply to the Sturmgewehr 44.

When setting up the assault rifle 44, remove the magazine and use a sandbag as support under the magazine well.

Key Points for the Marksmanship Instructor.

Aiming errors such as full, fine or jammed front sight have a more unfavorable effect on the grouping than with a rifle because of the short sight radius and the greater distance between the sight radius and the axis of the bore.

That is why even this station requires the greatest accuracy!

2. Station:

Aiming at Enemy Targets.

Point of aim, "6 o' clock hold a[n]d[338] center hold", changing of point of aim.

123. The training at this station shall[339] be conducted in the same way as with the rifle (compare No. 53-60).

Number 59 and Figure 14 are not valid for the assault rifle because of the different shape of the trajectory[340].

Key Points for the Marksmanship Instructor.

Since the sight can only be set from 100 to 100[341], more practice is needed in aiming at the intermediate distances and selecting the appropriate point of aim.

---

[337] Reference to original document: The sheet is prematurely cut off at the outer margin and it stands only "ebenfal" with a raised but also cut-off "s" above "ebenfal".

[338] Reference to original document: Instead of the "n" there was a space, probably the typewriter did not hit properly.

[339] Reference to original document: Here "beginnt" ("begins") was written which is crossed out, "hat" ("has to") is written over it with a typewriter.

[340] Reference to original document: Here a space was missing, but it was corrected by hand with a slash.

[341] Meant here are adjustments of the sight in 100 m intervals. In *D 1854/3* it is stated that the distances 250, 350 and 450 m should also be adjustable.

3. Station:

Erlernen der Tätigkeiten beim Anschlag.

124. Die Ziffern 61-76 für die 3. Station der Schießausbildung mit Gewehr gelten sinngemäß für das Sturmgewehr 44.

Der Eigenart der Waffe entsprechend ergeben sich folgende Änderungen:

Beim Anschlag umfaßt der Schütze mit der einen Hand das Griffstück, mit der anderen Hand das Magazin, Zeigefinger am Magazinhalter. Der Daumen ist von rückwärts um das Magazin gelegt und drückt es nach vorn. Hierdurch wird das einwandfreie Zuführen der Patrone begünstigt. Das Magazin dient als Unterstützung[342].

Merkpunkte für den Schießlehrer.

125. Für das Sturmgewehr 44 gibt es keinen Zielkontrollspiegel[343]. Die Zieltätigkeit ist daher durch Einrichten der Waffe vom Schießlehrer zu überwachen.

Der Druckpunkt des Sturmgewehres 44 ist lang und weich. Auf langsames und gleichmäßiger [sic!] Durchkrümmen ist besonderer Wert zu legen. Reißen verschlechtert das Ergebnis wegen des kurzen Laufes noch mehr als beim Gewehr.

[Hier sind anders als üblich mehrere Leerzeilen.]

4. Station:

Der Anschlag liegend.

126. Zum Anschlag liegend liegt der Schütze hinter eine [sic!] Deckung, die so beschaffen sein[344] muß, daß das mit dem Magazin hinter der Deckung aufgestützte Sturmgewehr 44 mit seiner Mündung über die Deckung hinwegreicht.

---

[342] Ursprünglich stand statt „Unterstützung" „Unterlage". Dieses Wort wurde jedoch mit der Schreibmaschine ausgekreuzt (mit „x").

[343] Hierbei handelt es sich um ein Gerät, welches es einer weiteren Person ermöglicht zu sehen wohin der Schütze zielt, üblicherweise wird dies von Schießausbildern verwendet.

[344] Hier war vor „sein" ein „ist", welches mit Schreibmaschine ausgekreuzt wurde (mit „x").

3. Station:

Learning the Activities of the Aiming Position.

124. The numbers 61-76 for the 3rd station of firing training with rifle apply analogously to the Sturmgewehr 44.

According to the characteristics of the weapon, the following changes have been made:

In the aiming position, the rifleman grasps the grip with one hand and the magazine with the other hand, index finger on the magazine well. The thumb is placed around the magazine from behind and pushes it forward. This helps to feed the cartridge correctly. The magazine serves as a support[345].

Key Points for the Marksmanship Instructor.

125. There is no aim-checking device[346] for the Sturmgewehr 44. Therefore, the aiming activity must be monitored by the marksmanship instructor by setting up the rifle.

The trigger pull[347] of the Sturmgewehr 44 is long and soft. Special attention should be paid to slow and even pulling. Jerking worsens the result because of the short barrel even more than with a rifle.

[Here, unlike usual, there are several blank lines].

4. Station:

The Aiming Position Lying.

126. The rifleman lies behind a cover, which must be[348] such that the Sturmgewehr 44, which is supported by the magazine behind the cover, extends with its muzzle over the cover.

---

[345] Reference to original document: Originally, the word "Unterstützung" ("support") was replaced by "Unterlage" ("carpet pad") but this word was crossed out with a typewriter (with "x").

[346] This is a device that allows another person to see where the shooter is aiming, usually used by shooting instructors.

[347] There is no equivalent for "Druckpunkt" in English, determining the "Druckpunkt" is "to take up the slack".

[348] Reference to original document: Here there was an "ist" ("is") before "sein" ("be"), which was crossed out with a typewriter (with "x").

Der Schütze preßt sich mit dem Oberkörper fest an den Boden und stellt das Visier. Die linke Hand hat das Sturmgewehr 44 am Magazin erfaßt, Zeigefinger am Magazinhalter.

Der Kolben liegt flach auf der rechten Innenseite des rechten Unterarmes – das Magazin zeigt nach links, die Mündung ist leicht angehoben (Bild 40).

Originale in Wünsdorf.[349]

Der Schütze hebt den linken Unterarm, richtet das Sturmgewehr auf[.] (Bild 41)

Originale in Wünsdorf.[350]

Magazin senkrecht nach unten, und zeiht [sic!] es mit beiden Händen in die rechte Schulter. (Bild 42)

---

[349] Vermerk in Handschrift und blauen Buntstift.
[350] Vermerk in Handschrift und blauen Buntstift.

The rifleman presses his upper body firmly against the ground and sets the rear sight. The left hand has grasped the Sturmgewehr 44 at the magazine, index finger at the magazine well.

The butt lies flat on the right inner side of the right forearm - the magazine points to the left, the muzzle is slightly raised (Figure 40).

Originals in Wünsdorf.[351]

The rifleman raises his left forearm, raises the assault rifle[.] (Figure 41)

Originals in Wünsdorf.[352]

Magazine vertically downwards, and pull it with both hands into the right shoulder. (Figure 42)

---

[351] Note in handwriting and blue colored pencil.
[352] Note in handwriting and blue colored pencil.

Bild 42[353]

BArch, RH 11-I/14: Entwurf zur Heeresdienstvorschrift 240/2, Bild 42.

Nach dem Schuß zieht der Schütze mit beiden Händen das Sturmgewehr 44 zurück, dreht es dabei rechts, sodaß Kolben wieder flach auf der Innenseite des rechten Unterarmes liegt und preßt den Oberkörper in die Deckung.

Merkpunkte für den Schießlehrer.

127. Beim Anschlag liegend dient das Magazin stets als Unterstützung. Eine[354] zu starke Schräglage des Körpers zum Ziel ist falsch, da hierdurch die rechte Schulter zu weit zurückgenommen wird und nicht fest in der Schulter, sondern auf dem rechten Oberarmknochen bzw. Oberarm ruht. Dies hat bei Abgabe von Feuerstößen ein Ausweichen der Mündung zur Folge.

Der Oberkörper ruht fest auf beiden Ellenbogen. Die Kolbenklappe liegt auf der Schulterwulst.

5. Station.

Anschläge kniend (sitzend) und stehend.

128. Der Anschlag **kniend oder sitzend** wird wie mit Gewehr ausgeführt (vergl. Ziff .85 [sic!] – 87).

Die linke Hand unterstützt das Sturmgewehr 44 **unter** dem Abzugsbügel.

---

[353] Vermerk in Handschrift und blauen Buntstift.

[354] Die letzten beiden Buchstaben sehe beide wie „n" aus, sind jedoch mit anderen Buchstaben überschrieben bzw. unterlegt.

Figure 42[355]

BArch, RH 11-I/14: Entwurf zur Heeresdienstvorschrift 240/2, Bild 42.

After the shot, the rifleman pulls back the Sturmgewehr 44 with both hands, turning it to the right, so that the butt lies flat again on the inside of the right forearm and presses the upper body into cover.

Key Points for the Marksmanship Instructor.

127. In the aiming position lying the magazine always serves as a support. Too[356] much slanting of the body towards the target is wrong, because this causes the right shoulder to be pulled back too far and rests not firmly in the shoulder but on the right humerus or upper arm. This causes the muzzle to swerve when bursts are fired.

The upper body rests firmly on both elbows. The butt rests on the shoulder pocket.

5. Station.

Aiming Positions kneeling (seated) and standing.

128. The aiming position **kneeling or sitting** is carried out like with the rifle (compare No. 85 – 87).

The left hand supports the Sturmgewehr 44 **under** the trigger guard.

---

[355] Note in handwriting and blue colored pencil.

[356] Reference to original document: The last two letters [of "Eine"] both look like "n", but are overwritten or underlaid with other letters.

Bild 43[357]

BArch, RH 11-I/14: Entwurf zur Heeresdienstvorschrift 240/2, Bild 43.

Beim Anschlag **kniend** (sitzend) **aufgelegt** oder mit Magazinunterstützung umfaßt die linke Hand das Magazin wie beim Anschlag liegend (Bild 43).

Der **Anschlag stehend freihändig** wird wie mit Gewehr ausgeführt. (Bild 44).(Ziff...88)

44[358]

BArch, RH 11-I/14: Entwurf zur Heeresdienstvorschrift 240/2, Bild 44.

---

[357] Vermerk in Handschrift und blauen Buntstift.

[358] Vermerk in Handschrift und blauen Buntstift. Im Gegensatz zu vorherigen Anmerkungen wurde hier das „Bild" weggelassen und nurmehr die Ziffer angegeben, erst bei Bild 49 im Abschnitt *Schießausbildung mit leMG* wird wieder „Bild" angegeben.

BArch, RH 11-I/14: Entwurf zur Heeresdienstvorschrift 240/2, Bild 43.

Support kneeling (seated) aiming position or support it at the magazine, as the left hand grasps the magazine as with the prone aiming position (Figure 43).

The **freehand standing aiming position** is executed as with a rifle. (Figure 44).(No...88)

44[360]

BArch, RH 11-I/14: Entwurf zur Heeresdienstvorschrift 240/2, Bild 44.

---

[359] Note in handwriting and blue colored pencil.

[360] Note in handwriting and blue colored pencil. Contrary to previous comments, "Bild" ("Figure") was omitted here and only the number was indicated. Only in the case of Figure 49 in the section *Firing Training with light MG* is "Bild" used again.

Beim Anschlag **stehend aufgelegt** oder mit Magazinunterstützung umfaßt die linke Hand das Magazin wie beim Anschlag liegend oder kniend (Bild 45).

45[361]

BArch, RH 11-I/14: Entwurf zur Heeresdienstvorschrift 240/2, Bild 45.

Der Anschlag stehend angestrichen erfolgt sinngemäß wie mit Gewehr (Bild 46).

46[362]

BArch, RH 11-I/14: Entwurf zur Heeresdienstvorschrift 240/2, Bild 46.

---

[361] Vermerk in Handschrift und blauen Buntstift.
[362] Vermerk in Handschrift und blauen Buntstift.

In a **supported standing** aiming position or when supported with the magazine the left hand grasps the magazine like the aiming position lying or kneeling (Figure 45).

45[363]

BArch, RH 11-I/14: *Entwurf zur Heeresdienstvorschrift 240/2, Bild 45.*

The leaning aiming position is conducted in the same way as with rifle (Figure 46).

46[364]

BArch, RH 11-I/14: *Entwurf zur Heeresdienstvorschrift 240/2, Bild 46.*

---

[363] Note in handwriting and blue colored pencil.
[364] Note in handwriting and blue colored pencil.

47[365]

BArch, RH 11-I/14: Entwurf zur Heeresdienstvorschrift 240/2, Bild 47.

Beim **Anschlag an einem Baum** ist wegen der Schwere der Waffe die Benutzung des[366] Riemens zweckmäßig. Er wird mit der Hand mit dem Daumen fest an den Baum gepreßt. (Bild 47)

Merkpunkt für den Schießlehrer.

130. Beim Inanschlaggehen darf das angesteckte Magazin nicht mit Gewalt auf den Boden gestoßen werden, da sonst Hemmungen die Folge sind.

Feuerstöße nur im Anschlag mit Magazinunterstützung oder aufgelegt abzugeben, da beim Anschlag freihändig die Mündung ausweicht und die Garbe nicht zusammengehalten werden kann.

Bei Abgabe von Feuerstößen ist das Sturmgewehr 44 **mit beiden Händen** fest in die Schulter einzuziehen[367].

131. Visierlinie und Seelenachse liegen beim Sturmgewehr 44 weiter auseinander als beim Gewehr. Deshalb ist beim Anschlag hinter einer Deckung darauf zu achten, daß die Mündung über die Deckung zeigt.

Im deckungsarmen Gelände hat der Schütze beim Anschlag mit Magazinunterstützung unter dem Magazin das Erdreich zu entfernen, damit er kein[368] großes Ziel bietet.

Beim Anschlag angestrichen[369] an einen Baume, Haus, Mauer usw. müssen Rechtsschützen das Sturmgewehr 44 vor dem Griff anstreichen, damit dieser beim Schießen vor- und zurückschnellen kann. Linksschützen müssen darauf achten, daß die Hülsenauswurföffnung frei bleibt, damit die Hülsen ausgeworfen werden können.

---

[365] Vermerk in Handschrift und blauen Buntstift.

[366] Nachdem „s" wurde ein Buchstabe mit „x" überschrieben.

[367] Zwischen „Schulter" und „einzuziehen" stand „einziehen", welches mit „x" ausgekreuzt wurde.

[368] Zwischen „er" und „kein" stand vermutlich „klein", welches mit „x" ausgekreuzt wurde.

[369] Siehe Glossar: Anstreichen.

47^{370}

When **using the tree in an aiming position** it is advisable to use the[371] sling because of the weight of the weapon. It is pressed firmly to the tree with the thumb. (Figure 47)

Key Points for the Marksmanship Instructor.

130. When going into aiming position, the magazine must not be pushed onto the ground with force, as this may cause stoppages.

Bursts should only be fired in the aiming position with magazine support or rested, as the muzzle will move freely with a freehand aiming position and the sheaf cannot be held together.

When firing shots, pull[372] the Sturmgewehr 44 **with both hands** firmly into the shoulder.

131. The sight radius and the axis of the bore are further apart in the Sturmgewehr 44 than in the rifle. Therefore, it is important to make sure that the muzzle points over the cover when aiming behind cover.

In terrain with limited cover, the rifleman must remove the soil under the magazine when aiming with magazine support so that he does not[373] offer a big target.

When using a tree, house, wall, etc. in an aiming position right-handed rifleman must rest[374] the Sturmgewehr 44 in front of the grip so that it can jump back and forth when firing. Left-handed riflemen must make sure that the case ejection opening remains free so that the cases can be ejected.

---

[370] Note in handwriting and blue colored pencil.

[371] Reference to original document: After "s" a letter was overwritten with "x".

[372] Reference to original document: Between "Schulter" ("shoulder") and "einzuziehen" ("to pull in") was "einziehen" ("pull in"), which was crossed out with "x".

[373] Reference to original document: Between "er" ("he") and "kein" ("none") "klein" ("mall") was probably written, which was crossed out with "x".

[374] See Glossary: Rest (Anstreichen).

6. Station[375]

Nahkampfanschläge[376]

Der Schellschuß.

132. Der Schnellschuß mit dem Sturmgewehr 44 erfolgt wie beim Gewehr (vergl. Ziff. 104 – 108).

Es wird beim Schnellschuß im Anschlag stehende nur Einzelfeuer geschossen.

Der Hüftanschlag.

133. Der Hüftanschlag mit dem Sturmgewehr 44 ist nur auf nächste Entfernun[g] unter 50 m anzuwenden. Es kann in der Bewegung geschossen werden (Feuerstöße von 2 – 3 Schuß).

Die rechte Hand umfaßt das Griffstück, die linke Hand das Magazin, Zeigefinger am Magazinhalter. Der Kolben wird mit dem rechten Unterarm fest an den Körper gepreßt. Der Daumen der linken Hand drückt von rückwärts gegen das Magazin. Das Sturmgewehr ist soweit vorzubringen, daß der Griff nicht frei gleiten kann. Das Auge visiert den Feind über die Laufmündung an. Die Mündung ist bewußt[377] tief zu halten (Bild 48).

48[378]

BArch, RH 11-I/14: Entwurf zur Heeresdienstvorschrift 240/2, Bild 48.

---

[375] Hier fehlte der Punkt am Ende.
[376] Hier fehlte der Punkt am Ende.
[377] Zwischen „ist" und „bewußt" stand „besonders", welches mit „x" ausgekreuzt wurde.
[378] Vermerk in Handschrift und blauen Buntstift.

6. Station[379]

Close Combat Aiming Positions[380]

The Hasty Shot.

132. The hasty shot with the Sturmgewehr 44 is carried out the same way as with the rifle (compare No. 104 – 108).

With the hasty shot in the standing position only semi-automatic fire is used.

The Hip Aiming Position.

133. The hip aiming position with the Sturmgewehr 44 is only used at the immediate ranges[381] below 50 m. It can be fire in motion (bursts of 2 – 3 shots).

The right hand grasps the grip, the left hand the magazine, index finger on the magazine well. The butt is pressed firmly against the body with the right forearm. The thumb of the left hand presses from behind against the magazine. The assault rifle must be brought forward so far that the grip cannot slide freely. The eye sights the enemy over the muzzle of the barrel. The muzzle is to be kept deliberately[382] low (Figure 48).

48[383]

BArch, RH 11-I/14: Entwurf zur Heeresdienstvorschrift 240/2, Bild 48.

---

[379] Here the dot at the end was missing.

[380] Here the dot at the end was missing.

[381] "Nahe" and "nächste Entfernung" refer to different distances. We translated "nahe Entfernung" to "close range" and "nächste Entfernung" to "immediate ranges".

[382] Reference to original document: Between "ist" ("is") and "bewußt" ("consciously") "besonders" ("special") was written, which was crossed out with "x".

[383] Note in handwriting and blue colored pencil.

Ergänzung 5: Merkblatt 25/3: Anleitung für den Nahkampf und die Handgranatenausbildung Nummern 73-86: Übungsbeispiele

Vorbemerkung

Hierbei handelt es sich um die erwähnten Nummern 73 bis 76 des Dokuments *Merkblatt 25/3: Anleitung für den Nahkampf und die Handgranatenausbildung* vom 15. April 1944.[384]

Die Nummern befinden sich auf Seite 52-53. Dieser Text hält sich an die generelle Formatierung der Quelle, jedoch wurde darauf verzichtet Seitenumbrüche zu übernehmen.

Text

e) Übungsbeispiele

Aufrollen von Gräben beim Kampf um Stellungen

73. Bei dem Aufrollen eines Grabens sichert vor den eingeteilten Handgranatenwerfern in der Regel der Gruppenführer oder ein Gewehrschütze. Dieser trägt ein Gewehr mit aufgepflanzten Seitengewehr[385], eine Maschinenpistole oder Pistole.

74. Die Handgranatenwerfer beginnen erst mit Werfen, wenn sie auf Widerstand stoßen.

75. Alle übrigen Schützen beobachten nach den Seiten und nach rückwärts, reichen Handgranaten zu oder nehmen Gegner, der sich zeigt, unter Feuer.

---

[384] BArch, RH 2/3684: *Merkblatt 25/3: Anleitung für den Nahkampf und die Handgranaten-ausbildung, 15.4.1944.*
[385] Seitengewehr ist ein altes Synonym für Bajonett.

Supplement 5: Pamphlet 25/3:
Instructions for the Close Combat and
Hand Grenade Training
Numbers 73-86: Training Examples

Preliminary Note

These are the mentioned numbers 73 to 76 of the document *Merkblatt 25/3: Anleitung für den Nahkampf und die Handgranatenausbildung* from April 15, 1944.[386]

These numbers are on pages 52-53. This text follows the general formatting of the source, although original page breaks have not been included.

Text

e) Training Examples

Rolling up Trenches in Combat for Positions

73. When rolling up a trench, the squad leader or a rifleman usually provides protection in front of the assigned hand grenade thrower[387]. This person carries a rifle with a bayonet[388], a submachine gun or pistol.

74. The hand grenade thrower only starts throwing when they encounter resistance.

75. All other riflemen watch to the flanks and rear, pass hand grenades or take enemies who show themselves under fire.

---

[386] BArch, RH 2/3684: *Merkblatt 25/3: Anleitung für den Nahkampf und die Handgranaten-ausbildung, 15.4.1944.*

[387] This is one of the rare occasions where a "Werfer" is actually a person throwing things.

[388] "Seitengewehr" is an old synonym for bayonet.

76. Das Vordringen der Werfer kann durch Feuer von e.M.G. [sic!]³⁸⁹, Granatwerfern, Gewehren und Maschinenpistolen unterstützt werden.

77. Die Gruppe darf sich nicht an einer Stelle zusammenballen, da sonst ein Ausweichen vor feindlichen Handgranaten erschwert wird.

78. Grabenstellen, die der Gegner flankiert, sind kriechend oder im Sprung³⁹⁰ zu überwinden.

79. Um unnötige Verluste zu vermeiden, kann an solchen Punkten ein Warnposten zurückgelassen werden.

80. Gestatten es Lage und Gelände, so verlassen Teile der aufrollenden Mannschaft den Graben zeitweilig, um den Feind zu umgehen oder das Feuer zu verstärken.

81. Es ist anzustreben, zunächst die Handgranaten zu werfen, die von hinten vorgereicht werden.

82. Der Handgranatennachschub bedarf eingehender Regelung.

83. Ist der Feind mit Handgranaten niedergekämpft, so macht sich alles fertig und stürzt auf Befehl des Gruppenführers vorwärts.

84. Der Befehl ist so zu geben, daß das Vorstürzen unmittelbar nach der Detonation der letzten Handgranate erfolgt.

85. Bei einem tief in die feindlichen Linien führenden Stoß stürzt die Gruppe ohne Rücksicht auf abzweigende Gräben vorwärts auf ihr Ziel.

Flankendeckung übernehmen nachfolgende Gruppen:

---

³⁸⁹ Hierbei sollte es „le.M.G." heißen, siehe Nummer 87.
³⁹⁰ Siehe Glossar: Sprung.

76. The advance of the throwers can be supported by fire from the light MG, mortars, rifles and submachine guns.

77. The squad most not cluster in one place, as this makes it difficult to avoid enemy hand grenades.

78. Trench positions, that the enemy flanks, are to be overcome by crawling or in a rush[391].

79. To avoid unnecessary losses, a guard can be left behind at such points.

80. If the situation and terrain allow it, parts of the rolling up crew temporarily leave the trench to avoid the enemy or to increase the fire.

81. It shall be aspired to throw hand grenades first, which shall be passed forward from behind.

82. The supply of hand grenades requires detailed arrangements.

83. If the enemy is defeated with hand grenades, everything gets ready and rushes forward on the order of the squad leader.

84. The order shall be given in such a way that the forward rush occurs immediately after the detonation of the last hand grenade.

85. In the event of a thrust deep into the enemy lines, the squad rushes forward on its target, with no regard of the trenches that branch off.

Following squads take over flank coverage:

---

[391] See Glossary: Rush (Sprung).

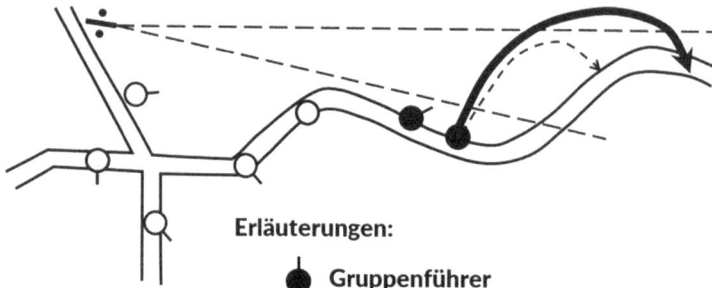

Erläuterungen:

- 🔴 **Gruppenführer**
- 🔴 **Handgranatenwerfer**
- ⚪ **Handgranatenträger**
- ⚪ **Gewehrschützen, Sicherer**
- •|• **I.M.G., welches Feind niederhält**

Bild 61

Beispiel für das Aufrollen von Gräben,
Hohlwegen[392] und langen Deckungen

86. Weitere Einzelheiten über den Kampf im Stellungskrieg enthält das Merkblatt 41 c 55 „Beispiele für Stoßtruppunternehmen als Unterlage für die Ausbildung im Ersatzheer", vom 2. Oktober 1943, und Erfahrungsberichte Abwehr (7), OKH/GenStdH/Ausb.Abt.[393] II, Nr. 3500/43, offen (7), vom 8. Oktober 1943.

---

[392] Ein Weg der sich durch jahrhundertelange Nutzung als auch durch Regenwasser in das Gelände eingeschnitten hat.
[393] Oberkommando des Heeres / General Stab des Heeres / Ausbildungsabteilung.

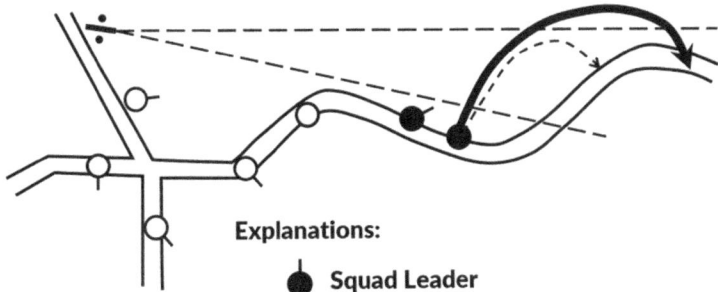

Explanations:

- Squad Leader
- Hand Grenade Thrower
- Hand Grenade Carrier
- Riflemen, Security
- LMG, which suppresses the enemy

Figure 61

Example for rolling up trenches,
sunken roads[394] and long covers

86. Further details about the combat in positional warfare are contained in pamphlet 41 c 55 "Examples for Raids as Basis for Training in the Replacement Army", from 2nd October 1943 and Experience Reports Defense (7), OKH/GenStdH/Ausb.Abt.[395] II, Nr. 3500/42, open (7), from 8, October 1943.

---

[394] A path that has cut into the terrain through centuries of use as well as through rainwater.
[395] Army High Command / General Staff of the Army / Training Department.

Ergänzung 6: Symbole

Vorbemerkung

Bei der folgenden Auflistung handelt es sich um eine Sammlung von Symbolen die in den hier übersetzten Originaldokumenten verwendet wurden. Sie basiert auf den Übersichten der *H.Dv. 130/2a* und *H.Dv. 130/2b* sowie dem *Merkblatt 25a/16: Der Sturmzug der Grenadier-Kompanie*. Dabei sei anzumerken das, obwohl es zwar die Vorschrift *H.Dv. 272: Muster für taktische Zeichen des Heeres* gab, die folgenden Symbole darin nicht aufgeführt sind. Zusätzlich konnten wir bei diversen Symbolen keine Legende finden, obwohl sie regelmäßig verwendet wurden. Dies zwang uns aus verschiedenen Handbüchern die wahrscheinlichste Interpretation zu rekonstruieren.

Des Weiteren ist zu beachten, dass es sich hierbei um generelle Symbole handelt. Es gab wohl diverse Abweichungen bzw. Spezialfälle, siehe zum Beispiel die Legende in der Ergänzung 5: *Merkblatt 25/3*, wo Handgranatenwerfer und Handgranatenträger eigene Symbole erhielten. Diese sind hier nicht aufgeführt.

Ein weitere Abweichung ist, dass im *Merkblatt 25a/16* für feindliche Einheiten Symbole oft nur die Umrisse gezeichnet wurden, wohingegen eigene Einheiten ausgemalt waren (siehe Abbildung 1). Diese Umriss-Darstellung wird allerdings zum Teil auch für freundliche Einheiten in den *H.Dv. 130/2a* und *130/2b* für bestimmte Rollen beim Kompanietrupp verwendet. Leider wissen wir nicht, ob es sich bei der Darstellung der feindlichen Einheiten im *Merkblatt 25a/16* um eine generelle bzw. neue Darstellungsform handelt oder um eine Ausnahme.

Es ist auch wichtig anzumerken, dass die generellen Dimensionen insbesondere die Strichbreiten etc. immer wieder abweichen. Zum Beispiel ist das MG in der *H.Dv. 272*, ganz anders als im *Merkblatt 25a/16*, mit dünnen Strichen und Punkten dargestellt.

⊥ Leichtes MG in Stellung

⊥ Feindliches leichtes MG in Stellung

⌀ Gewehrschütze

⊚ Feindlicher Gewehrschütze

Abbildung 1: Merkblatt 25a/16 Visuelle Syntax Freund / Feind

Supplement 6: Symbols

Preliminary Note

The following collection of symbols was used in the original documents translated here. They are based on the overviews of *H.Dv. 130/2a* and *H.Dv. 130/2b* as well as the *Pamphlet 25a/16: The Assault Platoon of the Grenadier-Company*. It should be noted that although there was a regulation *H.Dv. 272: Samples of Tactical Symbols of the Army*, the following symbols are not listed therein. In addition, we could not find a legend for several symbols although they were used regularly. This forced us to reconstruct the most likely interpretation from various manuals.

It should also be noted that these are general symbols. It seems that various deviations or special cases existed, see for example the legend in Supplement 5: *Pamphlet 25/3*, where a hand grenade thrower and hand grenade carriers received their own symbols. These are not listed here.

Another deviation is that in the *Pamphlet 25/3*, enemy unit symbols are often only drawn with outlines, whereas own units were filled (see Illustration 1). However, this outline representation is sometimes also used for friendly units in the *H.Dv. 130/2a* and *130/2b* for certain roles in company headquarters. Unfortunately, we do not know whether the depiction of enemy units *Pamphlet 25a/16* is a general or new form of depiction or an exception.

It is also important to note that the general dimensions, especially the line widths etc., are always different. For example, the MG in *H.Dv. 272* is shown with thin strokes and dots, quite different from those in the *Pamphlet 25a/16*.

    Light MG in Position

    Enemy Light MG in Position

    Rifleman

    Enemy Rifleman

Illustration 1: Pamphlet 25a/16 Visual Syntax Friend / Foe

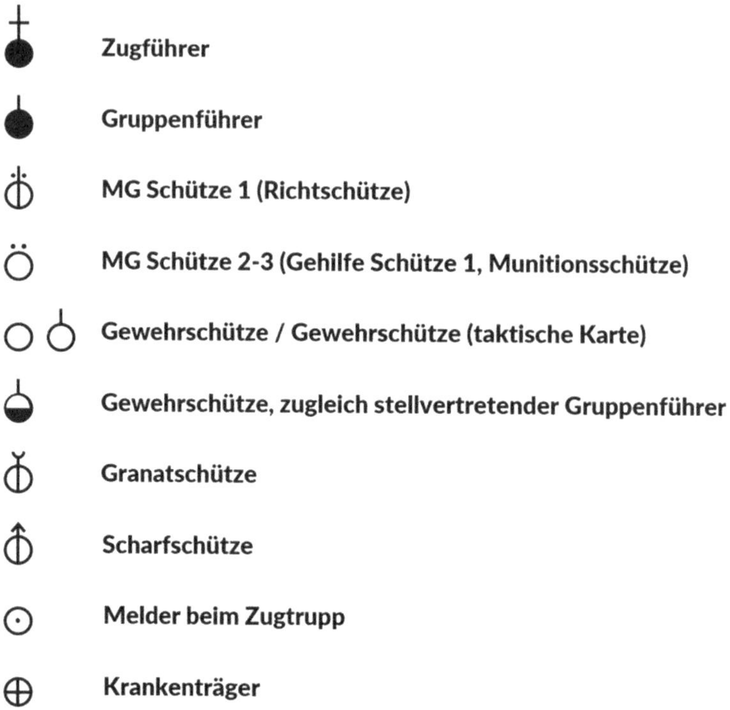

- ☦ **Zugführer**

- ☗ **Gruppenführer**

- ☥ **MG Schütze 1 (Richtschütze)**

- ☉ **MG Schütze 2-3 (Gehilfe Schütze 1, Munitionsschütze)**

- ○ ♂ **Gewehrschütze / Gewehrschütze (taktische Karte)**

- ♀ **Gewehrschütze, zugleich stellvertretender Gruppenführer**

- ☿ **Granatschütze**

- ♁ **Scharfschütze**

- ⊙ **Melder beim Zugtrupp**

- ⊕ **Krankenträger**

Abbildung 2: Symbole unterste taktische Ebene

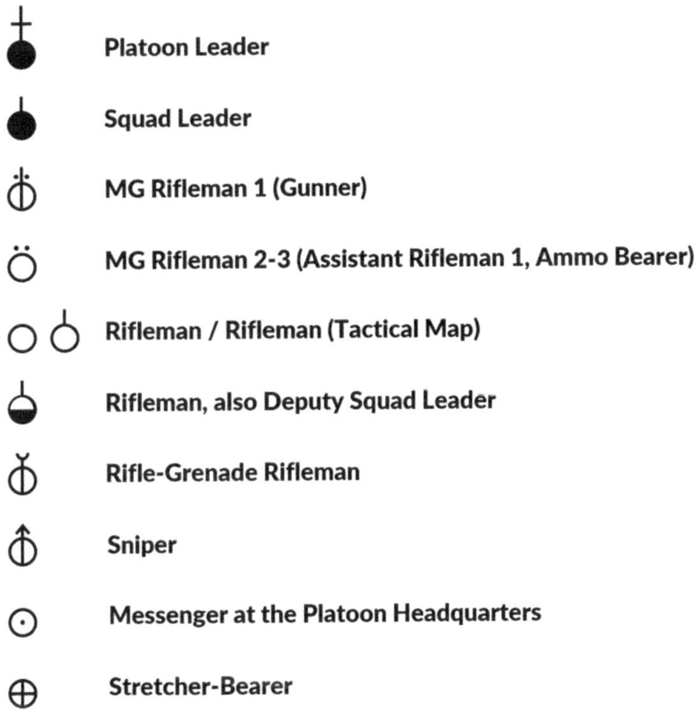

♁	**Platoon Leader**
●	**Squad Leader**
☿	**MG Rifleman 1 (Gunner)**
Ö	**MG Rifleman 2-3 (Assistant Rifleman 1, Ammo Bearer)**
○ ♂	**Rifleman / Rifleman (Tactical Map)**
♀	**Rifleman, also Deputy Squad Leader**
♀	**Rifle-Grenade Rifleman**
♂	**Sniper**
⊙	**Messenger at the Platoon Headquarters**
⊕	**Stretcher-Bearer**

Illustration 2: Symbols Lowest Tactical Level

Ergänzung 7: Kartensymbole

•|•	Leichtes Maschinengewehr
	Schweres Maschinengewehr / laut H. Dv. 272 (1944)
	Leichtes MG in Stellung / feindliches MG in Stellung
	Schweres Maschinengewehr in Stellung
42	Höhe 42
	Brücke
	Gebäude / Unterschlupf
	Laubwald
	Nadelwald
××××××	Flächendrahtsperre
××××	Spanische Reiter bzw. Drahtzaun laut H. Dv. 272 (1944)
	Gruppe* / Schützennest
	Feuernde Gruppe* / Schützennest
	Gruppe* in Entwicklung
	Feuernde Gruppe* in Entwicklung
	Feindliche Gruppe* / Schützennest
	Feindliche feuernde Gruppe* / Schützennest

*Je nach Situation / Karte kann es sich auch um größere Einheiten handeln.

Abbildung 3: Kartensymbole

Supplement 7: Map Symbols

•|•   Light Machinegun

•ᛋ|• :|•   Heavy Machinegun / according to H. Dv. 272 (1944)

🔨• 🔨•   Light MG in Position / Enemy MG in Position

🔨•   Heavy Machinegun in Position

⟨ 42   Height 42

≍   Bridge

▨   Building / Shelter

Ω Ω   Deciduous Forest

Λ Λ   Coniferous Forest

xxxxxx   Area Wire Barrier

-x-x-x-x-   Cheval-de-Frise or Wire Fence in H. Dv. 272 (1944)

⌒   Squad* / Riflemen Nest

⌒   Squad Firing* / Riflemen Nest Firing

⌒   Squad* during Full Deployment

⌒   Squad* Firing during Full Deployment

⌒   Enemy Squad* / Riflemen Nest

⌒   Enemy Squad* Firing / Riflemen Nest Firing

*Depending on the situation / map these can also be larger units.

Illustration 3: Map Symbols
EN-89

Ergänzung 8: Glossar

Abteilung / Bataillon: Beim deutschen Heer wurden Einheiten in der Stärke eines Bataillons, die Teil einer bestimmten Truppengattung waren (wie zum Beispiel Panzer, Artillerie oder Nachrichtentruppe) als „Abteilungen" bezeichnet. „Bataillon" wurde in erster Linie bei „infanterielastigen" Einheiten wie Pionier-, Infanterie- und Maschinengewehrbataillone genutzt.[1]

Anschluß / Anschlußmann: Der Anschluß / Anschlußmann war bei der Infanterie üblicherweise ein Schütze, eine Gruppe oder Zug, welcher als Referenz für Abstände und Zwischenräume genommen wurde: „Der Anschluß soll bis zum Eintritt in den Infanteriekampf die Bewegungen der Truppenteile in Einklang bringen und den Zusammenhang sicherstellen. Im Kampf hat stets der am weitesten Vorgedrungene den Anschluß."[2]

Anstreichen: Beim Anstreichen handelt es sich um das seitliche Anlehnen eines Gewehres zur Unterstützung beim Zielen an diverse Objekte zum Beispiel Wände, Bäume, etc.[3]

Blendkörper: Blendkörper waren ein spezieller Typ von Rauchgranaten. Blendkörper wurden insbesondere bei der Panzerbekämpfung eingesetzt. Die Panzerbesatzungen verloren bei korrekten Einsatz die Sicht, wodurch sie sowohl in der Fahrt als auch Waffenbedienung stark behindert wurden.

Bei den Blendkörpern BK 1 H und BK 2 H handelte es sich birnenförmige, mit einer Schraubkappe verschlossenen Glasbehälter. Hierbei war ein Reagenzglas im Glasbehälter durch die Schraubkappe fixiert. Der Glasbehälter enthielt eine Mischung aus Titantetrachlorid und Siliziumchlorid, das Reagenzglas Calciumchlorid. Beim Aufprall und der folgenden Vermischung entstand durch die chemische Reaktion eine Nebelwolke, die in etwa 15 bis 20 Sekunden anhielt. Eine BK 1 H wog 370 g, BK 2 H 400 g. Von der BK 1 H wurden in etwa 225 000 ausgeliefert, wohingegen von BK 2 H bis 1945 5,1 Millionen Stück produziert worden sind.[4]

---

[1] Siehe zum Beispiel: Gesterding, Schwatlo; Feyerabend, Hans-Joachim: *Unteroffizierthemen. Ein Handbuch für den Unteroffizierunterricht. Fünfte, neubearbeite Auflage.* E. S. Mittler & Sohn: Berlin, Germany, 1938, S. 21.

[2] Kühlwein, Fritz: *Die Gruppe im Gefecht. (Die neue Gruppe).* E. S. Mittler & Sohn: Berlin, 1940, S. 7.

[3] Haas, Walter: *Soldatenlexikon. Ein Merkbuch für den Infanteriedienst.* Franckh'sche Verlagshandlung: Stuttgart, Germany, o.J., S. 16.

[4] Fleischer, Wolfgang: *Deutsche Nahkampfmittel. Munition, Granaten und Kampfmittel bis 1945.* Motorbuch Verlag: Stuttgart, Germany, 2018, S. 153-155.

Supplement 8: Glossary

Battalion (Abteilung / Batallion): In the German army, units of some arms (e.g., tanks, artillery, signal, etc.) with the strength of a battalion were called "Abteilungen". "Batallion" was only used for "infantry-heavy" units like infantry, engineers and machine-gun battalions.[5]

Contact / Connecting File (Anschluß / Anschlußmann): The contact / connecting file in infantry units was usually a riflemen, squad or platoon, functioning as a reference for distance and spaces: "The contact shall bring the movements of the units into harmony until the start of the infantry combat and ensure the cohesion. During combat the most advanced always has the contact."[6]

[Rest / No equivalent] (Anstreichen): This is a special German word for lateral leaning of a rifle to support the aiming against various objects for example walls, trees, etc.[7]

Glass Smoke Grenade (Blendkörper): Blendkörper[8], were a special type of smoke grenades. Blendkörper were used specially to combat tanks. When used correctly, the tank crews became impaired in their visibility, which severely hindered them both in driving and weapon operation.

The glass smoke grenades BK 1 H and BK 2 H were pear-shaped glass containers closed with a screw cap. Here a test tube was fixed in the glass container by the screw cap. The glass container contained a mixture of titanium tetrachloride and silicon chloride, the test tube calcium chloride. On impact and subsequent mixing, the chemical reaction created a cloud of smoke that persisted for about 15 to 20 seconds. One BK 1 H weighed 370 g, BK 2 H 400 g. About 225,000 of the BK 1 H were delivered, whereas 5.1 million of BK 2 H were produced by 1945.[9]

---

[5] Example: Gesterding, Schwatlo; Feyerabend: *Unteroffizierthemen. Fünfte, neubearbeite Auflage.* E. S. Mittler & Sohn: Berlin, 1938, S. 21..

[6] Kühlwein, Fritz: *Die Gruppe im Gefecht. (Die neue Gruppe).* E. S. Mittler & Sohn: Berlin, 1940, S. 7.

[7] Haas, Walter: *Soldatenlexikon. Ein Merkbuch für den Infanteriedienst.* Franckh'sche Verlagshandlung: Stuttgart, Germany, o.J., S. 16.

[8] "Blendkörper" literally means "dazzle/blind body", the TM 30-506 translates "Blendkörper" with "frangible glass smoke grenade".

[9] Fleischer, Wolfgang: *Deutsche Nahkampfmittel. Munition, Granaten und Kampfmittel bis 1945.* Motorbuch Verlag: Stuttgart, Germany, 2018, S. 153-155.

Andere Rauchgranaten waren Nebelkerzen, Nebelgranaten oder die Rauchröhre.[10]

Durchbruch: Der Durchbruch ist die Fortführung des Einbruchs. Ziel ist es, den Zusammenhang der feindlichen Front zu brechen. Hierbei ist es wichtig bei der Durchbruchsstelle die jeweiligen Frontenden zu umfassen.[11] Siehe Abbildung 4: Einbruch und Durchbruch.

Einbruch: Der Einbruch ist das Ergebnis eines gelungenen Angriffs, der in die vorderste Stellung des Feindes eingedrungen ist.[12] Siehe Abbildung 4: Einbruch und Durchbruch.

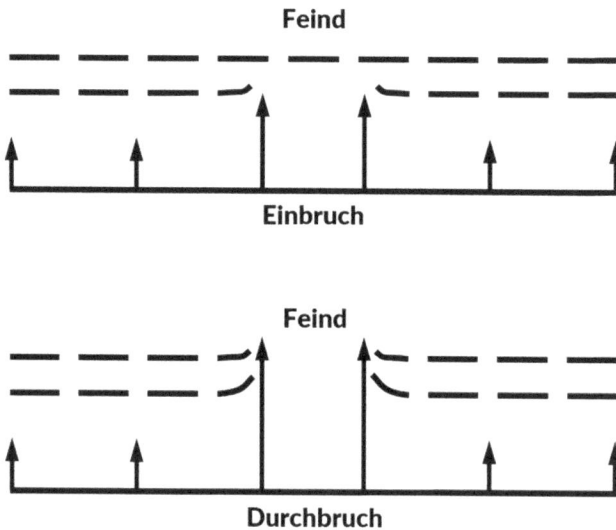

Abbildung 4: Einbruch und Durchbruch

---

[10] Fleischer, Wolfgang: *Deutsche Nahkampfmittel. Munition, Granaten und Kampfmittel bis 1945.* Motorbuch Verlag: Stuttgart, Germany, 2018, S. 155-156.

[11] Kühlwein, Fritz: *Die Gruppe im Gefecht. (Die neue Gruppe).* E. S. Mittler & Sohn: Berlin, 1940, S. 8.

[12] Kühlwein, Fritz: *Die Gruppe im Gefecht. (Die neue Gruppe).* E. S. Mittler & Sohn: Berlin, 1940, S. 8.

Other smoke grenades were Nebelkerzen[13], smoke grenades or the Rauchröhre[14].[15]

Penetration (Durchbruch): The penetration is the continuation of the break-in (Einbruch). The objective is to break the cohesion of the enemy front. Thereby it is important to encircle the respective front sections at the penetration point.[16] See Illustration 4: Break-In and Penetration.

Break-In (Einbruch): The break-in is the result of a successful attack that breached into the enemy's foremost lines.[17] See Illustration 4: Break-In and Penetration.

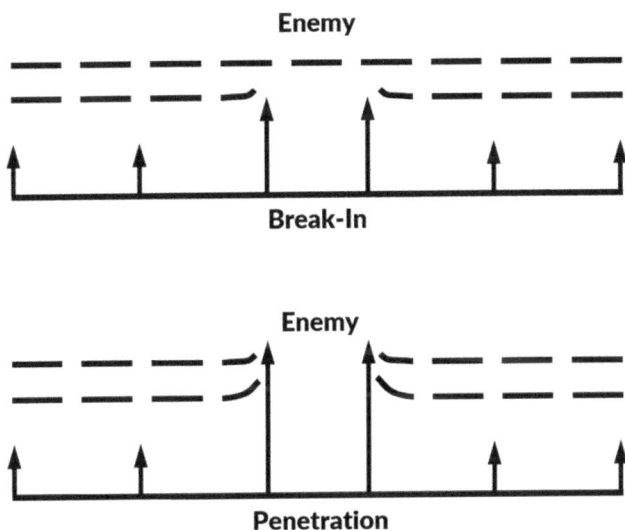

Illustration 4: Break-In and Penetration

---

[13] Literally "fog candles".
[14] Literally "fog tube".
[15] Fleischer, Wolfgang: *Deutsche Nahkampfmittel. Munition, Granaten und Kampfmittel bis 1945.* Motorbuch Verlag: Stuttgart, Germany, 2018, S. 155-156.
[16] Kühlwein, Fritz: *Die Gruppe im Gefecht. (Die neue Gruppe).* E. S. Mittler & Sohn: Berlin, 1940, S. 8.
[17] Kühlwein, Fritz: *Die Gruppe im Gefecht. (Die neue Gruppe).* E. S. Mittler & Sohn: Berlin, 1940, S. 8.

Einsatz, geschlossen: Der Begriff „geschlossener Einsatz" kommt häufig in deutschen Vorschriften des Zweiten Weltkrieges vor. Eine Einheit geschlossen einzusetzen, bedeutet ihre taktische Elemente gemeinsam einzusetzen, siehe folgende Beispiele für Infanterie (1944) und Panzer (1941 und 1943):

„In der Regel ist der M.P.-Zug geschlossen einzusetzen. Der Einsatz der einzelnen M.P.-Gruppen bildet die Ausnahme."[18]

„Die mittlere Panzerkompanie bildet mit ihren 14 Kampfwagenkanonen (7,5 cm) das Rückgrat der Panzerabteilung. Diese starke Feuerkraft gilt es – im allgemeinen durch geschlossenen Einsatz – schnell an entscheidender Stelle zu vernichtender Wirkung zu bringen."[19]

„Der geschlossene Einsatz [im Wald und im Gebirge] der Kompanie bildet die Ausnahme. In der Regel werden Halbzüge oder einzelne Wagen die angreifenden Schützen beim Vorgehen unterstützen."[20]

„In der Verteidigung halte die Wagen gedeckt und mindestens zugweise geschlossen zusammen, damit sie vom Fahrer und Bordschützen besetzt, wirksam zum Gegenstoss [sic!] antreten können."[21]

Aber auch in Befehlen vom Oberkommandos der Wehrmacht (OKW) wurde dieser Begriff verwendet:

„Für den diesen Einsatz gelten dabei folgende Richtlinien:

a) Die Luftwaffen-Feldbrigaden sind geschlossen einzusetzen. Ein Zerreißen der Verbände hat zu unterbleiben."[22]

---

[18] BArch, RH 11-I/83: *Merkblatt 25a/16: Vorläufiges Merkblatt „Der M.P.-Zug der Grenadier-Kompanie"*, 1.2.1944, S. 15.
[19] *H.Dv. 470/7: Ausbildungsvorschrift für die Panzertruppe. Heft 7: Die mittlere Panzerkompanie.* Reichsdruckerei, Berlin, Germany, 1. Mai 1941, S. 5.
[20] *H.Dv. 470/7: Die mittlere Panzerkompanie*, S. 68.
[21] TsAMO, F 500, Op. 12480, D 137: *Nachrichtenblatt der Panzertruppen. Nr. 1*, 15. Juli 1943, S. 10.
[22] Schramm, Percy E. (Hrsg.): *Kriegstagebuch des OKW. Eine Dokumentation: 1942. Band 4. Teilband 2.* Bechtermünz: Augsburg, Germany, 2005, S. 1299. Anlage 24: Führerbefehl vom 13. September 1942 betr. Ablösung abgekämpfter Divisionen aus dem Osten.

Employment of the Whole Unit (Einsatz, geschlossen): The term "geschlossener Einsatz"[23] is often used in German regulations of the Second World War. To employ a unit as "geschlossen", means to employ its tactical elements together, see the following examples for infantry (1944) and tanks (1941 and 1943):

"As a rule, the SMG[24]-platoon should be used as a whole. The use of the individual SMG-squads is the exception."[25]

"The medium tank company with its 14 vehicle-mounted guns (7.5 cm) forms the backbone of the tank battalion[26]. This strong firepower must be brought - in general by employing the unit as a whole - quickly to a decisive point and applied for destructive effect."[27]

"The employment as a whole company [in forests and mountains] is the exception. As a rule, half-platoons or individual vehicles will support the attacking riflemen."[28]

"In the defense, keep the vehicles covered and together at minimum at a platoon strength, so that they, manned by the driver and gunner, can effectively take up the hasty counterattack[29]."[30]

But this term was also used in orders from the High Command of the Wehrmacht (OKW):

"The following guidelines apply for the employment:
a) The Luftwaffe-field brigades are to be employed as a whole. The units must not be torn apart."[31]

---

[23] The literal translation of "geschlossener Einsatz" would be "closed employment".

[24] Technically, this was not a submachine gun. For details see Supplement 9.

[25] BArch, RH 11-I/83: *Merkblatt 25a/16: Vorläufiges Merkblatt „Der M.P.-Zug der Grenadier-Kompanie"*, 1.2.1944, S. 15.

[26] In the German Army, units of some arms (like tanks, artillery, etc.) with the strength of a battalion, were called "Abteilung" (literally detachment/department) not "Battalions".

[27] *H.Dv. 470/7: Ausbildungsvorschrift für die Panzertruppe. Heft 7: Die mittlere Panzerkompanie.* Reichsdruckerei, Berlin, Germany, 1. Mai 1941, S. 5.

[28] *H.Dv. 470/7: Die mittlere Panzerkompanie*, S. 68.

[29] The Germans distinguished between a hasty counterattack ("Gegenstoß") and regular counterattack ("Gegenangriff"). See Glossary: Hasty Counterattack (Gegenstoß).

[30] TsAMO, F 500, Op. 12480, D 137: *Nachrichtenblatt der Panzertruppen. Nr. 1*, 15. Juli 1943, S. 10.

[31] Schramm, Percy E. (Hrsg.): *Kriegstagebuch des OKW. Eine Dokumentation: 1942. Band 4. Teilband 2.* Bechtermünz: Augsburg, Germany, 2005, S. 1299. Anlage 24: Führerbefehl vom 13. September 1942 betr. Ablösung abgekämpfter Divisionen aus dem Osten.

Ein Problem ist jedoch, dass es wir noch keine passende englische Übersetzung für „geschlossener Einsatz" gefunden haben. In unserer Übersetzung der *H.Dv. 470/7* hatten wir uns nach langem hin und her für „combined employment" entschieden. Dies halten wir inzwischen für falsch, da „combined" die Kombination von mehreren verschiedenen Elementen impliziert. Wir haben uns mit mehreren Personen zu dem Thema ausgetauscht, so schlug zum Beispiel Dr. Leo Niehorster „massed employment" vor.[32] Dies würde auch mit dem *Field Manual 17-32: The Tank Company, Light and Medium* vom August 1942 einhergehen, wo es bezüglich dem Einsatz im Dschungel heißt:

„In general, because of their sensitiveness to terrain, tanks are unsuited for mass employment in jungles."[33]

Allerdings ist hier das Problem ist, dass es auch den „massierten Einsatz" – wenn auch seltener – in deutschen Vorschriften gab und hier handelte es sich um den konzentrierten Einsatz von Truppen an einer gewissen Stelle.

Im Englischen finden sich eher „Negativ-Definitionen" wie zum Beispiel:

„They [larger units of the Armored Force] are to be employed on decisive missions. They must not be frittered away."[34]

„Tank attacks will be costly or will result in failure to reach their objective unless employed in decisive numbers."[35]

„The piecemeal employment of tank units is wrong; they must be used in large numbers in a coordinated effort."[36]

---

[32] Email Leo Niehorster vom 28. Juli 2020.

[33] *FM 17-32: Armored Force Field Manual: The Tank Company, Light and Medium.* War Department: Washington, USA, August, 1942, p. 77.

[34] *FM 17-10: Armored Force Field Manual: Tactics and Technique.* War Department: Washington, USA, March, 1942, p. 3.

[35] *FM 17-10: Armored Force Field Manual: Tactics and Technique.* War Department: Washington, USA, March, 1942, p. 90.

[36] *FM 17-10: Armored Force Field Manual: Tactics and Technique.* War Department: Washington, USA, March, 1942, p. 131.

One problem is that we have not yet found a suitable English translation for "geschlossener Einsatz". In our translation of the *H.Dv. 470/7* we had decided after a long back and forth for "combined employment". We now think that this is wrong, because "combined" implies the combination of several different elements. We exchanged views with several people on the subject, for example Dr. Leo Niehorster suggested "massed employment".[37] This would also be in line with *Field Manual 17-32: The Tank Company, Light and Medium* of August 1942, which states with regard to the use in the jungle:

"In general, because of their sensitiveness to terrain, tanks are unsuited for mass employment in jungles."[38]

However, this created another problem because "massive employment" is also used - albeit less frequently - in German regulations, pointing to the concentrated employment of troops at a certain point.

In English "negative definitions" are common, for example:

"They [larger units of the Armored Force] are to be employed on decisive missions. They must not be frittered away."[39]

"Tank attacks will be costly or will result in failure to reach their objective unless employed in decisive numbers."[40]

"The piecemeal employment of tank units is wrong; they must be used in large numbers in a coordinated effort."[41]

---

[37] Email Leo Niehorster from 28. July 2020.
[38] *FM 17-32: Armored Force Field Manual: The Tank Company, Light and Medium.* War Department: Washington, USA, August, 1942, p. 77.
[39] *FM 17-10: Armored Force Field Manual: Tactics and Technique.* War Department: Washington, USA, March, 1942, p. 3.
[40] *FM 17-10: Armored Force Field Manual: Tactics and Technique.* War Department: Washington, USA, March, 1942, p. 90.
[41] *FM 17-10: Armored Force Field Manual: Tactics and Technique.* War Department: Washington, USA, March, 1942, p. 131.

Sonstige Alternativen, die wir angedacht haben waren:

- Unified Employment: Das Problem hierbei ist, dass eine Einheit schon „vereinigt" ist.
- Cohesive Employment: Ähnliches Problem wie bei „unified employment".
- Closed Employment: Dies könnte leicht mit „close order" (geschlossene Ordnung) verwechselt werden und ist auch wenig aussagekräftig.
- Non-piecemeal Employment: Ist eine „Negativ-Definition".

Basierend darauf haben wir uns entschieden „geschlossener Einsatz" mit „employment of the whole unit" bzw. „employing the unit as a whole" zu übersetzen, was auch nicht einer gewissen Ironie entbehrt.

Entfaltung: Die Entfaltung dient dazu die Gefechtsbereitschaft zu erhöhen. Dementsprechend findet sie statt, wenn damit gerechnet werden muss, dass es zu einem Zusammenstoß mit dem Feind kommt. Die Entfaltung ist die Umgliederung von der Marschkolonne in mehrere Kolonnen, die eine breitere Front bilden. Dementsprechend führt die Entfaltung zu einer Verlangsamung der entfaltenden Einheiten. Ebenso wird die für den Kampf nötige Tiefengliederung vorbereitet. Der Entfaltung folgt die Entwicklung.[42]

Entwicklung: Die Entwicklung folgt üblicherweise auf die Entfaltung. Dabei werden die Einheiten weiter aufgegliedert, um sich für den Kampf vorzubereiten. Die Entwicklung kann auch direkt aus der Marschkolonne heraus erfolgen, wenn keine Zeit zur Entfaltung ist.[43]

---

[42] Kühlwein, Fritz: *Die Gruppe im Gefecht. (Die neue Gruppe).* E. S. Mittler & Sohn: Berlin, 1940, S. 8; sowie *H.Dv. 300/1: Truppenführung I. Teil.* E. S. Mittler & Sohn: Berlin, 1936 (1933), S. 95-96.

[43] Kühlwein, Fritz: *Die Gruppe im Gefecht. (Die neue Gruppe).* E. S. Mittler & Sohn: Berlin, 1940, S. 8.

Other alternatives that we have considered were:

- Unified Employment: The problem here is that a unit is already "unified".
- Cohesive Employment: Similar problem as with "unified employment".

- Closed Employment: This could easily be confused with "close order" (geschlossene Ordnung) and is not very descriptive.

- Non-piecemeal Employment: Is a "negative-definition".

Based on this, we have decided to translate "geschlossener Einsatz" with "employment of the whole unit" or "employing the unit as a whole", which is not without a certain irony.

Preliminary Deployment – "development" according to TM 30-506 (Entfaltung): Preliminary deployment serves to increase the combat readiness. Thus, it takes place if an encounter with the enemy is likely. Preliminary deployment is the regrouping of the marching column into several columns offering a wider front. Accordingly, the preliminary deployment slows down the movement of the corresponding units. Additionally, the necessary distribution in depth required for combat is prepared. The preliminary deployment precedes the full deployment (Entwicklung).[44]

Full Deployment – "deployment" according to TM 30-506 (Entwicklung): The full deployment usually follows the preliminary deployment (Entfaltung). The units are further spread out to prepare for battle. Full deployment can also take place directly from the marching column, if there is no time for a preliminary deployment.[45]

---

[44] Kühlwein, Fritz: *Die Gruppe im Gefecht. (Die neue Gruppe).* E. S. Mittler & Sohn: Berlin, 1940, S. 8; also *H.Dv. 300/1: Truppenführung I. Teil.* E. S. Mittler & Sohn: Berlin, 1936 (1933), S. 95-96.

[45] Kühlwein, Fritz: *Die Gruppe im Gefecht. (Die neue Gruppe).* E. S. Mittler & Sohn: Berlin, 1940, S. 8.

Ersatzheer: Aufgabe des Ersatzheeres war es für das Feldheer personellen und materiellen Ersatz zur Verfügung zu stellen. Dementsprechend waren die Aufgaben die Bereitstellung und Ausbildung von Soldaten, als auch die Beschaffung und Bereitstellung von Material. Zusätzlich war es auch ihre Aufgabe das Heimatgebiet zu sichern. Dementsprechend setzte sich das Ersatzheer aus vier Hauptteilen zusammen 1) den Kommandobehörden und Verwaltungsdiensstellen, 2) Wachtruppen, 3) Ersatztruppen und 4) Schulen, Lehr- und Versuchstruppen.[46]

Feuerüberfall: „Schlagartiger Einsatz einer mehr oder minder großen Zahl für einen bestimmten Kampfzweck zusammengefaßter Waffen. Er ist bei allen Kampflagen anzustreben und verspricht besonderen Erfolg gegen lohnende, kurze sichtbare Ziele oder zur Einleitung einer Überraschung, z. B. beim Angriff."[47]

Für die MG-Kompanie ist der Feuerüberfall wie folgt beschrieben „[...] überraschendes Feuer von kurzer Dauer auf ein Ziel"[48]. Für die Artillerie folgendermaßen: „Feuerüberfall: (Feuerschlag) ist der Ausdruck für ein überraschend beginnendes mit höchster Feuergeschwindigkeit abgegebenes Wirkungsschießen, das hinsichtlich Raum, Zeit und Geschützzahl nicht den Einschränkungen des 'Vernichtungsfeuers' unterliegt. Schlagartige Feuereröffnung ist notwendig. Die Wirkung ist am größten, wenn die Schüsse aller beteiligten Kaliber gleichzeitig am Ziel einschlagen. Der Feuerüberfall wird gegen Augenblicksziele, beim Niederhalten des Feindes, beim Störungsfeuer, bei der Einleitung von Feuervorbereitungen, Täuschung des Feindes u. ä. angewendet."[49]

---

[46] Mueller-Hillebrand, Burkhart: *Das Deutsche Heer 1933-1945. Band I.* E. S. Mittler & Sohn: Frankfurt am Main, Germany, 1954, S. 80-83.

[47] Haas, Walter: *Soldatenlexikon. Ein Merkbuch für den Infanteriedienst.* Franckh'sche Verlagshandlung: Stuttgart, Germany, o.J., S. 57.

[48] Altrichter, Friedrich: *Der Reserveoffizer. Ein Handbuch für den Offizier und Offizieranwärter des Beurlaubtenstandes aller Waffen.* Vierzehnte, durchgesehene Auflage. Verlag von E. S. Mittler & Sohn: Berlin, Germany, 1941, S. 228.

[49] BArch, RH 17/809: Schule VII für Fahnenjunker der Infanterie: *Taktische Grundbegriffe und Ausdrücke*, August 1944, S. 4.

Replacement Army: The task of the Replacement Army was to provide the Field Army with personnel and material replacements. Accordingly, the tasks were the provisioning and training of soldiers, as well as the procuring and provisioning of material. Additionally, its task was to secure the home area. Accordingly, the replacement army consisted of four main parts 1) the command authorities and administrative offices, 2) guard troops, 3) replacement troops and 4) schools, training and trial troops.[50]

Surprise Fire (Feuerüberfall): "Abrupt employment of a more or less large number of weapons combined for a specific combat purpose. It is to be aimed at in all combat situations and promises special success against worthwhile, short visible targets or to initiate a surprise, e.g. when attacking."[51]

For the MG-company, surprise fire is described as follows: "[...] surprising fire of short duration at a target"[52]. For the artillery as follows: "Surprise Fire: (Fire Strike) is an expression for a surprising fire for effect bombardment at the highest firing speed, which is not subject to the restrictions of the 'annihilation fire' regarding space, time and number of guns. Sudden opening of fire is necessary. The effect is greatest when the shots of all calibers involved hit the target simultaneously. Surprise Fire is used against momentary targets, suppressing the enemy, harassing fire, initiating fire preparations, deceiving the enemy, etc."[53]

---

[50] Mueller-Hillebrand, Burkhart: *Das Deutsche Heer 1933-1945. Band I.* E. S. Mittler & Sohn: Frankfurt am Main, Germany, 1954, S. 80-83.

[51] Haas, Walter: *Soldatenlexikon. Ein Merkbuch für den Infanteriedienst.* Franckh'sche Verlagshandlung: Stuttgart, Germany, o.J., S. 57.

[52] Altrichter, Friedrich: *Der Reserveoffizer. Ein Handbuch für den Offizier und Offizieranwärter des Beurlaubtenstandes aller Waffen.* Vierzehnte, durchgesehene Auflage. Verlag von E. S. Mittler & Sohn: Berlin, Germany, 1941, S. 228.

[53] BArch, RH 17/809: Schule VII für Fahnenjunker der Infanterie: *Taktische Grundbegriffe und Ausdrücke,* August 1944, S. 1.

Feuergruppe: Die Feuergruppe ist eine der 3 Gruppen des Sturmzuges. Sie besteht aus einem Gruppenführer und 7 Schützen. 2 dieser Schützen sind MG-Schützen (Schütze 1), 4 dieser Schützen sind Munitionsschützen. Ein weiterer Schütze ist der stellvertretende Gruppenführer. Die Hauptaufgabe der Feuergruppe ist es Feuerunterstützung zu geben. Die Feuergruppe war im *Vorläufigen Merkblatt: Der M.P.-Zug der Grenadier-Kompanie* von 1. Februar 1944 noch nicht vorhanden. Hier bestand der Zug noch aus 3 Gruppen, die mit dem MP 43/1 ausgestattet waren. Das Vorwort vermerkte explizit, dass der Zug ohne leichtes MG gegliedert war. Es gab weitere Truppenversuche mit verschiedenen Verteilungen von leichten MG, zum Beispiel einen mit je 1 leichtes MG pro Gruppe.[54] Der Erfahrungsbericht zur MP 44 vom September 1944 der 1. Infanterie-Division kam zu dem Schluß, dass für den Angriff 2 leichte MG zu viel seien und nur zwei in der Verteidigung nötig sind.[55] Die Konzentration der leichten MG in der Feuergruppe wurde als die beste Lösung angesehen, da dadurch die MGs in einer Gruppe konzentriert waren und dies die Führung erleichterte.[56]

Feuerkraft: „Feuerkraft bezeichnete dabei die durch die Feuerwaffen erzielbare Wirkung, also das Verwunden und Töten von gegnerischen Soldaten, aber auch den dadurch erzielten Effekt sie in Deckung zu zwingen (Feuerüberlegenheit)."[57] Siehe auch Stoßkraft.

Gefechtsfahrzeug: Eine zeitgenössische Publikation beschreibt das Gefechtsfahrzeug folgendermaßen: „Die Gefechtsfahrzeuge (in der Regel pferdebespannt) führen alles das auf dem Gefechtsfeld mit, was die Truppe braucht: Munition und Kampfmittel aller Art, Ersatzteile und Werkzeuge für kleinere Instandsetzungen, Sanitäts- und Veterinärgerät."[58] Siehe auch Gefechtstroß.

---

[54] Handrich, Dieter: *Sturmgewehr 44. Vorgänger, Entwicklung und Fertigung der revolutionärsten Infanteriewaffen.* 2. überarbeitete und erweiterte Auflage. dwj Verlags-GmbH: Blaufelden, Germany, 2016, S. 242.

[55] BArch, RH 12-2/139: 1.Inf.Div: *Erfahrungsberichte über Grossversuch mit M.Pi. 44.* S. 2-4, Bl. 30-32.

[56] Handrich, Dieter: *Sturmgewehr 44,* S. 267.

[57] Raths, Ralf: *Vom Massensturm zur Stoßtrupptaktik. Die deutsche Landkriegstaktik im Spiegel von Dienstvorschriften und Publizistik 1906 bis 1918.* Zentrum für Militärgeschichte und Sozialwissenschaften der Bundeswehr: Potsdam, Germany, 2019, S. 31.

[58] Bieringer, Ludwig: *Nachschubfibel. Zweite verbesserte Auflage.* Verlag „Offene Worte", Berlin, 1938, S. 20.

Fire Squad (Feuergruppe): The fire squad is one of the three squads of the assault platoon. It is composed out of one platoon leader and 7 riflemen. 2 of these riflemen are MG-gunners (rifleman 1), and 4 of these riflemen are ammo bearers. An additional rifleman is the deputy squad leader. The primary role of the fire squad is to provide fire support. The fire squad was not yet present in the *Preliminary Pamphlet: The SMG-Platoon of the Grenadier-Company* from 1. February 1944. At that point, the platoon consisted of three squads, that were equipped with the MP 43/1. The foreword made explicit mention of the fact that the platoon was organized without a MG. troop trials with different allocations of light MGs were conducted, for example the use of one light MG per squad.[59] The experience report about the MP 44 from September 1944 of the 1st Infantry Division came to the conclusion that for the attack, two MGs are too many and only required during defense.[60] The concentration of the light MG in the fire squad was considered as the best solution, as this allowed the MGs to be placed in a single squad which simplified its command.[61]

Firepower (Feuerkraft): "Firepower refers to the effect achievable by firearms, that is, the wounding and killing of enemy soldiers, but also the effect achieved by forcing them into cover (fire superiority)."[62] See also Shock Action (Stoßkraft).

Combat Supply Vehicle (Gefechtsfahrzeug): A contemporary publication described the combat supply vehicle in the following manner: "The combat supply vehicles (usually horse-drawn) carry everything that the troops need on the battlefield: ammunition and ordnance of all kinds, spare parts and tools for minor repairs, medical and veterinary equipment."[63] See also Combat Train (Gefechtstroß).

---

[59] Handrich, Dieter: *Sturmgewehr 44. Vorgänger, Entwicklung und Fertigung der revolutionärsten Infanteriewaffen.* 2. überarbeitete und erweiterte Auflage. dwj Verlags-GmbH: Blaufelden, Germany, 2016, S. 242.

[60] BArch, RH 12-2/139: 1.Inf.Div: *Erfahrungsberichte über Grossversuch mit M.Pi. 44.* S. 2-4, Bl. 30-32.

[61] Handrich, Dieter: *Sturmgewehr 44*, S. 267.

[62] Raths, Ralf: *Vom Massensturm zur Stoßtrupptaktik. Die deutsche Landkriegstaktik im Spiegel von Dienstvorschriften und Publizistik 1906 bis 1918.* Zentrum für Militärgeschichte und Sozialwissenschaften der Bundeswehr: Potsdam, Germany, 2019, S. 31.

[63] Bieringer, Ludwig: *Nachschubfibel. Zweite verbesserte Auflage.* Verlag „Offene Worte", Berlin, 1938, S. 20.

Gefechtstroß: Der Gefechtstroß setzte sich aus geländegängigen Transportfahrzeugen, Feldküche und Handpferden – hierbei handelt es sich um Pferde, die mit der Hand gehalten werden - zusammen. Die Transportfahrzeuge führten das Material, das die Truppe auf dem Gefechtsfeld brauchte, mit sich: Munition, Betriebsstoff, Kampfmittel aller Art, Ersatzteile, Werkzeuge für kleinere Instandsetzungen, Sanitäts- und Veterinärgerät.[64]

Gegenangriff: „Gegenangriff ist ein planmäßig mit Art.- usw. Unterstützung eingehend vorbereiteter Angriff stärkerer rückwärts liegender Reserven."[65] Ergänzend dazu ein Auszug aus der zentralen Vorschriftenreihe für die Infanterie von 1945: „Hat sich der Feind bereits im H.K.F. [Hauptkampffeld] eingerichtet, so ist er nur im sorgfältig vorbereiteten Gegenangriff zu werfen."[66] Der Unterschied zum Gegenstoß wird dabei nochmal klar hervorgehoben: „Der Gegenangriff darf nicht überhastet werden. Er ist erst durchzuführen, wenn die Feuerunterstützung sichergestellt ist oder die zugesagten Sturmgeschütze oder Panzer eingetroffen sind."[67]

Gegenstoß: „Gegenstoß ist der sofort beim Eindringen des Angreifers angesetzte Stoß der dicht hinter der H.K.L. [Hauptkampflinie] bereit gehaltenen örtlichen Reserven des Verteidigers, um den in die H.K.L. eingedrungenen Angreifer in sofortigem Draufgehen wieder über die H.K.L. zu werfen."[68] Ergänzend dazu ein Auszug aus der zentralen Vorschriftenreihe für die Infanterie von 1945: „Der Gegenstoß muß den Feind noch in der Bewegung treffen. Es kommt nicht auf die Anzahl, sondern auf die Umsicht, Tatkraft und Schnelligkeit der Kämpfer an. Der Gegenstoß ist mit allen verfügbaren Waffen zu unterstützen."[69]

---

[64] Bieringer, Ludwig: *Nachschubfibel. Zweite verbesserte Auflage.* Verlag „Offene Worte", Berlin, 1938, S. 20.

[65] Kühlwein, Fritz: *Die Gruppe im Gefecht. (Die neue Gruppe).* E. S. Mittler & Sohn: Berlin, 1940, S. 11.

[66] BArch, RH 1/1217: *H.Dv. 130/20: Ausbildungsvorschrift für die Infanterie. Heft 20. Die Führung des Grenadier-Regiments.* Vom 21. 3. 1945. Verlage „Offene Worte": Berlin, Germany, 1945, S. 95.

[67] BArch, RH 1/1217: *H.Dv. 130/20: Ausbildungsvorschrift für die Infanterie. Heft 20. Die Führung des Grenadier-Regiments,* S. 94.

[68] Kühlwein, Fritz: *Die Gruppe im Gefecht. (Die neue Gruppe).* E. S. Mittler & Sohn: Berlin, 1940, S. 11.

[69] BArch, RH 1/1217: *H.Dv. 130/20: Ausbildungsvorschrift für die Infanterie. Heft 20. Die Führung des Grenadier-Regiments,* S. 92.

Combat Train (Gefechtstroß): The combat train was composed of cross-country capable transport vehicles, field kitchen and near horses – these are horses that are held with the hand. The transport vehicles carried everything that was needed by the troops on the battlefield: ammunition, fuel, ordnance of all kinds, spare parts, tools for smaller maintenance, medical and veterinary equipment.[70]

Counterattack (Gegenangriff): "Counterattack is a planned attack with artillery and other support of thoroughly prepared attack of stronger rearward lying reserves."[71] This is supplemented by an extract from the central series of regulations for the infantry of 1945: "If the enemy has already established himself in the main defensive area, he may be defeated[72] only in a carefully prepared counterattack."[73] The difference to the hasty counterattack is again clearly emphasized: "The counterattack must not be rushed. It is not to be carried out until fire support is ensured or the promised assault guns or tanks have arrived."[74]

Hasty Counterattack (Gegenstoß): "[The] hasty counterattack is the immediate thrust of the defender's local reserves held in readiness just behind the main line of resistance, in order to drive back[75] the attacker who has intruded the main line of resistance back over the main line of resistance in an immediate attack[76]."[77] In addition, an excerpt from the central series of regulations for the infantry of 1945: "The hasty counterattack must hit the enemy while still in motion. It does not depend on the number, but on the prudence, energy and speed of the fighters. The hasty counterattack must be supported with all available weapons."[78]

---

[70] Bieringer, Ludwig: *Nachschubfibel. Zweite verbesserte Auflage.* Verlag "Offene Worte", Berlin, 1938, S. 20.

[71] Kühlwein, Fritz: *Die Gruppe im Gefecht. (Die neue Gruppe).* E. S. Mittler & Sohn: Berlin, 1940, S. 11.

[72] The literal translation of "zu werfen" is "to throw".

[73] BArch, RH 1/1217: *H.Dv. 130/20: Ausbildungsvorschrift für die Infanterie. Heft 20. Die Führung des Grenadier-Regiments.* Vom 21. 3. 1945. Verlage „Offene Worte": Berlin, Germany, 1945, S. 95.

[74] BArch, RH 1/1217: *H.Dv. 130/20: Ausbildungsvorschrift für die Infanterie. Heft 20. Die Führung des Grenadier-Regiments,* S. 94.

[75] The literal translation of "über [...] zu werfen" is "to throw over [...]".

[76] "Draufgehen" literally means "going down", here it means "go against / onto". In another context, colloquially it also means "dying".

[77] Kühlwein, Fritz: *Die Gruppe im Gefecht. (Die neue Gruppe).* E. S. Mittler & Sohn: Berlin, 1940, S. 11.

[78] BArch, RH 1/1217: *H.Dv. 130/20: Ausbildungsvorschrift für die Infanterie. Heft 20. Die Führung des Grenadier-Regiments,* S. 92.

General der Infanterie: General der Infanterie war sowohl ein Dienstrang als auch eine verkürzte Bezeichung für eine Dienststellung. Die vollständige Bezeichnung der Dienststellung war General der Infanterie beim Oberbefehlshaber des Heeres. Der General der Infanterie beim Oberbefehlshaber des Heeres wurde im Oktober 1939 mit anderen Waffengeneralen beim Oberbefehlshaber des Heeres nach dem Polenfeldzug aufgestellt.[79] Im Verlauf des Krieges wurden seine Aufgaben erweitert und die Strukturen angepasst. Bei einer solchen Umstellung im Herbst 1944 wurde diese Bezeichnung in General der Infanterie im Oberkommando des Heeres (OKH) verändert.[80] Aus der Dienstanweisung für die Waffengenerale im OKH: „1. Die Waffengenerale im O.K.H. sind die höchsten Waffenvorgesetzten ihrer Waffe und alleinigen Vertreter ihrer Belange im Oberkommando des Heeres."[81] Es sei angemerkt, dass eine solche Doppeldeutigkeit von Dienstrang und Dienststellung in der Wehrmacht keine Besonderheit war.

Gepäcktroß: Beim Gepäcktroß befand sich all das Gepäck, welches die kämpfende Truppe nicht unbedingt zum Marsch und Gefecht benötigte. Dementsprechend sollte sich etwa 75 % des Gepäcks der Truppe beim Gepäcktroß befinden während die Mannschaften den restliche Teil als Marschgepäck selbst transportierten. Typisch für den Gepäcktroß waren der Transport von zusätzlicher Kleidung und Vorräte für die Truppe.[82]

---

[79] Mueller-Hillebrand, Burkhart: *Das Deutsche Heer 1933-1945. Band II.* E. S. Mittler & Sohn: Frankfurt am Main, Germany, 1956, S. 96.

[80] Mueller-Hillebrand, Burkhart: *Das Deutsche Heer 1933-1945. Band III.* E. S. Mittler & Sohn: Frankfurt am Main, Germany, 1969, S. 193-194.

[81] *Allgemeine Heeresmitteilungen. 11. Jahrgang, 27. Ausgabe. 7. Dezember 1944.* Berlin, Germany, 1944, S. 357.

[82] Bieringer, Ludwig: *Nachschubfibel. Zweite verbesserte Auflage.* Verlag „Offene Worte", Berlin, 1938, S. 23.

General of the Infantry (General der Infanterie): General of the Infantry was both a rank and a shortened title for an administrative position. The complete title of the position was General of the Infantry at the Commander-in-Chief of the Army. The General of Infantry at the Commander-in-Chief of the Army was posted with other arms generals at the Commander-in-Chief of the Army after the Polish campaign in October 1939.[83] Over the course of the war, his tasks were expanded and the structures adapted. During one of these restructuring phases in fall 1944, the title was changed to General of the Infantry at the Army High Command (OKH).[84] From the service instructions for the arms generals in the OKH: "1. The arms generals in the O.K.H. are the highest weapon superiors of their respective arm and the sole representatives of their interests in the High Command of the Army."[85] It should be noted that such a double meaning of rank and administrative position was not an exception in the Wehrmacht.

Baggage Train (Gepäcktroß): The baggage train transported all the baggage, which was not necessarily needed by the men during march and engagements. Accordingly, about 75 % of the baggage should be carried by the baggage train, whereas the remainining part was carried in the field packs with the troops. It was typical for the baggage trains to transport additional clothes and supplies for the troops.[86]

---

[83] Mueller-Hillebrand, Burkhart: *Das Deutsche Heer 1933-1945. Band II.* E. S. Mittler & Sohn: Frankfurt am Main, Germany, 1956, S. 96.

[84] Mueller-Hillebrand, Burkhart: *Das Deutsche Heer 1933-1945. Band III.* E. S. Mittler & Sohn: Frankfurt am Main, Germany, 1969, S. 193-194.

[85] *Allgemeine Heeresmitteilungen. 11. Jahrgang, 27. Ausgabe. 7. Dezember 1944.* Berlin, Germany, 1944, S. 357.

[86] Bieringer, Ludwig: *Nachschubfibel. Zweite verbesserte Auflage.* Verlag "Offene Worte", Berlin, 1938, S. 23.

Gewehrgranatgerät: Auch „Schießbecher für Gewehr" genannt.[87] Dies war eine Vorrichtung die auf das Standard-Gewehr der Wehrmacht, den Karabiner 98k, aufgeschraubt werden konnte. Sie bestand aus einer Halterung und einem Drallrohr mit 3 cm Kaliber. Anstatt der regulären Patrone wurde eine Gewehr-Kartusche verwendet. Diese diente dazu Granaten, die sich im Schießbecher befanden, abzufeuern.[88] Verschiedene Typen von Granaten wurden eingesetzt und erfüllten im Kampf unterschiedliche Rollen. So gab es bis 1945 16 verschiedene Granattypen mit bis zu 7 Unterarten, darunter die Gewehr-Sprenggranate, Gewehr-Propagandagranate und Gewehr-Panzergranate.[89]

Nachdem die Gewehrgranate vom Gasdruck befördert wurde und der Gasdruck bei vollautomatischen Waffen wie dem StG 44 zum erheblichen Teil im Gaszylinder abgeleitet wird, mussten entsprechende Anpassungen vorgenommen werden. Damit der Gasdruck nicht im Gaszylinder sondern Gewehrgranatgerät landet, versuchte man ihn durch einen verstellbaren Gasstopfen zu leiten.[90] Der Gasstopfen war beim Truppenversuch erfolgreich, jedoch gab es erhebliche Probleme mit dem Granatvisier. Das StG 44 war jedoch dazu gedacht den Karabiner 98k idealerweise komplett zu ersetzen.[91] Deshalb wurde ursprünglich die MP 43/1 durch die MP 43 ersetzt, da hier das Laufende und Kornträger so umkonstruiert wurde, dass das Gewehrgranatgerät anzubringen war. Allerdings wurde die Einführung schließlich nicht wirklich vorangetrieben, da man die Waffe, nun MP 44 genannt, auf die Dauer zu stark belastet hätte. Die Produktion der Treibpatrone wurde daher abgelehnt.[92] Ebenso hätte die Produktion dieser Patrone zu einer Verringerung der regulären Munition geführt hätte. Das StG 44 kam daher im Lauf des Krieges nicht mit dem Gewehrgranatgerät zum regulären Einsatz.[93]

---

[87] Merkblatt 41/23: Merkblatt über Handhabung, Mitführung und Verwendung der Gewehrgranate. Vom 20. 10. 42, OKH: Berlin, 1942. (Reprint), S. 6.
[88] Merkblatt 41/23: Merkblatt über Handhabung, Mitführung und Verwendung der Gewehrgranate. Vom 20. 10. 42, OKH: Berlin, 1942. (Reprint), S. 5-12.
[89] Fleischer, Wolfgang: Deutsche Nahkampfmittel. Munition, Granaten und Kampfmittel bis 1945. Motorbuch Verlag: Stuttgart, Germany, 2018, S. 104.
[90] Handrich, Dieter: Sturmgewehr 44. Vorgänger, Entwicklung und Fertigung der revolutionärsten Infanteriewaffen. 2. überarbeitete und erweiterte Auflage. dwj Verlags-GmbH: Blaufelden, Germany, 2016, S. 460-461.
[91] Handrich, Dieter: Sturmgewehr 44. Vorgänger, Entwicklung und Fertigung der revolutionärsten Infanteriewaffen. 2. überarbeitete und erweiterte Auflage. dwj Verlags-GmbH: Blaufelden, Germany, 2016, S. 118.
[92] BArch, RH 11-I/54: General der Infanterie: Gewehrgranatgerät für MP 44, 23. Juli 1944, Bl. 67.
[93] Handrich, Dieter: Sturmgewehr 44. Vorgänger, Entwicklung und Fertigung der revolutionärsten Infanteriewaffen. 2. überarbeitete und erweiterte Auflage. dwj Verlags-GmbH: Blaufelden, Germany, 2016, S. 462.

Rifle-Grenade Launcher (Gewehrgranatgerät): Also called "shooting cup for rifle".[94] This was a device that could be screwed onto the standard Wehrmacht rifle, the Karabiner 98k. It consisted of a mount and a spin tube with 3 cm caliber. A rifle-grenade cartridge was used instead of the regular cartridge. This was used to fire rifle-grenades that were in the shooting cup.[95] Different types of grenades were used and fulfilled different roles on the battlefield. Up until 1945 16 different grenade types with up to 7 subtypes existed, among these were the high-explosive rifle-grenade, propaganda rifle-grenade and anti-tank rifle-grenade.[96]

Since the rifle-grenade was transported by the gas pressure and the gas pressure in fully automatic weapons such as the StG 44 is diverted to a considerable extent in the gas tube, appropriate adjustments had to be made. So that the gas pressure does not land in the gas tube but in the rifle-grenade device, an attempt was made to direct it through an adjustable gas plug.[97] The gas plug was successful in the troop trials, but there were considerable problems with the grenade sights. Yet, the StG 44 was intended to replace the Karabiner 98k completely.[98] Therefore, the MP 43/1 was originally replaced by the MP 43, as the barrel and front sight were redesigned to accommodate the rifle-grenade launcher. However, in the end, the introduction was not really pushed forward, as the weapon, now called MP 44, would have been too heavily stressed in the long run. The production of the propellant rifle-grenade cartridge was therefore rejected.[99] Similarly, the production of this rife-grenade cartridge would have led to a reduction in the production of regular ammo. The StG 44 was therefore not used in regular service with the rifle-grenade during the war.[100]

---

[94] *Merkblatt 41/23: Merkblatt über Handhabung, Mitführung und Verwendung der Gewehrgranate.* Vom 20. 10. 42, OKH: Berlin, 1942. (Reprint), S. 6.

[95] *Merkblatt 41/23: Merkblatt über Handhabung, Mitführung und Verwendung der Gewehrgranate.* Vom 20. 10. 42, OKH: Berlin, 1942. (Reprint), S. 5-12.

[96] Fleischer, Wolfgang: *Deutsche Nahkampfmittel. Munition, Granaten und Kampfmittel bis 1945.* Motorbuch Verlag: Stuttgart, Germany, 2018, S. 104.

[97] Handrich, Dieter: *Sturmgewehr 44. Vorgänger, Entwicklung und Fertigung der revolutionärsten Infanteriewaffen.* 2. überarbeitete und erweiterte Auflage. dwj Verlags-GmbH: Blaufelden, Germany, 2016, S. 460-461.

[98] Handrich, Dieter: *Sturmgewehr 44. Vorgänger, Entwicklung und Fertigung der revolutionärsten Infanteriewaffen.* 2. überarbeitete und erweiterte Auflage. dwj Verlags-GmbH: Blaufelden, Germany, 2016, S. 118.

[99] BArch, RH 11-I/54: General der Infanterie: *Gewehrgranatgerät für MP 44,* 23. Juli 1944, Bl. 67.

[100] Handrich, Dieter: *Sturmgewehr 44. Vorgänger, Entwicklung und Fertigung der revolutionärsten Infanteriewaffen.* 2. überarbeitete und erweiterte Auflage. dwj Verlags-GmbH: Blaufelden, Germany, 2016, S. 462.

Granatschütze: Der Granatschütze war ein Schütze der mit einem Gewehr und einem entsprechenden Gewehrgranatgerät ausgestattet war. Er verfügte über verschiedene Gewehrgranaten, die ihm erlaubten sowohl Infanterie wie auch im beschränkten Maße Panzer zu bekämpfen. Die generelle Aufgabe ergibt sich aus folgenden Auszug aus dem Merkblatt zur Verwendung von Gewehrgranaten: „Die Gewehr-Sprenggranate dient zur Bekämpfung von Nahzielen, vor allem hinter Deckungen, die von schweren Infanteriewaffen und der Artillerie ohne Gefährdung der eigenen Truppen nicht gekämpft oder anderen Nahkampfmitteln nicht vernichtet werden können. Als Handgranate verwandt ersetzt sie die Stiel- und Eihandgranate."[101] Da das Sturmgewehr 44 nicht mit einem „Schießbecher" (siehe auch Eintrag: Gewehrgranatgerät) ausgestattet wurde, verblieb der Granatschütze im Sturmzug meist mit dem Karabiner 98k. Siehe auch Gewehrgranatgerät.

Granattrupp: In der Gliederung des Sturmzug, bestand der Granattrupp aus 3 Granatschützen. Er war im Zugtrupp gegliedert und unterstand dem Zugführer. Wie die Feuergruppe unterstützte der Granattrupp die Sturmgruppen bei ihren verschiedenen Aufgaben und war das einzige Element im Sturmzug welcher mittels Steilfeuer auf den Feind wirken konnte. Diese Bewaffnung wurde zum Teil auch zur Namensgebung des Trupps benutzt. Im *Zwischenbericht zum M.P.-Truppenversuch* der Infanterieschule Döberitz vom September 1944 fand sich zum Beispiel der Begriff „3 Gewehrgranatschützen (Steilfeuertrupp)"[102].

Der Granattrupp war im *Vorläufigen Merkblatt: Der M.P.-Zug der Grenadier-Kompanie* noch nicht vorhanden. Hier war ein einziger Granatschütze (Schütze 1) auf jede Gruppe zugeordnet. Später wurden diese Schützen aus den Gruppen ausgegliedert und in den Granattrupp innerhalb des Zugtrupps gegliedert.

---

[101] *Merkblatt 41/23: Merkblatt über Handhabung, Mitführung und Verwendung der Gewehrgranate.* Vom 20. 10. 42, OKH: Berlin, 1942. (Reprint), S. 5.
[102] RH 11-1/54: Infanterieschule, Abteilung IIIa: *M.P.-Versuch*, 14. Sept. 44, S. 1, Bl. 109.

Rifle-Grenade Rifleman (Granatschütze): The rifle-grenade rifleman was a rifleman who was equipped with a rifle and an appropriate rifle-grenade launcher. He had several rifle-grenades that allowed him to engage both infantry and, to a limited extend, tanks. The general task derives from the following excerpt from the pamphlet on the use of rifle-grenades: "The high-explosive rifle-grenade is used to combat close-range targets, especially behind cover, which cannot be engaged by heavy infantry weapons and artillery without endangering friendly troops or other close-range weapons. Used as a hand grenade, it replaces the stick and egg hand grenade."[103] As the Sturmgewehr 44 was not equipped with a "shooting cup", the rifle-grenade rifleman usually retained the older Karabiner 98k. See also: Rifle-Grenade Launcher (Gewehrgranatgerät).

Rifle-Grenade Section (Granattrupp): The rifle-grenade section consisted of 3 rifle-grenade riflemen within the organization for the assault platoon. It was part of the platoon headquarters and subordinated to the platoon leader. Like the fire squad, the rifle-grenade section supported the assault squads in their various tasks and was the only element in the assault platoon that could engage the enemy with indirect fire[104]. This weaponry also sometimes influenced the name of the section. For example, in the *Intermediate Report about the SMG-Troop Trial* of the infantry school Döberitz from September 1944 it was indicated as "3 rifle-grenade rifleman (indirect fire section)"[105].

The rifle-grenade section was not yet present in the *Preliminary Pamphlet: The SMG-Platoon of the Grenadier-Company*. Here a single rifle-grenade rifleman (rifleman 1) was assigned to each squad. Later, these riflemen were separated from the squads and incorporated into the rifle-grenade section within the platoon headquarters.

---

[103] *Merkblatt 41/23: Merkblatt über Handhabung, Mitführung und Verwendung der Gewehrgranate.* Vom 20. 10. 42, OKH: Berlin, 1942. (Reprint), S. 5.

[104] The literal translation of "Steilfeuer" would be "high-angle fire" or "steep fire". The complementary word was "Flachfeuer" meaning "flat-trajectory fire" so direct fire.

[105] RH 11-1/54: Infanterieschule, Abteilung IIIa: *M.P.-Versuch*, 14. Sept. 44, S. 1, Bl. 109.

Granatwerfer, leicht: Dies war üblicherweise der 5-cm leichte Granatwerfer 36. Es handelt sich hierbei um einen Mörser und nicht um einen Granatwerfer nach heutigem Sprachgebrauch, welcher manchmal unterhalb eines Sturmgewehres angebracht ist. Eine zeitgenössische Beschreibung erläutert den typischen Einsatz dieser Waffe: „Schußweite 50-450 m. Er ist die Steilfeuerwaffe des Schützenzuges und bekämpft aus einer Deckung Einzelziele, die von Gewehr und M. G. nicht gefaßt werden können."[106] Die Produktion dieses Granatwerfers und seiner Munition wurde 1943 eingestellt, da seine Schussweite und Wirkung zu gering waren.[107] Es sei angemerkt das der Granatwerfer nicht vom Granattrupp des Sturmzuges benutzt wurde.

Grenadier: Die Bezeichnung Grenadier geht auf das 17. Jahrhundert zurück, wo dieser Truppentyp Granaten, die in der Benutzung der heutigen Handgranate ähneln, durch Wurf einsetzte. So wurden zur Zeit Friedrich des Großen nur speziell ausgewählte Soldaten in Grenadier-Bataillone organisiert. Diese Soldaten zeichneten sich dadurch aus, dass sie besonders verlässlich und aggressiv waren.[108] Im Zweiten Weltkrieg wurde dieser Begriff inflationärer benutzt, so wurden im Juli 1942 zuerst die motorisierten Schützen in Panzergrenadiere umbenannt und dann, im Oktober 1942 wurden auch alle regulären Infanterie-Regimenter in Grenadier-Regimenter umbenannt.[109]

Gruppe: Siehe Schützengruppe.

---

[106] Altrichter, Friedrich: *Der Reserveoffizer. Ein Handbuch für den Offizier und Offizieranwärter des Beurlaubtenstandes aller Waffen.* Vierzehnte, durchgesehene Auflage. Verlag von E. S. Mittler & Sohn: Berlin, Germany, 1941, S. 210.
[107] Fleischer, Wolfgang: *Militärtechnik des Zweiten Weltkriegs. Entwicklung, Einsatz, Konsequenzen.* Motorbuch Verlag: Stuttgart, Germany, 2020, S. 183.
[108] Duffy, Christopher: *The Army of Frederick the Great. Second Edition.* Helion & Company: Warwick, UK, 2020 (1996), p. 124.
[109] *Allgemeine Heeresmitteilungen. 9. Jahrgang, 17. Ausgabe.* 21. Juli 1942. Berlin, Germany, 1942, S. 307. *Allgemeine Heeresmitteilungen. 9. Jahrgang, 25. Ausgabe.* 7. November 1942. Berlin, Germany, 1942, S. 509.

Mortar, light (Grantwerfer, leicht): This was usually the 5 cm leichte Granatwerfer[110] 36. This is a mortar and not a grenade launcher in the modern sense, which is sometimes mounted below an assault rifle. A contemporary description explains the typical use of this weapon: "Range 50-450 m. It is the indirect fire weapon of the rifle platoon and engages from cover single targets, which cannot be engaged by rifle and MG."[111] Production of this mortar and its ammunition was discontinued in 1943, since its range and effect were too limited.[112] It should be noted that the mortar was not used by the rifle-grenade section of the Assault platoon.

Grenadier (Grenadier): The name Grenadier dates back to the 17th century, when this type of troops used grenades similar in use to today's hand grenades by throwing them. At the time of Frederick the Great only specially selected soldiers were organized into grenadier battalions. These soldiers distinguished themselves by being particularly reliable and aggressive.[113] In the Second World War this term was used more frequently. First, in July 1942 the motorized riflemen were renamed to Panzergrenadiere and then, in October 1942, all regular infantry regiments were renamed to grenadier regiments.[114]

Squad (Gruppe): See Rifle Squad (Schützengruppe).

---

[110] This is a bit tricky, since in modern German a "Granatwerfer" is a "grenade launcher", yet back in World War 2 the term "Granatwerfer" was used for the mortar.

[111] Altrichter, Friedrich: *Der Reserveoffizer. Ein Handbuch für den Offizier und Offizieranwärter des Beurlaubtenstandes aller Waffen.* Vierzehnte, durchgesehene Auflage. Verlag von E. S. Mittler & Sohn: Berlin, Germany, 1941, S. 210.

[112] Fleischer, Wolfgang: *Militärtechnik des Zweiten Weltkriegs. Entwicklung, Einsatz, Konsequenzen.* Motorbuch Verlag: Stuttgart, Germany, 2020, S. 183.

[113] Duffy, Christopher: *The Army of Frederick the Great. Second Edition.* Helion & Company: Warwick, UK, 2020 (1996), p. 124.

[114] *Allgemeine Heeresmitteilungen. 9. Jahrgang, 17. Ausgabe.* 21. Juli 1942. Berlin, Germany, 1942, S. 307. *Allgemeine Heeresmitteilungen. 9. Jahrgang, 25. Ausgabe.* 7. November 1942. Berlin, Germany, 1942, S. 509.

Hauptkampffeld (HKF): Eine Verteidigungsstellung bestand aus drei Teilen: den Gefechtsvorposten, den vorgeschobenen Stellungen und dem Hauptkampffeld.[115] Das Hauptkampffeld ist dabei der wichtigste Teil der Stellung.

Hauptkampflinie (HKL): Die vorderste Linie des Hauptkampffeldes war die Hauptkampflinie (HKL).[116] Diese wurde von den Truppenführern gemessen der geografischen Lage aufgestellt und definierte so den Rand der zu verteidigenden Zone. So beschrieb Kühlwein die Hauptkampflinie als „ [...] eine Linie, durch die der Truppenführer den Zusammenhang der Verteidigung sicherstellt und eindeutig das Gelände bezeichnet, das festgehalten werden soll. Sie ist der vorderste Rand des Hauptkampffeldes in der Verteidigung. Vor ihr soll der Angriff des Feindes im zusammengefaßten Feuer aller Waffen spätestens zusammenbrechen bzw. sie soll nach Abschluß des Kampfes vom Verteidiger wieder in Besitz genommen sein."[117] Die Hauptkampflinie war daher in der Verteidigung von zentraler Bedeutung.

Hohlweg: Ein Weg der sich durch jahrhundertelange Nutzung als auch durch Regenwasser in das Gelände eingeschnitten hat.

Heer: Das Heer war, neben der Luftwaffe und Kriegsmarine, eine der drei Teilstreitkräfte der Wehrmacht. Oft wird das Heer jedoch mit der Wehrmacht verwechselt. Die Wehrmacht hingegen war die gesamte Streitkraft die sich wiederrum in Heer, Luftwaffe und Kriegsmarine gliederte.

---

[115] *H.Dv. 300/1: Truppenführung (T.F.) I. Teil. Abschnitt I – XIII.* Verlag Mittler & Sohn: Berlin, 1936, S. 179.
[116] *H.Dv. 300/1: Truppenführung (T.F.) I. Teil. Abschnitt I – XIII.* Verlag Mittler & Sohn: Berlin, 1936, S. 182.
[117] Kühlwein, Fritz: *Die Gruppe im Gefecht. (Die neue Gruppe).* E. S. Mittler & Sohn: Berlin, 1940, S. 12.

Main Defensive Area (Hauptkampffeld): A defensive position consisted of three parts: combat outposts, positions of advanced covering forces and the main defensive area.[118] The main defensive area was the most important part of the position.

Main Line of Resistance (Hauptkampflinie): The foremost line of the main defensive area as the main line of resistance (HKL).[119] It was set by the commanders based on the geographical situation and thus defined the edge of the area that is to be defended. Kühlwein described the main line of resistance as "[...] a line with which the commander ensures the coherence of the defense and clearly identifies the terrain to be held. It is the foremost line of the main defensive area in the defense. In front of it the enemy's attack shall collapse in the combined fire of all weapons at the latest, or it shall be taken back by the defender after the end of the combat."[120] The main line of resistance was therefore of central importance in the defense.

Sunken Road (Hohlweg): A path that has cut into the terrain through centuries of use, as well as through rainwater.

German Army (Heer): The German Army was, next to the Luftwaffe (German Air Force) and Kriegsmarine (German Navy), one of the three branches of the Wehrmacht. The German Army (Heer) is often confused with the Wehrmacht. The Wehrmacht however was the armed forces as a whole, composed out of the three branches of German Army, German Air Force and Germany Navy.

---

[118] *H.Dv. 300/1: Truppenführung (T.F.) I. Teil. Abschnitt I – XIII.* Verlag Mittler & Sohn: Berlin, 1936, S. 179.
[119] *H.Dv. 300/1: Truppenführung (T.F.) I. Teil. Abschnitt I – XIII.* Verlag Mittler & Sohn: Berlin, 1936, S. 182.
[120] Kühlwein, Fritz: *Die Gruppe im Gefecht. (Die neue Gruppe).* E. S. Mittler & Sohn: Berlin, 1940, S. 12.

Kartusche: „Kartusche" war eine verkürzte Bezeichnung für Gewehr-Kartuschen sowie Gewehr-Treibpatronen, die für das Abfeuern von Gewehrgranaten mit dem Gewehrgranatgerät notwendig waren. Kartuschen unterschieden sich je nach eingesetzter Gewehrgranate, da jeweils eine andere Pulverladung nötig war. Die Gewehr-Kartusche war oftmals etwas kürzer als eine reguläre Gewehrpatrone[121], konnte aber in einigen Fällen vom Aussehen, wie zum Beispiel bei der Gewehr-Treibpatrone die für das Verschießen der Gewehr-Panzergranaten gedacht war, einer reguläre Patrone ähneln.[122]

Kompanie: Siehe Schützenkompanie.

Koppel: Die „Koppel" ist eine Bezeichnung für Gürtel die einer Uniform zugehörig sind. Die Gürtelschnalle heißt „Koppelschloss".[123]

Maschinenkarabiner 42 (H): Siehe Ergänzung 9.

Maschinenkarabiner 42 (W): Siehe Ergänzung 9.

Munitionsausstattung: Die erste Munitionsausstattung war jene Menge an Munition, die die kämpfende Truppe in ihren eigenen Gefechts- und Nachschubfahrzeugen mitführen konnte.[124] Siehe Gefechtsfahrzeug.

---

[121] *Merkblatt 41/23: Merkblatt über Handhabung, Mitführung und Verwendung der Gewehrgranate.* Vom 20. 10. 42, OKH: Berlin, 1942. (Reprint), S. 12-13.

[122] *Merkblatt 41/23: Merkblatt über Handhabung, Mitführung und Verwendung der Gewehrgranate.* Vom 20. 10. 42, OKH: Berlin, 1942. (Reprint), S. 13.

[123] Schlicht, Adolf; Angolia, John R.: *Die deutsche Wehrmacht. Uniformierung und Ausrüstung 1933-1945. Band 1: Das Heer.* Motorbuch Verlag: Stuttgart, Germany, 2000, S. 379-380.

[124] Donat, Gerhard: *Beispiele für den Munitionsverbrauch der deutschen Wehrmacht im zweiten Weltkrieg.* In: Allgemeine schweizerische Militärzeitschrift, Band 129, Jahr 1963, Heft 2, S. 76. (Elektronische Version); sowie Bieringer, Ludwig: *Nachschubfibel. Zweite verbesserte Auflage.* Verlag „Offene Worte", Berlin, 1938, S. 36.

Rifle-Grenade Cartridge (Kartusche): "Kartusche" was a short term for rifle-grenade cartridges as well as rifle-grenade propelling cartridges[125], which were required for firing rifle-grenades with the rifle-grenade launcher. Rifle-grenade cartridges differed depending on the used rifle-grenade, since a different powder charge was required for each. The rifle-grenade cartridge was generally a bit shorter than a regular rifle cartridge[126] but could, in case of the rifle-grenade propelling cartridge that was used for firing the anti-tank rifle-grenade, resemble a regular cartridge.[127]

[Note that this translation is very tricky since the German word "Patrone" is usually translated with "cartridge". At the same time, when describing the use of rifle-grenades, "Kartusche", is also often translated with "cartridge" or "blank cartridge". This is complicated further as, in this context, "Gewehrtreibpatrone" is also often used for a longer "Kartusche".]

Company (Kompanie): See Rifle Company (Schützenkompanie).

Belt (Koppel): The "Koppel" is a term for belts that belongs to a uniform. The belt buckle is called "Koppelschloss" [literally belt lock].[128]

Maschinenkarabiner 42 (H): See Supplement 9.

Maschinenkarabiner 42 (W): See Supplement 9.

Ammunition Complement (Munitionsaausstattung): The first ammunition complement was the amount of ammunition that the fighting troops could carry in their own combat supply and supply vehicles.[129] See Combat Supply Vehicle (Gefechtsfahrzeug).

---

[125] The word "Treibpatrone" literally means "propelling cartridge" unlike the other blank cartridges used for rifle-grenades it looked very similar to a regular rifle cartridge.

[126] *Merkblatt 41/23: Merkblatt über Handhabung, Mitführung und Verwendung der Gewehrgranate.* Vom 20. 10. 42, OKH: Berlin, 1942. (Reprint), S. 12-13.

[127] *Merkblatt 41/23: Merkblatt über Handhabung, Mitführung und Verwendung der Gewehrgranate.* Vom 20. 10. 42, OKH: Berlin, 1942. (Reprint), S. 13.

[128] Schlicht, Adolf; Angolia, John R.: *Die deutsche Wehrmacht. Uniformierung und Ausrüstung 1933-1945. Band 1: Das Heer.* Motorbuch Verlag: Stuttgart, Germany, 2000, S. 379-380.

[129] Donat, Gerhard: *Beispiele für den Munitionsverbrauch der deutschen Wehrmacht im zweiten Weltkrieg.* In: Allgemeine schweizerische Militärzeitschrift, Band 129, Jahr 1963, Heft 2, S. 76. (Elektronische Version); sowie Bieringer, Ludwig: *Nachschubfibel. Zweite verbesserte Auflage.* Verlag „Offene Worte", Berlin, 1938, S. 36.

Panzerfaust: Die Panzerfaust war eine Waffe, die der Panzerbekämpfung diente. Während des Krieges gab es mehrere Entwicklungen der Panzerfaust, weshalb unter diesen Namen nicht nur eine einzelne Waffe, sondern eine ganze Waffenreihe fällt. Hierbei handelt es sich um eine Waffe, die einen Gefechtskopf mit einer Hohlladung verschießt. Eine Hohlladung ist ein Sprengkopf, der die Explosionsenergie fokussiert und das Metall im Sprengkopf in eine Art Metallstachel umwandelt. Durch die hohe Geschwindigkeit durchdringt dieser Stachel selbst Panzerstahl. Es ist hierbei wichtig anzumerken, dass der Stachel sich nicht durchbrennt, sondern den Stahl durchstößt.

Die Panzerfaust gab es in mehreren Variationen. Darunter fallen die Panzerfaust 30, 60 und 100. Die jeweilige Nummer bezeichnet hierbei die effektive Reichweite in Meter. Die Waffe selber hatte eine Länge von etwas mehr als einem Meter und ein Gewicht von 5,2 kg, wobei der Gefechtskopf 2,9 kg wog. Die Durchschlagsleistung war bei etwa 200 mm Panzerstahl.[130] Die Durchschlagsleistung des Gefechtskopfes ist aufgrund des Hohlladungsprinzip unabhängig von der Geschwindigkeit und von daher auf jede Entfernung dieselbe, anders als bei konventionellen panzerbrechenden Geschossen. Insgesamt wurden um die 8,2 Millionen Panzerfäuste bis März 1945 produziert.[131]

MP 43/1: Siehe Ergänzung 9.

MP 43: Siehe Ergänzung 9.

MP 44: Siehe Ergänzung 9.

MP Zug: Siehe Sturmzug.

---

[130] Fleischer, Wolfgang: *Deutsche Nahkampfmittel. Munition, Granaten und Kampfmittel bis 1945*. Motorbuch Verlag: Stuttgart, Germany, 2018, S. 187.
[131] Fleischer, Wolfgang: *Deutsche Nahkampfmittel. Munition, Granaten und Kampfmittel bis 1945*. Motorbuch Verlag: Stuttgart, Germany, 2018, S. 200.

Panzerfaust: The Panzerfaust[132] was a weapon that was used to combat tanks. During the war there were several developments of the Panzerfaust, which is why this name does not only refer to a single weapon, but to a whole line of weapons. This is a weapon that shoots a warhead with a hollow charge. A hollow charge is a warhead that focuses the explosion energy and converts the metal in the warhead into a kind of metal spike. Due to the high velocity this spike penetrates even armored steel. It is important to note that the spike does not burn through, but pierces the steel.

There were several variations of the Panzerfaust. Among them are the Panzerfaust 30, 60 and 100. The respective number indicates the effective range in meters. The weapon itself had a length of just over one meter and a weight of 5.2 kg, with the warhead weighing 2.9 kg. The penetrating power was about 200 mm of armored steel.[133] Due to the hollow charge principle, the penetrating power of the warhead is independent of velocity and therefore the same at any distance, unlike with conventional armor piercing projectiles. A total of about 8.2 million Panzerfaust were produced by March 1945.[134]

MP 43/1: See Supplement 9.

MP 43: See Supplement 9.

MP 44: See Supplement 9.

SMG[135] Platoon (MP Zug): See Assault Platoon (Sturmzug).

---

[132] The literal translation of "Panzerfaust" is "tank fist", "armor fist" or "armored fist", although in contemporary depictions it is shown as an armored fist smashing tanks.

[133] Fleischer, Wolfgang: *Deutsche Nahkampfmittel. Munition, Granaten und Kampfmittel bis 1945.* Motorbuch Verlag: Stuttgart, Germany, 2018, S. 187.

[134] Fleischer, Wolfgang: *Deutsche Nahkampfmittel*, S. 200.

[135] SMG means submachine gun. Technically, this was not a submachine gun, but the designation machine carbine was abolished, and the designation assault rifle was only introduced at the end of 1944. Regarding the naming and general development see Supplement 9.

Nest: Die *H.Dv. 316: Pionierdienst aller Waffen* beschreibt ein Nest wie folgt: „Verbindet man mehrere Schützenlöcher durch Gräben, so entstehen Nester, die durch den Einbau von Unterschlupfen verstärkt werden können."[136] Allerdings benutzt Kühlwein eine etwas offenere Definition: „Einige zu gemeinsamen Handeln unter einheitlichen Befehl auf engem Raum zusammengefaßte Schützen mit oder ohne M.G."[137] Diese Nester dienen also im allgemeinen dem Schutze der Soldaten, stellen dabei aber auch Feuerstellungen bzw. Positionen von denen sich Soldaten gegenseitig unterstützen können dar und konnten, je nach Lage und Bedarf auf Dauer zu verstärkten Stellung ausgebaut werden.

Panjewagen: Hierbei handelt es sich um einen von einem oder mehreren Pferden gezogenen Wagen. Der Name leitet sich vom Panjepferd ab. Dies war eine Pferderasse, welche vor allem in Osteuropa stark vertreten war. Das Panjepferd ist generell kleiner als andere europäische Pferderassen, zeichnet sich aber durch seine Zähigkeit aus. Diese Pferde wurden in großer Zahl von der Wehrmacht und Roten Armee im Zweiten Weltkrieg genutzt.[138] Panjewagen waren nicht standardisiert und meist lokal requiriert.[139]

---

[136] *H.Dv. 316: Pionierdienst aller Waffen.* Nachdruck 1936. Vom 11. 2. 1935. Verlag E.S. Mittler & Sohn: Berlin, 1936, S. 268.

[137] Kühlwein, Fritz: *Die Gruppe im Gefecht. (Die neue Gruppe).* E. S. Mittler & Sohn: Berlin, 1940, S. 13.

[138] DiNardo, R.L.: *Mechanized Juggernaut or Military Anachronism. Horses and the German Army of WWII.* Stackpole Books: Mechanicsburg, USA, 2009, S. 47.

[139] Filips, Katherina: *Typical Russian Words in German War-Memoir Literature.* In: The Slavic and East European Journal, vol. 8, no. 4, 1964, JSTOR, www.jstor.org/stable/304421, last access: 31st October 2020, p. 409.

Nest (Nest): The *H.Dv. 316: Pioneer Service of All Arms* describes a nest as follows: "If several foxholes are connected by trenches, nests are formed which can be strengthened by the installation of shelters."[140] However, Kühlwein uses a somewhat more open definition: "A number of riflemen, with or without MG, grouped together for joint action under uniform command in a confined space."[141] As such, these nests generally provided protection for the soldiers but also constituted firing positions or positions from which the riflemen could support each other and that could, if necessary, be reinforced.

Panje Carriage (Panjewagen): This is a carriage drawn by one or more horses. The name derives from the panje horse. This was a horse breed that was especially well represented in Eastern Europe. It is generally smaller than other European horse breeds but renowned for its toughness. These horses were used in large numbers by the Wehrmacht and Red Army during the Second World War.[142] Panje carriages were not standardized and mostly locally requisitioned.[143]

---

[140] *H.Dv. 316: Pionierdienst aller Waffen.* Nachdruck 1936. Vom 11. 2. 1935. Verlag E.S. Mittler & Sohn: Berlin, 1936, S. 268.

[141] Kühlwein, Fritz: *Die Gruppe im Gefecht. (Die neue Gruppe).* E. S. Mittler & Sohn: Berlin, 1940, S. 13.

[142] DiNardo, R.L.: *Mechanized Juggernaut or Military Anachronism. Horses and the German Army of WWII.* Stackpole Books: Mechanicsburg, USA, 2009, S. 47.

[143] Filips, Katherina: *Typical Russian Words in German War-Memoir Literature.* In: The Slavic and East European Journal, vol. 8, no. 4, 1964, JSTOR, www.jstor.org/stable/304421, last access: 31st October 2020, p. 409.

Schützengruppe: Die Schützengruppe oder Gruppe war eine Teileinheit der deutschen Infanterie im 2. Weltkrieg[144] und wurde mehrfach umstrukturiert. Auch vor dem Krieg gab es mehrere Varianten. So bestand zum Beispiel eine Gruppe in 1936 aus 14 Mann, darunter der Gruppenführer, Truppführer, leichten M.G.-Trupp (4 Schützen) und dem Schützentrupp (7 Schützen).[145] Im September 1939 bestand die Gruppe nur noch aus 12 Mann.[146] Diese und ähnliche Gliederungen waren laut Elser kaum führbar.[147] Daher wurde die Gruppe nach dem Polenfeldzug im Oktober 1939 umstrukturiert. Das *Merkblatt für Gliederung und Kampfweise der Schützenkompanie zu 12 Gruppen* vom 13. Oktober 1939 gibt an:

„1. Die Gruppe besteht aus Gruppenführer und 9 Schützen.

2. Die Einteilung in l.M.G.- und Schützentrupp sowie die Verwendung eines besonderen Unteroffiziers als Truppführer fallen fort."[148]

Diese Gliederung wurde lange Zeit beibehalten. Im Zuge der Umgliederung der Infanterie-Division zur Infanterie-Division neuer Art (n.A.) im Jahre 1943 kam es auch zur Umgliederung der Schützenkompanien und ihrer Einheiten. Laut der *Kriegsstärkenachweisung 131 n Schützenkompanie (n.A.)* vom 1. Oktober 1943 bestand die Gruppe nunmehr aus einem Gruppenführer und 8 Schützen.[149]

Betrachtet man die Gruppen aus *Vorläufigen Merkblatt: Der M.P.-Zug der Grenadier-Kompanie* vom Februar 1944 so bestand die Gruppe weiterhin aus einem Gruppenführer und 8 Schützen.

---

[144] Kühlwein, Fritz: *Die Gruppe im Gefecht. (Die neue Gruppe).* E. S. Mittler & Sohn: Berlin, 1940, S. 19.

[145] Siwinna, Carl (Hrsg.);von Heygendorff, ohne Vorname: *Das Kommandobuch. Band 1: Die Schützenkompanie.* 16. Auflage. Neubearbeitet. Mars-Verlag: Berlin, Germany, 1936, S. 24.

[146] Niehorster, Leo W.G.: *German World War II Organizational Series. Volume 1/II-1: 1st and 2nd Welle Army Infantry Divisions (1 September 1939).* The Military Press: Buckinghamshire, UK, 2007 (2006), p. 20.

[147] Elser, Gerhard: *Von der „Einheitsgruppe" zum „Sturmzug". Zur Entwicklung der deutschen Infanterie 1922 – 1945,* in: Der Infanterist, Heft 1, 2003, S. 85.

[148] *Merkblatt für Gliederung und Kampfweise der Schützenkompanie zu 12 Gruppen.* Zum Einlegen in die H. Dv. 130/2b. Verlage „Offene Worte", Berlin, Germany, 1939, S. 5.

[149] *Kriegsstärkenachweisung 131 n Schützenkompanie (n.A.)* vom 1. Oktober 1943.

Rifle Squad (Schützengruppe): The rifle squad or squad was a sub-subunit of the German infantry in the Second World War[150] and was restructured several times. Also, before the war there were several variants. For example, a squad in 1936 consisted of 14 men, including the squad leader, section leader, light M.G. section (4 riflemen) and the rifle section (7 riflemen).[151] In September 1939 the squad still consisted of 12 men.[152] According to Elser, these and similar organization were hard to command.[153] Therefore, after the Polish campaign in October 1939, the squad was restructured. The *Pamphlet for the Organization and Fighting Method of the Rifle Company into 12 Squads* from October 13, 1939, states:

"1. The squad consists of squad leaders and 9 riflemen.

2. The separation into light MG and rifle section as well as the use of a special non-commissioned officer as section leader are dropped."[154]

This structure was maintained for a long time. In the course of the reorganization of the Infantry Division into the Infantry Division new type (n.A.) in 1943, the rifle companies and their units were also reorganized. According to the *Kriegsstärkenachweisung*[155] *131 n Schützenkompanie (n.A.)* of October 1, 1943, the squad now consisted of a squad leader and 8 riflemen.[156]

Looking at the squads from the *Preliminary Pamphlet: The SMG-Platoon of the Grenadier-Company* of February 1944, the squad still consisted of a squad leader and 8 riflemen.

---

[150] Kühlwein, Fritz: *Die Gruppe im Gefecht. (Die neue Gruppe).* E. S. Mittler & Sohn: Berlin, 1940, S. 19.

[151] Siwinna, Carl (Hrsg.);von Heygendorff, ohne Vorname: *Das Kommandobuch. Band 1: Die Schützenkompanie.* 16. Auflage. Neubearbeitet. Mars-Verlag: Berlin, Germany, 1936, S. 24.

[152] Niehorster, Leo W.G.: *German World War II Organizational Series. Volume 1/II-1: 1st and 2nd Welle Army Infantry Divisions (1 September 1939).* The Military Press: Buckinghamshire, UK, 2007 (2006), p. 20.

[153] Elser, Gerhard: *Von der „Einheitsgruppe" zum „Sturmzug". Zur Entwicklung der deutschen Infanterie 1922 – 1945,* in: Der Infanterist, Heft 1, 2003, S. 85.

[154] *Merkblatt für Gliederung und Kampfweise der Schützenkompanie zu 12 Gruppen.* Zum Einlegen in die H. Dv. 130/2b. Verlage „Offene Worte", Berlin, Germany, 1939, S. 5.

[155] The literal translation of "Kriegsstärkenachweisung" is "war strength certificate", it is a table of organization and equipment.

[156] *Kriegsstärkenachweisung 131 n Schützenkompanie (n.A.) vom 1. Oktober 1943.*

Allerdings bestand die Gruppe im *Merkblatt: Der Sturmzug der Grenadier-Kompanie* vom November 1944 nun nur noch aus einem Gruppenführer mit 7 Schützen. Dies liegt daran, dass die 3 Granatschützen nun im Zugtrupp zusammengefasst waren und nicht wie im Februar noch auf die 3 Gruppen aufgeteilt waren. Daher veränderte sich die Größe des Schützenzuges im Zuge dieser Umstrukturierung nicht.[157]

Schützenkette: Die Schützenkette ist neben der Schützenreihe eine der zwei Grundformationen der geöffneten Ordnung der Gruppe.[158] Hierbei befinden sich die Schützen nebeneinander in Stellung. Zur Ausrichtung dient hierbei der Schütze 1 (Maschinengewehr-Schütze). Bei der regulären Schützenkette befindet er sich in der Mitte, bei Schützenkette rechts befinden sich die anderen Schützen rechts von ihm, bei Schützenkette links entsprechend links von ihm.[159]

Der Abstand zwischen den Schützen ist – wenn nicht anders befohlen – 5 Schritt.[160] Die Schützenkette wird angewendet zum Feuerkampf der „ganzen" Gruppe oder wenn die Feuerbereitschaft des leichten Maschinengewehrs und der Gewehrschützen notwendig ist um das schnelle Überwinden von Geländestreifen die vom Gegner eingesehen werden können zu ermöglichen.[161]

---

[157] Vielen Dank an Gary Kennedy für diesen Hinweis. Email vom 9. Oktober 2020.
[158] *H.Dv. 130/2a: Ausbildungsvorschrift für die Infanterie. Heft 2a. Die Schützenkompanie.* Entwurf. Vom 16. März 1941. Verlag „Offene Worte": Berlin, Germany, 1941, S. 108.
[159] Zimmermann, Bodo: *Infanteriedienst. Für den Einzelschützen der aktiven Truppe, der Reserve und der Landwehr.* 18. Auflage (Kriegsausgabe) der „Soldatenfibel". Verlag „Offene Worte": Berlin, Germany, 1940, S. 92-93.
[160] *H.Dv. 130/2a: Ausbildungsvorschrift für die Infanterie. Heft 2a. Die Schützenkompanie.* Entwurf. Vom 16. März 1941. Verlag „Offene Worte": Berlin, Germany, 1941, S. 108-110.
[161] Zimmermann, Bodo: *Infanteriedienst-* Berlin, Germany, 1940, S. 92.

However, in the *Pamphlet: The Assault Platoon of the Grenadier-Company* of November 1944 the squad now consisted of only one squad leader with 7 riflemen. This is because the 3 rifle-grenade riflemen were now combined in the platoon headquarters and not distributed into the 3 squads as in February. As such the size of the platoon as a whole did not change due to this restructuring.[162]

Skirmishing Line (Schützenkette): The skirmishing line is next to the squad column one of the two basic formations of the extended order of the squad.[163] Here the riflemen are in position next to each other. For alignment, the rifleman 1 (machine gunner) is used. With the regular skirmishing line he is in the center, with the skirmishing line right the other riflemen are on his right, and with the skirmishing line left correspondingly on his left.[164]

The spaces between the riflemen is - if not ordered otherwise - 5 paces.[165] The skirmishing line is used for firefighting of the "whole" squad or when the readiness to fire of the light machine gun and the rifleman is necessary to enable the quick crossing of terrain that can be observed by the opponent.[166]

---

[162] Many thanks to Gary Kennedy for this note. Email from 9th October 2020.

[163] *H.Dv. 130/2a: Ausbildungsvorschrift für die Infanterie. Heft 2a. Die Schützenkompanie. Entwurf.* Vom 16. März 1941. Verlag „Offene Worte": Berlin, Germany, 1941, S. 108.

[164] Zimmermann, Bodo: *Infanteriedienst. Für den Einzelschützen der aktiven Truppe, der Reserve und der Landwehr.* 18. Auflage (Kriegsausgabe) der „Soldatenfibel". Verlag „Offene Worte": Berlin, Germany, 1940, S. 92-93.

[165] *H.Dv. 130/2a: Ausbildungsvorschrift für die Infanterie. Heft 2a. Die Schützenkompanie. Entwurf.* Vom 16. März 1941. Verlag „Offene Worte": Berlin, Germany, 1941, S. 108-110.

[166] Zimmermann, Bodo: *Infanteriedienst-* Berlin, Germany, 1940, S. 92.

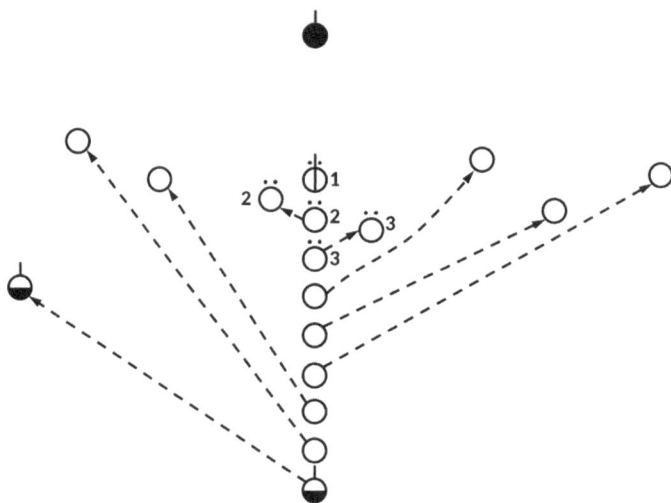

Abbildung 5: Umbildung von Schützenreihe auf Schützenkette

Schützenkompanie: Die *H.Dv. 130/2a: Ausbildungsvorschrift für die Infanterie. Heft 2a: Die Schützenkompanie,* beschreibt die Schützenkompanie folgendermaßen: „Die Schützenkompanie bildet den Kern des Infanterieregiments. Ihr Kampfgeist ist ausschlaggebend für den Wert des ganzen Heeres."[167] Zu Beginn des Krieges bestand eine Infanteriedivision aus 3 Infanterieregimentern, 1 Artillerieregiment und mehreren Abteilungen/Bataillonen. Das Infanterieregiment bestand zum Großteil aus 3 Infanteriebataillonen, welche sich je aus 3 Schützenkompanien und einer Maschinengewehrkompanie zusammensetzten. Eine Schützenkompanie bestand laut *H.Dv. 130/2a* von 1941 aus:

---

[167] *H.Dv. 130/2a: Ausbildungsvorschrift für die Infanterie. Heft 2a: Die Schützenkompanie.* Verlag „Offene Worte", Berlin, 16. März 1941, S. 189.

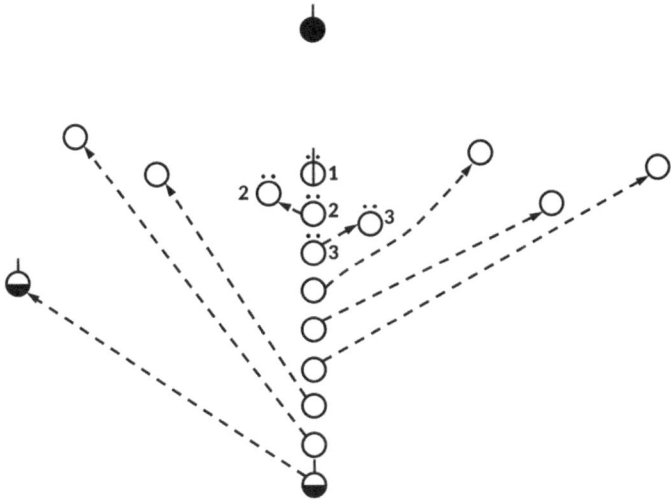

Illustration 5: Change from Squad Column to Skirmishing Line

Rifle Company (Schützenkompanie): The *H.Dv. 130/2a: Training Regulation for the Infantry. Booklet 2 a: The Rifle Company*, describes the rifle company in the following manner: "The rifle company forms the core of the infantry regiment. Its fighting spirit is essential for the value of the whole Army."[168] At the beginning of the war an infantry division consisted of 3 infantry regiments, 1 artillery regiment and several battalions. The infantry regiment consisted mainly of 3 infantry battalions, which consisted of 3 rifle companies and one machine gun company each. According to *H.Dv. 130/2a* from 1941 one rifle company consisted of:

---

[168] *H.Dv. 130/2a: Ausbildungsvorschrift für die Infanterie. Heft 2a: Die Schützenkompanie.* Verlag „Offene Worte", Berlin, 16. März 1941, S. 189.

„[...]dem Kompanieführer
dem Kompanietrupp
dem Pz.B.[169]-Trupp
3 Schützenzügen mit je 2 Infanteriekarren
dem Gefechtstroß, [sic!]
dem Verpflegungstroß
dem Gepäcktroß.“[170]

Je nach Gliederung hatte die Schützenkompanie zwischen 1939 und 1943 eine autorisierte Stärke um die 190 Mann.[171] Nach der Umgliederung zur Infanterie-Division neuer Art im Herbst 1943 wurde diese Zahl auf etwa 140 reduziert, allerdings verfügte die Kompanie über eine Granatwerfergruppe.[172] Dies stellt einen Unterschied zur Kompanie der Volksgrenadierdivision dar, da hier die Granatwerfergruppe entfiel und sie dadurch nur noch eine autorisierte Stärke um die 120 Mann hatte.

Im Oktober 1942 kam es außerdem zu einer Umbenennung der Infanterie. So heißt es in den Allgemeinen Heeresmitteilungen 1942, Heft 25 vom 7. November 1942 mit Verweis auf eine Anordnung vom 15. Oktober 1942:

„1. Sämtliche Infanterie-Regimenter mit Ausnahme der Jäger- und Gebirgsjäger-Regimenter erhalten mit sofortiger Wirkung die Bezeichnung

‚Grenadier-Regimenter‘.

Die Angehörigen der Grenadier-Regimenter der unteren Mannschaftsdienstgrade erhalten die Bezeichnung

‚Grenadier‘ und ‚Obergrenadier‘.“[173]

---

[169] Panzerbüchsen.
[170] *H.Dv. 130/2a: Ausbildungsvorschrift für die Infanterie. Heft 2a: Die Schützenkompanie.* Verlag „Offene Worte“, Berlin, 16. März 1941, S. 189.
[171] Niehorster, Leo W.G.: *German World War II Organizational Series. Volume 1/II-1: 1st and 2nd Welle Army Infantry Divisions (1 September 1939).* The Military Press: Buckinghamshire, UK, 2007 (2006), p. 20. And *H.Dv. 130/2a: Ausbildungsvorschrift für die Infanterie. Heft 2a: Die Schützenkompanie.* Verlag „Offene Worte“, Berlin, 16. März 1941.
[172] *Kriegsstärkenachweisung 131 n Schützenkompanie (n.A.) vom 1. Oktober 1943.*
[173] *Allgemeine Heeresmitteilungen. 9. Jahrgang, 25. Ausgabe. 7.* November 1942. Berlin, Germany, 1942, S. 509.

"[...] the company commander
the company headquarters
the anti-tank rifle section
3 rifle platoons with 2 infantry carriages each
the combat train, [sic!]
the ration train
the baggage train."[174]

Depending on its organization, the rifle company had an authorized strength of about 190 men between 1939 and 1943.[175] After the reorganization into the Infantry Division new type in autumn 1943, this number was reduced to about 140, but the company had a mortar squad.[176] This is different from the company of the Volksgrenadierdivision, because here the mortar squad was dropped, leaving them with only an authorized strength of about 120 men.

In October 1942, the infantry was also renamed. This is stated in the General Army Announcement 1942, issue 25 of November 7, 1942, with reference to an order of October 15, 1942:

"1. All infantry regiments, with the exception of the light infantry[177] and mountain troop[178] regiments, shall be designated with immediate effect

'Grenadier Regiment'.

The members of the grenadier regiments of the lower ranks are called

'Grenadier' and 'Obergrenadier'."[179]

---

[174] H.Dv. 130/2a: Ausbildungsvorschrift für die Infanterie. Heft 2a: Die Schützenkompanie. Verlag „Offene Worte", Berlin, 16. März 1941, S. 189.

[175] Niehorster, Leo W.G.: German World War II Organizational Series. Volume 1/II-1: 1st and 2nd Welle Army Infantry Divisions (1 September 1939). The Military Press: Buckinghamshire, UK, 2007 (2006), p. 20. And H.Dv. 130/2a: Ausbildungsvorschrift für die Infanterie. Heft 2a: Die Schützenkompanie. Verlag „Offene Worte", Berlin, 16. März 1941.

[176] Kriegsstärkenachweisung 131 n Schützenkompanie (n.A.) vom 1. Oktober 1943.

[177] The term "Jäger" literally means "hunter", these were light infantry. Be aware that in early war there were "leichte Divisionen" (light divisions) these were "weak" panzer divisions.

[178] The term "Gebirgsjäger" literally means "mountain hunter".

[179] Allgemeine Heeresmitteilungen. 9. Jahrgang, 25. Ausgabe. 7. November 1942. Berlin, Germany, 1942, S. 509.

Es ist wichtig hier anzumerken, dass in internen Dokumenten wie zum Beispiel in Kriegsstärkenachweisungen die Bezeichnung Schützenkompanien etc. lange weiterverwendet wurden.[180]

Schützenreihe: Die Schützenreihe ist neben der Schützenkette eine der zwei Grundformationen der geöffneten Ordnung der Gruppe.[181] Bei der Schützenreihe folgen die Schützen aufeinander. Dabei befindet sich der Gruppenführer üblicherweise an der vordersten Position gefolgt von Schütze 1 (Maschinengewehr-Schütze). Allerdings ist die Position des Gruppenführers von diesem frei wählbar.[182] Für den Abstand zwischen den Schützen waren in der Vorschrift 5 Schritt als Basiswert angegeben, natürlich konnte ein anderer Wert befohlen werden.[183]

Die Schützenreihe bietet der Einheit eine flexible Formation. So schreibt Zimmermann: „Die Schützenreihe eignet sich am besten zur Annäherung an den Feind bei schmalen Deckungen, im durchschnittenen Gelände, auf Bergpfaden, in der Nacht. Im beobachteten Artl.-Feuer auf der deckungsarmen Ebene bietet sie ein schlechteres Ziel als die breiten Schützenketten."[184] Die Schützenreihe ist auch für den Feuerkampf geeignet, wenn das leichte Maschinengewehr alleine feuert.[185]

---

[180] Zum Beispiel in der *Kriegsstärkenachweisung 131 n* vom 1. Mai 1944 heißt es *Schützenkompanie (n.A.)*. Ebenso *Kriegsstärkenachweisung 130 n: Stabskompanie eines Infanterieregiments(n.A.)*. Das „n.A." steht für neue Art, die Leerzeichen bzw. deren fehlen sind entsprechend den Dokumenten.

[181] *H.Dv. 130/2a: Ausbildungsvorschrift für die Infanterie. Heft 2a. Die Schützenkompanie.* Entwurf. Vom 16. März 1941. Verlag „Offene Worte": Berlin, Germany, 1941, S. 106.

[182] *H.Dv. 130/2a: Ausbildungsvorschrift für die Infanterie. Heft 2a. Die Schützenkompanie.* Entwurf. Vom 16. März 1941. Verlag „Offene Worte": Berlin, Germany, 1941, S. 108-110.

[183] *H.Dv. 130/2a: Ausbildungsvorschrift für die Infanterie. Heft 2a. Die Schützenkompanie.* Entwurf. Vom 16. März 1941. Verlag „Offene Worte": Berlin, Germany, 1941, S. 108-110.

[184] Zimmermann, Bodo: *Infanteriedienst. Für den Einzelschützen der aktiven Truppe, der Reserve und der Landwehr.* 18. Auflage (Kriegsausgabe) der „Soldatenfibel". Verlag „Offene Worte": Berlin, Germany, 1940, S. 95.

[185] Zimmermann, Bodo: *Infanteriedienst. Für den Einzelschützen der aktiven Truppe, der Reserve und der Landwehr.* 18. Auflage (Kriegsausgabe) der „Soldatenfibel". Verlag „Offene Worte": Berlin, Germany, 1940, S. 92.

It is important to note here that in internal documents such as the table of organization and equipment, the term 'rifle companies' etc. was used for a long time.[186]

Squad Column (Schützenreihe): The squad column is beside the skirmishing line one of the two basic formations of the extended order of the squad.[187] In the squad column the riflemen follow each other. The squad leader is usually in the front position followed by rifleman 1 (machine gunner). However, the squad leader can choose his position freely.[188] For the distance between the riflemen the base value of 5 paces was given in the regulation, of course a different value could be ordered.[189]

The squad column provides the unit with a flexible formation. Zimmermann describes this as follows: "The squad column is best suited for approaching the enemy in narrow cover, in intersected terrain, on mountain paths, at night. Under observed artillery fire on the low-coverage plain, it offers a worse target than the wide skirmishing lines."[190] The squad column is also suitable for firefights when the light machine gun fires alone.[191]

---

[186] For example in the *Kriegsstärkenachweisung 131 n* from 1, May 1944 it is noted *Schützenkompanie (n.A.)*. Also *Kriegsstärkenachweisung 130 n: Stabskompanie eines Infanterieregiments(n.A.)*. The "n.A." is short for "neue Art" [which means "new type"], the spaces or missing spaces are according to the documents.

[187] *H.Dv. 130/2a: Ausbildungsvorschrift für die Infanterie. Heft 2a. Die Schützenkompanie. Entwurf.* Vom 16. März 1941. Verlag „Offene Worte": Berlin, Germany, 1941, S. 106.

[188] *H.Dv. 130/2a: Ausbildungsvorschrift für die Infanterie. Heft 2a. Die Schützenkompanie. Entwurf.* Vom 16. März 1941. Verlag „Offene Worte": Berlin, Germany, 1941, S. 108-110.

[189] *H.Dv. 130/2a: Ausbildungsvorschrift für die Infanterie. Heft 2a. Die Schützenkompanie. Entwurf.* Vom 16. März 1941. Verlag „Offene Worte": Berlin, Germany, 1941, S. 108-110.

[190] Zimmermann, Bodo: *Infanteriedienst. Für den Einzelschützen der aktiven Truppe, der Reserve und der Landwehr.* 18. Auflage (Kriegsausgabe) der „Soldatenfibel". Verlag „Offene Worte": Berlin, Germany, 1940, S. 95.

[191] Zimmermann, Bodo: *Infanteriedienst. Für den Einzelschützen der aktiven Truppe, der Reserve und der Landwehr.* 18. Auflage (Kriegsausgabe) der „Soldatenfibel". Verlag „Offene Worte": Berlin, Germany, 1940, S. 92.

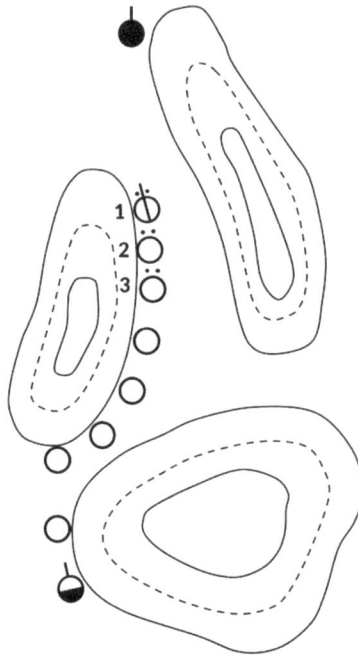

Abbildung 6: Schützenreihe

Schützenzug: Der Schützenzug bestand 1936 aus dem Zugführer, Zugtrupp und 3 Gruppen.[192] Im September 1939 bestand die Gliederung aus dem Zugführer, Zugtrupp, 3 Gruppen und einem leichten Granatwerfertrupp.[193] Nachdem Polenfeldzug kam es im Oktober 1939 zu einer Umstrukturierung. Dabei wurde zum einen die Gruppen verkleinert und einfacher strukturiert. Zum anderen wurden die Anzahl der Gruppen pro Schützenzug von 3 auf 4 erhöht.[194] Der Schützenzug umfasste zu dieser Zeit um die 50 Mann.[195]

---

[192] H.Dv. 130/2b: Ausbildungsvorschrift für die Infanterie. Heft 2. Die Schützenkompanie. Teil b. Der Schützenzug und die Schützenkompanie. Vom 24. März 1936. Verlag „Offene Worte": Berlin, Germany, 1936.

[193] Niehorster, Leo W.G.: German World War II Organizational Series. Volume 1/II-1: 1st and 2nd Welle Army Infantry Divisions (1 September 1939). The Military Press: Buckinghamshire, UK, 2007 (2006), p. 20.

[194] Merkblatt für Gliederung und Kampfweise der Schützenkompanie zu 12 Gruppen. Zum Einlegen in die H. Dv. 130/2b. Verlage „Offene Worte", Berlin, Germany, 1939, S. 9.

[195] Merkblatt für Gliederung und Kampfweise der Schützenkompanie zu 12 Gruppen. Zum Einlegen in die H. Dv. 130/2b. Verlage „Offene Worte", Berlin, Germany, 1939, S. 10.

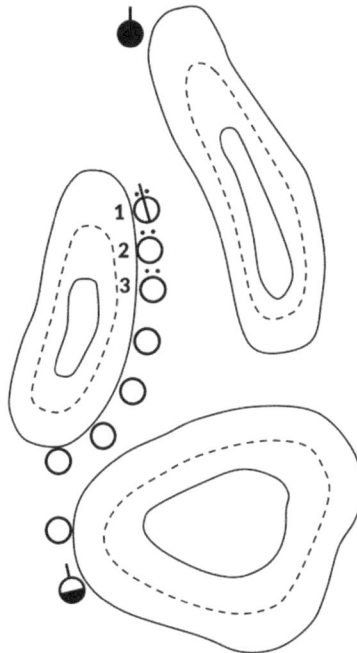

Illustration 6: Squad Column

Rifle Platoon (Schützenzug): In 1936 the rifle platoon consisted of the platoon leader, platoon headquarters and 3 squads.[196] In September 1939 the organization consisted of the platoon leader, platoon headquarters, 3 squads and a light mortar section.[197] After the Polish campaign, a restructuring took place in October 1939. On the one hand, the squads were reduced in size and structured in a simpler way. On the other hand, the number of squads per rifle platoon was increased from 3 to 4.[198] At this time the rifle platoon had about 50 men.[199]

---

[196] H.Dv. 130/2b: Ausbildungsvorschrift für die Infanterie. Heft 2. Die Schützenkompanie. Teil b. Der Schützenzug und die Schützenkompanie. Vom 24. März 1936. Verlag „Offene Worte": Berlin, Germany, 1936.

[197] Niehorster, Leo W.G.: German World War II Organizational Series. Volume 1/II-1: 1st and 2nd Welle Army Infantry Divisions (1 September 1939). The Military Press: Buckinghamshire, UK, 2007 (2006), p. 20.

[198] Merkblatt für Gliederung und Kampfweise der Schützenkompanie zu 12 Gruppen. Zum Einlegen in die H. Dv. 130/2b. Verlage „Offene Worte", Berlin, Germany, 1939, S. 9.

[199] Merkblatt für Gliederung und Kampfweise der Schützenkompanie zu 12 Gruppen. Zum Einlegen in die H. Dv. 130/2b. Verlage „Offene Worte", Berlin, Germany, 1939, S. 10.

Nach der Umgliederung zur Infanterie-Division neuer Art im Herbst 1943 sank die autorisierte Stärke des Schützenzuges auf 31 Mann, der leichte Granatwerfertrupp war entfallen und die Zahl der Gruppen wurde auf 3 reduziert worden, wobei deren Größe auch auf 9 Mann gesunken war.[200] Der Schützenzug der Volksgrenadierdivision hatte um die 33 Mann.

Schwerpunkt: Der Begriff Schwerpunkt hat insbesondere in der englischsprachigen Literatur und Diskussion sehr viel Staub aufgewirbelt.[201] Ein kurzer Blick auf Clausewitz *Vom Kriege* zeigt auf, dass er den Begriff meist im (groß)strategischen Kontext benutzt, so zum Beispiel:

„Aus ihnen [vorherrschenden Verhältnis zweier Staaten] wird sich ein gewisser Schwerpunkt, ein Zentrum der Kraft und Bewegung bilden, von welchem das Ganze abhängt, und auf diesen Schwerpunkt des Gegners muß der gesammelte Stoß aller Kräfte gerichtet sein."[202]

Und auch bei der weiteren Ausführung hier:

„Alexander, Gustav Adolf, Karl XII., Friedrich der Große hatten ihren Schwerpunkt in ihrem Heer, wäre dies zertrümmert worden, so würden sie ihre Rolle schlecht ausgespielt haben; bei Staaten, die durch innere Parteiungen zerrissen sind, liegt er meistens in der Hauptstadt; bei kleinen Staaten, die sich an mächtige stützen, liegt er im Heer dieser Bundesgenossen; bei Bündnissen liegt er in der Einheit des Interesses;"[203]

---

[200] *Kriegsstärkenachweisung 131 n Schützenkompanie (n.A.)* vom 1. Oktober 1943.

[201] Vego, Milan: *Clausewitz's Schwerpunkt. Mistranslated from German – Misunderstood in English.* In: Military Review, January-February 2007, p. 101.

[202] Grassi, Ernesto (Ed.): von Clausewitz, Carl: *Vom Kriege.* Rowohlt: Hamburg, Germany, 2005, S. 211.

[203] Corff, Oliver (Ed.): von Clausewitz, Carl: *Vom Kriege.* Erstausgabe von 1832-1834. A4 Version basierend auf Textdaten bibliotheca Augustana. Clausewitz-Gesellschaft e.V.: Berlin, Germany, 2010, S. 459.

After the reorganization into the Infantry Division new type in the fall of 1943, the authorized strength of the Rifle Platoon decreased to 31 men, the light mortar section was eliminated and the number of squads was reduced to 3, and their size had also decreased to 9 men.[204] The Rifle Platoon of the Volksgrenadierdivision had about 33 men.

Weight of Effort (Schwerpunkt): The term Schwerpunkt [which we translated as weight of effort] has stirred up quite a debate, especially in the English language literature and discussion.[205] A brief look at Clausewitz *On War* shows that he usually uses the term in (grand) strategic context, for example:

"From them [the prevailing relation of two states] a certain weight of effort, a center of force and motion, on which the whole depends, will be formed, and on this weight of effort of the adversary the combined thrust of all forces must be directed."[206]

And also, in the further elaboration here:

"Alexander, Gustav Adolf, Charles XII, Frederick the Great had their weight of effort in their army; if this had been shattered, they would have played their role badly; in states torn apart by internal parties, it is usually in the capital; in small states supported by powerful ones, it is in the army of these allies; in alliances, it is in the unity of interest;"[207]

---

[204] *Kriegsstärkenachweisung 131 n Schützenkompanie (n.A.)* vom 1. Oktober 1943.

[205] Vego, Milan: *Clausewitz's Schwerpunkt. Mistranslated from German – Misunderstood in English.* In: Military Review, January-February 2007, p. 101.

[206] Grassi, Ernesto (Ed.): von Clausewitz, Carl: *Vom Kriege.* Rowohlt: Hamburg, Germany, 2005, S. 211.

[207] Corff, Oliver (Ed.): von Clausewitz, Carl: *Vom Kriege.* Erstausgabe von 1832-1834. A4 Version basierend auf Textdaten bibliotheca Augustana. Clausewitz-Gesellschaft e.V.: Berlin, Germany, 2010, S. 459.

In *Vom* Kriege kommt das Wort „Schwerpunkt" und seine Variationen insgesamt 49-mal vor. Allerdings nutzt Clausewitz den Begriff lange bevor er ihn genauer spezifiziert. So schreibt er zum Beispiel:

„Wie dieser Gedanke von dem Schwerpunkt der feindlichen Macht bei dem ganzen Kriegsplan wirksam wird, werden wir im letzten Buche betrachten, denn dahin gehört der Gegenstand überhaupt, und wir haben ihn von daher nur entlehnt, um keine Lücke in der Vorstellungsreihe zu lassen."[208]

Es fällt auf, dass der Begriff nicht immer dieselbe Bedeutung hat. Die Begriffe „Schwerpunkt" und „Schwerpunktbildung" werden vom Militärhistoriker Gerhard Groß in seinem Buch zum operativen Denken des Deutschen Heeres wiederholt erwähnt, selten im strategischen, sondern in erster Linie im operativen Sinne.[209]

In der *Truppenführung* wird Schwerpunkt und wie er sich kennzeichnet angesprochen:

„Der Schwerpunkt [im Angriff] wird gekennzeichnet: beim Ansatz des Angriffs durch schmale Gefechtsstreifen, durch Maßnahmen für die Feuervereinigung aller Waffen, auch als benachbarten Gefechtsstreifen, und durch Verstärkung des Feuers durch besonders zugewiesene schwere Infanteriewaffen und Artillerie; während der Durchführung des Angriffs durch Steigern des Feuers und Einsetzen von Kampfwagen und Reserven. Die Wahl des Schwerpunktes wird durch die Artillerie, manchmal auch durch die Kampfwagen weitgehend beeinflußt."[210]

---

[208] Corff, Oliver (Ed.): von Clausewitz, Carl: *Vom Kriege.* Erstausgabe von 1832-1834. A4 Version basierend auf Textdaten bibliotheca Augustana. Clausewitz-Gesellschaft e.V.: Berlin, Germany, 2010, S. 364.
[209] Groß, Gerhard P.: *Mythos und Wirklichkeit: Die Geschichte des operativen Denkens im deutschen Heer von Moltke d. Ä. bis Heusinger.* Zeitalter der Weltkriege, Band 9. Ferdinand Schönigh: Paderborn, Germany, 2012, S. 67-68, 156, 166, 171, 173, 201.
[210] *H.Dv. 300/1: Truppenführung (T.F.) I. Teil. Abschnitt I – XIII.* Verlag Mittler & Sohn: Berlin, 1936, S. 123.

In *On War* the word "Schwerpunkt" and its variations occur a total of 49 times. However, Clausewitz uses the term long before he specifies it more precisely. He writes, for example:

"How this idea of the weight of effort of enemy power becomes effective in the whole war plan, we shall consider in the last book, for that is where the object belongs in the first place, and so we have only borrowed it in order to leave no gap in the series of ideas."[211]

It is noticeable that the term does not always have the same meaning. The terms "Schwerpunkt" and "Schwerpunktbildung"[212] are mentioned repeatedly by the military historian Gerhard Groß in his book on the operational thinking of the German Army, rarely in a strategic, and primarily in an operational sense.[213]

In *Unit Command* the weight of effort is addressed and characterized:

"The weight of effort [in the attack] is characterized: in the commencement of the attack in narrow combat sectors, by measures for concentration fire of all weapons, also as adjacent combat sectors, and by the reinforcement of the fire by specially assigned heavy infantry weapons and artillery; during the execution of the attack by increasing the fire and using combat vehicles and reserves. The choice of the weight of effort is largely influenced by the artillery, sometimes also by the combat vehicles."[214]

---

[211] Corff, Oliver (Ed.): von Clausewitz, Carl: *Vom Kriege*. Erstausgabe von 1832-1834. A4 Version basierend auf Textdaten bibliotheca Augustana. Clausewitz-Gesellschaft e.V.: Berlin, Germany, 2010, S. 364.

[212] The term "Bildung" means "creation" in this context, but it can also mean "education".

[213] Groß, Gerhard P.: *Mythos und Wirklichkeit: Die Geschichte des operativen Denkens im deutschen Heer von Moltke d. Ä. bis Heusinger*. Zeitalter der Weltkriege, Band 9. Ferdinand Schönigh: Paderborn, Germany, 2012, S. 67-68, 156, 166, 171, 173, 201.

[214] *H.Dv. 300/1: Truppenführung (T.F.) I. Teil. Abschnitt I – XIII.* Verlag Mittler & Sohn: Berlin, 1936, S. 123.

Hierbei wird eindeutig nicht mehr die strategische, sondern die taktisch-operative Ebene angesprochen. Ebenso Kühlwein:

„Der Schwerpunkt wird im Angriff (mindestens im Btl.-Verbande) an die Stelle gelegt, wo man die Entscheidung herbeiführen will. Hier werden die Hauptkräfte und die Masse der Munition eingesetzt. Er wird gekennzeichnet durch schmale Gefechtsstreifen und durch Feuervereinigung aller Waffen, auch aus benachbarten Gefechtsstreifen (Flankierung). Für die Wahl des Schwerpunktes ist die Feindbesetzung (gutes Vorwärtskommen) und hauptsächlich die Gunst des Geländes maßgebend."[215]

Eine Definition von 1944 orientiert sich hier auch ganz klar an *Truppenführung*:

„Schwerpunkt: wird durch schmale Gefechtsstreifen, vermehrten Einsatz von schweren Waffen und Nachführen von Reserven sowie Munition an der Stelle gebildet, wo die Entscheidung fallen soll."[216]

In *Truppenführung* fällt der Begriff Schwerpunkt noch öfter:

„Reicht die unmittelbar mit der Infanterie zusammenarbeitende Artillerie für die Unterstützung nicht aus, so muß der Artillerieführer mit der übrigen Artillerie aushelfen, vorzugsweise durch Unterstützung der im Schwerpunkt angreifenden Infanterie."[217]

Darauf kommentierten Condell und Zabecki in ihrer Übersetzung:

„In the original, the term Schwerpunkt is used. What was really meant, however, was decisive point [entscheidende Stelle], not center of gravity as Clausewitz defined the term."[218]

---

[215] Kühlwein, Fritz: *Die Gruppe im Gefecht. (Die neue Gruppe)*. E. S. Mittler & Sohn: Berlin, 1940, S. 14-15.

[216] BArch, RH 17/809: Schule VII: *Taktische Grundbegriffe*, August 1944, S. 4

[217] H.Dv. 300/1: *Truppenführung (T.F.) I. Teil. Abschnitt I – XIII*. Verlag Mittler & Sohn: Berlin, 1936, S. 144.

[218] Condell, Bruce (ed.); Zabecki, David T. (ed.): *On the German Art of War. Truppenführung*. Stackpole Books: Mechanicsburg, PA, USA, 2009 (2001), p. 102.

This clearly no longer addresses the strategic, but the tactical-operational level. Likewise Kühlwein:

"The weight of effort is put in the attack (at least at battalion-level) at the place where one wants to bring about the decisive outcome[219]. Here the main forces and the mass of ammunition are used. It is characterized by narrow combat sectors and by fire concentration of all weapons, also from adjacent combat sectors (flanking). The choice of the weight of effort is determined by the enemy's position (good advancement) and mainly by the favor of the terrain."[220]

A definition from 1944 also clearly orients itself on *Unit Command*:

"Weight of Effort: is formed by narrow combat sectors, increased use of heavy weapons and replenishment of reserves and ammunition at the point where the decisive outcome[221] is to be made."[222]

In *Unit Command*, the term weight of effort is used even more often:

"If the artillery working directly with the infantry is not sufficient for support, the artillery commander must help out with the rest of the artillery, preferably by supporting the infantry attacking at the weight of effort."[223]

Condell and Zabecki commented on this in their translation:

"In the original, the term Schwerpunkt is used. What was really meant, however, was decisive point [entscheidende Stelle], not center of gravity as Clausewitz defined the term."[224]

---

[219] Note the literal translation of "Entscheidung" would be "decision", but in this case it refers to the "Entscheidung" in the sense of decisive outcome, like it is used in "Entscheidungsschlacht" which is translated and well-known as "decisive battle".

[220] Kühlwein, Fritz: *Die Gruppe im Gefecht. (Die neue Gruppe).* E. S. Mittler & Sohn: Berlin, 1940, S. 14-15.

[221] Note the literal translation of "Entscheidung" would be "decision", but in this case it refers to the "Entscheidung" in the sense of decisive outcome, like it is used in "Entscheidungsschlacht" which is translated and well-known as "decisive battle".

[222] BArch, RH 17/809: Schule VII: *Taktische Grundbegriffe*, August 1944, S. 4

[223] *H.Dv. 300/1: Truppenführung (T.F.) I. Teil. Abschnitt I – XIII.* Verlag Mittler & Sohn: Berlin, 1936, S. 144.

[224] Condell, Bruce (ed.); Zabecki, David T. (ed.): *On the German Art of War. Truppenführung.* Stackpole Books: Mechanicsburg, PA, USA, 2009 (2001), p. 102.

Dies geht natürlich davon aus, dass sich jemand an die ziemlich schwammige Verwendung von Schwerpunkt bei Clausewitz hielt und sie gleichzeitig von der (groß)strategischen Ebene auf die taktisch-operative Ebene anwendete.

Die Durchsicht von offiziellen und semi-offiziellen[225] Publikationen der Zeit vermittelt den Eindruck, dass es sich bei Schwerpunkt um einen sehr praktischen Begriff handelte, der in erster Linie auf der taktischen Ebene benutzt wurde. Ein solch pragmatischer Ansatz kommt auch klar hervor, wenn Altrichter im *Reserveoffizier* unter „Schwerpunktbildung" 1941 schreibt:

„Wahl des Schwerpunktes dort, wo nach Feindlage und Gelände die besten Voraussetzungen für den Erfolg vorliegen. Ist die entscheidende Stelle nicht von vornherein zu erkennen, so muß der Schwerpunkt ins Ungewisse gebildet und erforderlichenfalls später verlegt werden."[226]

Und darauf folgt dann die konkrete Handlungsanweisung:

„Bildung des Schwerpunktes wird erreicht durch:
Zuweisung schmaler Gefechtsstreifen,
Feuervereinigung aller Waffen, auch aus Nachbargefechtsstreifen,
Verstärkung des Feuers durch besonders zugewiesene Artillerie und schwere Infanteriewaffen,
Steigerung des Feuers,
Einsatz von Panzerverbänden und Reserven,
Einsatz von Luftstreitkräften."[227]

Dr. Roman Töppel, der sich in seiner Forschung jahrzehntelang mit Operationsbefehlen, Kriegstagebüchern, Einsatzberichten und sonstigen Quellen beschäftigt hat und auch Veteranen zum Thema Schwerpunkt befragt hat, gab auf die Frage zu einer Definition für Schwerpunkt für die deutschen Streitkräfte im 2. Weltkrieg folgende Definition:

„Schwerpunkt ist der Punkt, an dem die Masse der Kräfte zur Erreichung des operativen Hauptziels eingesetzt wird."[228]

---

[225] In vielen Fällen sind ganze Textpassagen, Grafiken und Sonstiges 1:1 oder fast 1:1 identisch, allerdings ist ohne eingehender Recherche schwer festzustellen, wer von wem „abgeschrieben" hat bzw. ob es in manchen Fällen nicht ein und derselbe Autor war.
[226] Altrichter, Friedrich: *Der Reserveoffizer. Ein Handbuch für den Offizier und Offizieranwärter des Beurlaubtenstandes aller Waffen.* Vierzehnte, durchgesehene Auflage. Verlag von E. S. Mittler & Sohn: Berlin, Germany, 1941, S. 259.
[227] Altrichter, Friedrich: *Der Reserveoffizer. Ein Handbuch für den Offizier und Offizieranwärter des Beurlaubtenstandes aller Waffen.* Vierzehnte, durchgesehene Auflage. Verlag von E. S. Mittler & Sohn: Berlin, Germany, 1941, S. 259.
[228] Email von Dr. Roman Töppel, 8. November 2020.

This, of course, assumes that someone kept to the rather vague use of weight of effort by Clausewitz and at the same time applied it from the (grand) strategic level to the tactical-operational level.

Looking through official and semi-official[229] publications of the time gives the impression that emphasis was a very practical term, used primarily at the tactical level. This pragmatic approach is also evident when Altrichter writes in the Reserve Officer's 1941 "Schwerpunktbildung"[230]:

"Choice of the weight of effort where, according to enemy position and terrain, the best conditions for success are available. If the decisive point cannot be recognized from the outset, the weight of effort must be formed in the unknown and, if necessary, moved later."[231]

And this is followed by specific instructions for action:

"Formation of the weight of effort is achieved by:
allocation of narrow combat sectors,
fire concentration of all weapons, also from neighboring combat sectors,
reinforcement of fire with specially assigned artillery and heavy infantry weapons,
intensification of the fire,
employment of tank units and reserves,
employment of air forces."[232]

Dr. Roman Töppel, who has spent decades in his research dealing with operation orders, war diaries, mission reports and other sources and who has also interviewed veterans on the subject of weight of effort, when asked about a definition for weight of effort for the German armed forces in the Second World War provided the following definition:

"Weight of effort is the point at which the mass of forces is used to achieve the main operational objective."[233]

---

[229] In many cases, entire text passages, graphics and miscellaneous are 1:1 or almost 1:1 identical, but without detailed research it is difficult to determine who "copied" from whom or whether in some cases it was not one and the same author.

[230] The term "Bildung" means "creation" in this context, but it can also mean "education".

[231] Altrichter, Friedrich: *Der Reserveoffizer. Ein Handbuch für den Offizier und Offizieranwärter des Beurlaubtenstandes aller Waffen.* Vierzehnte, durchgesehene Auflage. Verlag von E. S. Mittler & Sohn: Berlin, Germany, 1941, S. 259.

[232] Altrichter, Friedrich: *Der Reserveoffizer. Ein Handbuch für den Offizier und Offizieranwärter des Beurlaubtenstandes aller Waffen.* Vierzehnte, durchgesehene Auflage. Verlag von E. S. Mittler & Sohn: Berlin, Germany, 1941, S. 259.

[233] Email from Dr. Roman Töppel, 8. November 2020.

Diese Definition und auch die anderen aus zeitgenössischen Quellen angeführten Definitionen haben mit der Clausewitz'schen Verwendung wenig bis gar nichts zu tun, denn dabei stimmen weder die Ebene noch der praktische Ansatz überein.

Letztlich sei anzumerken das im deutschen Sprachgebrauch Schwerpunkt auch generell benutzt wird. Als Beispiel sei folgendes Zitat aus dem auch in diesem Buch abgedruckten *Vorläufigen Merkblatt: Der M.P.-Zug der Grenadier-Kompanie* aufgeführt: „Der Schwerpunkt der Ausbildung liegt in der Handhabung der Waffe und im Schulgefechtsschießen."[234] Es handelt sich hierbei also um sowohl einen taktisch-operativ-strategischen Begriff, so wie um ein Alltagswort das einen gewissen „Fokus" beschreibt.

Seelenachse: Die Seelenachse entspricht der Richtung, den das Geschoss folgen würde also der Abgangsrichtung, wenn es keinen physikalischen Effekte wie zum Beispiel der Schwerkraft unterliegen würde. Die Bohrung eines Laufes wird auch als Seele bezeichnet daher der Name.

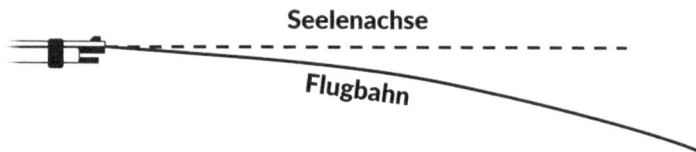

Abbildung 7: Seelenachse

Seitengewehr: Alte Bezeichnung für ein Bajonett. Ein Bajonett ist eine Stichwaffe, die an einer Schusswaffe normalerweise einem Gewehr befestigt wird. Daraus ergibt sich auch der Name. Ein Seitengewehr war für den Nahkampf geeignet. So schreibt Reibert: „Zweck: Blanke Waffe zum Nahkampf, allein oder auf den Karabiner aufgepflanzt angewendet."[235]

---

[234] BArch, RH 11-I/83: Merkblatt 25a/16: Vorläufiges Merkblatt „Der M.P.-Zug der Grenadier-Kompanie", 1.2.1944, S. 10.
[235] Gesterding, Schwatlo; Feyerabend, Hans-Joachim: *Unteroffizierthemen. Ein Handbuch für den Unteroffizierunterricht.* Siebente, neubearbeite Auflage. E. S. Mittler & Sohn: Berlin, Germany, 1943, S. 96.

This definition and the other definitions cited from contemporary sources have little or nothing to do with Clausewitz' use, as neither the level nor the practical approach is consistent.

Finally, it should be noted that "Schwerpunkt" is often used in the German language in a more general manner. The following quotations originating from the *Preliminary Pamphlet: The SMG-Platoon of the Grenadier-Company* also printed in this book makes this clear: "The focus [Schwerpunkt] of the training is on the handling of the weapon and in basic live fire combat exercise."[236] Thus, this word is used on a tactical, operational and strategic level, while at the same time being a word of daily relevance, as it can simple describe a certain "focus".

Axis of the Bore (Seelenachse): The axis of the bore corresponds to the direction the bullet would follow, namely the flight direction, if it were not subject to physical effects such as gravity. The rifling of a barrel is also called the soul, hence the name.[237]

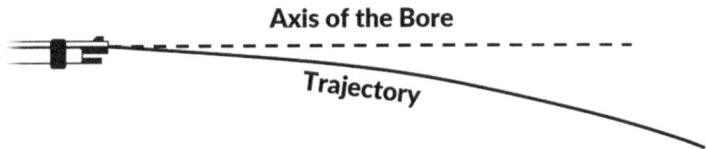

Illustration 7: Axis of the Bore

Bayonet (Seitengewehr): Old name for a bayonet.[238] A bayonet is a stabbing weapon, which is usually attached to a rifle. This is also the origin of its name. A bayonet is useful in close quarter combat. As Reibert notes: "Purpose: Cold weapon for close combat, used alone or attached to the carbine."[239]

---

[236] BArch, RH 11-I/83: Merkblatt 25a/16: Vorläufiges Merkblatt „Der M.P.-Zug der Grenadier-Kompanie", 1.2.1944, S. 10.

[237] Note that the literal translation of "Seelenachse" is "axis of the soul".

[238] Note that the literal translation of "Seitengewehr" is "side rifle".

[239] Gesterding, Schwatlo; Feyerabend, Hans-Joachim: *Unteroffizierthemen. Ein Handbuch für den Unteroffizierunterricht. Siebente, neubearbeite Auflage.* E. S. Mittler & Sohn: Berlin, Germany, 1943, S. 96.

Sprung: Vorarbeiten wurde unter Feuer bzw. von Feind einsehbarem Gelände meist kriechend oder sprungweise durchgeführt.[240] Der Sprung ist ein schnelles Vorwärtsbewegen für kurze Zeit, er wird normalerweise koordiniert durchgeführt. Je nach Situation, zum Beispiel, wenn der Feind nahe genug ist, kann er auch einzeln ausgeführt werden.[241] Die Länge des Sprungs ist von der Situation abhängig, insbesondere vom Gelände, feindlichen Feuer und eigener Feuerunterstützung.[242] Auf Kommando bereiten sich der Maschinengewehrschütze und die Schützen auf den Sprung vor:

„Die Schützen nehmen das Gewehr in die linke Hand, stützen die rechte Hand auf den Boden und ziehen das rechte Bein möglichst nahe an den Leib heran[.] Sie dürfen sich bei den Vorbereitungen für den Sprung nicht aufrichten [...]."[243]

Das Ziel des Sprungs kann vor dem Durchführungskommando angekündigt werden zum Beispiel mit „Nächster Sprung: Waldrand!" Auf das Kommando „Auf! Marsch! Marsch!" beginnt der Sprung nach vorne. Dies wird auch als vorwärts stürzen bezeichnet. Der Sprung kann durch Zeichen oder die Kommandos „Volle Deckung!" oder „Stellung!" beendet werden.[244]

In der Praxis war die Situation wohl eher fließend, so schreibt Reibert:

„Die Kommandos zum Sprung werden oft durch Zeichen oder Befehle (z. B. „Folgen!") ersetzt. Häufig werden die Schützen auch ohne Befehl dem Beispiel des vorstürzenden Führers folgen."[245]

---

[240] Reibert, Wilhelm: *Der Dienstunterricht im Heere. Ausgabe für den Schützen der Schützenkompanie. Zwölfte, völlig neubearbeitete Auflage.* Jahrgang 1940. Verlag von E. S. Mittler & Sohn: Berlin, Germany, 1940. Reprint by The Naval & Military Press Ltd, S. 279.
[241] Haas, Walter: *Soldatenlexikon. Ein Merkbuch für den Infanteriedienst.* Franckh'sche Verlagshandlung: Stuttgart, Germany, o.J., S. 149-150.
[242] Reibert, Wilhelm: *Dienstunterricht. Schützen,* S. 279.
[243] Reibert, Wilhelm: *Dienstunterricht. Schützen,* S. 279-280.
[244] Reibert, Wilhelm: *Dienstunterricht. Schützen,* S. 280-281.
[245] Reibert, Wilhelm: *Dienstunterricht. Schützen,* S. 281.

Rush (Sprung): An advance under fire or in terrain observed by the enemy was usually made in a crawl or in a rush.[246] The rush is a rapid advance for a short duration which is usually conducted in a coordinated manner. Depending on the situation, for example if the enemy is close enough, it can also be conducted individually.[247] The length of the rush is dependent on the situation and especially the terrain, enemy fire and own fire support.[248] The MG gunners and rifleman prepare to rush on command:

"The rifleman take the rifle into their left hand, brace themselves with their right hand against the ground, and tuck the right knee as close as possible towards their body. They may not stand up while preparing for the rush [...]."[249]

The aim of the rush can be indicated before the command, for example with: "Next rush: edge of the forest!" On the command "Up! March! March!" the rush to the front commences. This is also referred to as a forward rush. The rush can be ended by sign or the command "Full cover!" or "Position!".[250]

In practice it was likely more fluid, as Reibert notes:

"The commands for the rush were often substituted via calls and orders (e.g., "Follow!"). Often the rifleman would also follow the example of their forward rushing leader."[251]

---

[246] Reibert, Wilhelm: *Der Dienstunterricht im Heere. Ausgabe für den Schützen der Schützenkompanie. Zwölfte, völlig neubearbeitete Auflage.* Jahrgang 1940. Verlag von E. S. Mittler & Sohn: Berlin, Germany, 1940. Reprint by The Naval & Military Press Ltd, S. 279.

[247] Haas, Walter: *Soldatenlexikon. Ein Merkbuch für den Infanteriedienst.* Franckh'sche Verlagshandlung: Stuttgart, Germany, o.J., S. 149-150.

[248] Reibert, Wilhelm: *Dienstunterricht. Schützen*, S. 279.

[249] Reibert, Wilhelm: *Dienstunterricht. Schützen*, S. 279-280.

[250] Reibert, Wilhelm: *Dienstunterricht. Schützen*, S. 280-281.

[251] Reibert, Wilhelm: *Dienstunterricht. Schützen*, S. 281.

sS Munition: Dies war die Standardmunition für Gewehre und Maschinengewehre des deutschen Heeres im 2. Weltkrieg. Dabei steht „sS" für „schweres Spitzgeschoss".[252] Der Patronenboden war durch einen grünen Ring gekennzeichnet. Das Geschoss war aus Blei.

Stoßkraft: Die Stoßkraft steht für die vorantragende Kraft im Angriff. So schreibt Raths: „Stoßkraft hingegen meinte den durch den Schwung der Soldaten im Sturm vorgetragenen Impuls des Angriffs, der letztlich die Gegner aus der zu erobernden Position werfen sollte."[253] In Zimmermanns *Infanteriedienst* von 1940 heißt es letztlich: „Die Stoßkraft der Schützen, die mit Bajonett und Handgranate und dem gefürchteten deutschen ‚Hurra' zum Sturm auf den Feind antreten, entscheidet den Kampf."[254]

Sturmgewehr: Bezeichnung die von Hitler 1944 zur Einführung der Maschinenpistole 44, welche in Sturmgewehr 44 umbenannt wurde, vergeben wurde. Der Name hat schließlich diesen Typ von vollautomatischer Schusswaffe geprägt. Siehe Ergänzung 9, Punkt: Hitlers Ablehnungen und Namensgebung.

Sturmgruppe: Die Sturmgruppen machten 2 der 3 Gruppen des Sturmzuges aus. Eine Sturmgruppe besteht aus einem Gruppenführer und 7 Schützen, wovon einer stellvertretender Gruppenführer ist, alle waren einheitlich mit dem Sturmgewehr 44 ausgestattet. Die Hauptaufgabe der Sturmgruppe im Angriff ist der Einbruch in die feindliche Stellung. In der Verteidigung dient eine Sturmgruppe als Gegenstoßreserve.

---

[252] Hahn, Fritz: *Waffen und Geheimwaffen des deutschen Heeres 1933-1945. Band 1.* Dörfler Verlag: Eggolsheim, o.J., S. 25. Siehe auch: Zimmermann, Bodo: *Infanteriedienst. Für den Einzelschützen der aktiven Truppe, der Reserve und der Landwehr. 18. Auflage (Kriegsausgabe) der „Soldatenfibel".* Verlag „Offene Worte": Berlin, Germany, 1940, S. 25.
[253] Raths, Ralf: *Vom Massensturm zur Stoßtrupptaktik. Die deutsche Landkriegstaktik im Spiegel von Dienstvorschriften und Publizistik 1906 bis 1918.* Zentrum für Militärgeschichte und Sozialwissenschaften der Bundeswehr: Potsdam, Germany, 2019, S. 31.
[254] Zimmermann, Bodo: *Infanteriedienst. Für den Einzelschützen der aktiven Truppe, der Reserve und der Landwehr. 18. Auflage (Kriegsausgabe) der „Soldatenfibel".* Verlag „Offene Worte": Berlin, Germany, 1940, S. 35.

sS Ammunition (sS Munition): This was the standard ammunition for rifles and machine guns of the German Army in Second World War. The abbreviation "sS" stands for "schweres Spitzgeschoss"[255].[256] The cartridge base was marked by a green ring. The bullet was made of lead.

Shock Action[257] (Stoßkraft): The Shock action describes the protruding force of an attack and was defined by Raths as: "Shock action, on the other hand, meant the impulse of the attack, carried forward by the momentum of the soldiers in the assault, which was ultimately intended to throw the enemy from the position to be conquered."[258] In Zimmermann's *Infantry Service* of 1940 it is described as: "The power of the riflemen, who attack the enemy with bayonets and hand grenades and the dreaded German 'Hurray', decides the combat."[259]

Assault Rifle (Sturmgewehr): Designation given by Hitler in 1944 for the introduction of the Maschinenpistole 44, which was subsequently renamed Sturmgewehr 44. The name finally coined this type of fully automatic firearm. See Supplement 9, point: Hitler's Rejections and Choice of Name.

Assault Squad (Sturmgruppe): The assault squads made up 2 of the 3 squads of the assault platoon. One assault squad consisted of a squad leader and 7 riflemen, one of whom was a deputy squad leader, all riflemen were uniformly equipped with the Sturmgewehr 44. The main task of the assault squad in attack is the break-in[260] into the enemy position. In the defense, an assault squad serves as a hasty counterattack[261] reserve.

---

[255] Literally translated "schweres Spitzegeschoss" means "heavy pointed projectile". "Pointed projectile" is also called "spitzer" in English.

[256] Hahn, Fritz: *Waffen und Geheimwaffen des deutschen Heeres 1933-1945. Band 1.* Dörfler Verlag: Eggolsheim, o.J., S. 25. Siehe auch: Zimmermann, Bodo: *Infanteriedienst. Für den Einzelschützen der aktiven Truppe, der Reserve und der Landwehr.* 18. Auflage (Kriegsausgabe) der „Soldatenfibel". Verlag „Offene Worte": Berlin, Germany, 1940, S. 25.

[257] Note that there are various translations for "Stoßkraft" like "shock power", "striking power" etc. We went with "shock action" since this was used in contemporary US Army field manuals of the Armored Force, like *FM 17-32* and *FM 17-10*.

[258] Raths, Ralf: *Vom Massensturm zur Stoßtrupptaktik. Die deutsche Landkriegstaktik im Spiegel von Dienstvorschriften und Publizistik 1906 bis 1918.* Zentrum für Militärgeschichte und Sozialwissenschaften der Bundeswehr: Potsdam, Germany, 2019, S. 31.

[259] Zimmermann, Bodo: *Infanteriedienst. Für den Einzelschützen der aktiven Truppe, der Reserve und der Landwehr.* 18. Auflage (Kriegsausgabe) der „Soldatenfibel". Verlag „Offene Worte": Berlin, Germany, 1940, S. 35.

[260] There is no English equivalent for the military term "Einbruch". See Glossary: Break-In (Einbruch).

[261] The Germans distinguished between a hasty counterattack ("Gegenstoß") and regular counterattack ("Gegenangriff"). See Glossary: Hasty Counterattack (Gegenstoß) and Counterattack (Gegenangriff).

Im *Vorläufigen Merkblatt: Der M.P.-Zug der Grenadier-Kompanie* von 1. Februar 1944 hieß die Sturmgruppe noch MP-Gruppe. Es bestanden zudem 3 MP-Gruppen und sie waren anders gegliedert. Die MP-Gruppe hatte 9 statt 8 Mann, des Weiteren hatte jede MP-Gruppe einen Granatschützen. Diese Granatschützen wurden den Gruppen entnommen und in den Zugtrupp des Sturmzuges gegliedert. Dies hatte unter anderem den Vorteil, dass der Gruppenführer sowohl in der Führung wie Ausbildung entlastet wurde.[262]

Sturmzug: Der Sturmzug war das Ergebnis mehrerer Truppenversuche für eine optimale Gliederung, sowie den materiellen Beschränkungen, insbesondere die begrenzte Anzahl von MP 44 / StG 44, als auch ein Mangel an Munition für diese Waffe. Denn die Kampfkraft der mit der MP 44 ausgestatteten Einheiten war sehr hoch:

„Die Erfahrungen haben gezeigt, daß die Kampfkraft der Infanterie-Kompanien (Grenadier-, Füsilier-, Jäg.- und Geb.Jäg.Kpn.) durch die Umbewaffnung mit MP 44 wesentlich gesteigert werden kann. Mit dieser Waffe ausgestattete Stoßzüge haben sich infolge ihrer überlegenen Feuerkraft im Angriff und in der Verteidigung besonders bewährt."[263]

Aber die Möglichkeiten zur vollständigen Ausstattung sehr beschränkt:

„Die Umbewaffnung aller Inf.Kompanien mit MP 44 kann jedoch nur allmählich erfolgen."[264]

---

[262] BArch, RH 11-1/54: Feld-Uffz.-Schule d.Inf: *Stellungnahme auf Grund der durchgeführten M.P.-Versuche,* 30.10.44, S. 1, Bl. 176.
[263] BArch, RH 11-1/54: OKH, General der Infanterie: *Erhöhung der Kampfkraft der Inf.Kompanien durch bevorzugte Bewaffnung mit Selbstlader und MP 38/40,* 7.10.44, S. 1, Bl. 146.
[264] BArch, RH 11-1/54: OKH, General der Infanterie: *Erhöhung der Kampfkraft der Inf.Kompanien durch bevorzugte Bewaffnung mit Selbstlader und MP 38/40,* 7.10.44, S. 1, Bl. 146.

In the *Preliminary Pamphlet: The SMG-Platoon of the Grenadier-Company* of February 1, 1944, the assault squad was still called the SMG[265]-squad. There were also 3 SMG-squads and they were structured differently. The SMG-squad had 9 men instead of 8, and each SMG-squad also had rifle-grenade rifleman. These rifle-grenade riflemen were removed from the squads and assigned to the assault platoon. One of the advantages of this was that the squad leader was relieved of both leadership and training.[266]

Assault Platoon (Sturmzug): The assault platoon was the result of several troop trials for an optimal structure, as well as the material limitations, especially the limited number of MP 44 / StG 44, as well as a lack of ammunition for this weapon. After all, the combat effectiveness[267] of the units equipped with the MP 44 was very high:

"Experience has shown that the combat effectiveness of infantry companies (grenadier, fusilier, light infantry[268] and mountain troop[269] companies) can be considerably increased by rearming them with MP 44. Shock platoons equipped with this weapon have proven to be particularly effective in attack and defense due to their superior firepower."[270]

But the possibilities for complete equipment are very limited:

"However, the rearmament of all infantry companies with MP 44 can only take place gradually."[271]

---

[265] SMG means submachine gun. Technically, this was not a submachine gun, but the designation machine carbine was abolished, and the designation assault rifle was only introduced at the end of 1944. Regarding the naming and general development see Supplement 9.

[266] BArch, RH 11-1/54: Feld-Uffz.-Schule d.Inf: *Stellungnahme auf Grund der durch-geführten M.P.-Versuche*, 30.10.44, S. 1, Bl. 176.

[267] The literal translation of "Kampfkraft" is "combat strength".

[268] The term "Jäger" literally means "hunter", these were light infantry. Be aware that in early war there were "leichte Divisionen" (light divisions) these were "weak" panzer divisions.

[269] The term "Gebirgsjäger" literally means "mountain hunter".

[270] BArch, RH 11-1/54: OKH, General der Infanterie: *Erhöhung der Kampfkraft der Inf.Kompanien durch bevorzugte Bewaffnung mit Selbstlader und MP 38/40*, 7.10.44, S. 1, Bl. 146.

[271] BArch, RH 11-1/54: OKH, General der Infanterie: *Erhöhung der Kampfkraft der Inf.Kompanien durch bevorzugte Bewaffnung mit Selbstlader und MP 38/40*, 7.10.44, S. 1, Bl. 146.

Bei den Versuchen wurden auch Züge zum Vergleich mit MP 38/40 und Selbstladern statt der MP 44 ausgestattet. Bei Selbstladern waren die Nachteile, dass zu oft Hemmungen auftraten, 10 Schuss pro Magazin nicht ausreichten, es nicht möglich war Feuerstöße abzugeben und sie Unhandlich im Nahkampf waren. Bei der MP 38/40 war, die Ungenauigkeit über 100 m Entfernung von Nachteil, welches durch die Beschränkung das kein Einzelfeuer abgegeben werden konnte noch weiter verstärkt wurde.[272] Ebenso wurde angeführt:

„Vergleichsschießen im Einzelschuß bewiesen die Überlegenheit der M.Pi.44 in der Schußleistung gegenüber dem Selbstlader und der M.Pi.38/40."[273]

Die endgültige Gliederung des Sturmzuges bestand aus 2 Sturmgruppen, 1 Feuergruppe und dem Zugtrupp.

Eine vorherige Gliederung wie in Ergänzung 1: *Vorläufiges Merkblatt: Der M.P.-Zug der Grenadier-Kompanie* vom 1. Februar 1944 ersichtlich ist, hatte noch keine Feuergruppe. Die 3 MP-Gruppen waren mit dem MP 43/1 ausgestattet, sowie einen Granatschützen. Diese Gliederung hatte einige Nachteile und wurde daher verändert. Die Granatschützen wurden in den Zugtrupp konzentriert, des Weiteren wurde eine Feuergruppe mit leichten Maschinengewehren hinzugefügt.

Der *Zwischenbericht zum M.P.-Truppenversuch* vom 14. September 1944 führt bezüglich dieser Veränderung an:

„Die Gliederung des Zuges in Feuer- und Sturmgruppen sowie die Zusammenfassung der Gewehrgranatgeräte in Zugtrupp wird für zweckmäßig gehalten. Bereits bei der kurzen Versuchszeit hat sich diese Gliederung praktisch voll bewährt und stellt ausbildungs- und führungsmäßig eine Vereinfachung dar."[274]

---

[272] BArch, RH 11-1/54: Feld-Uffz.-Schule d.Inf: *Stellungnahme auf Grund der durch-geführten M.P.-Versuche*, 30.10.44, S. 1, Bl. 176.

[273] BArch, RH 11-1/54: Feld-Uffz.-Schule d.Inf: *Stellungnahme auf Grund der durch-geführten M.P.-Versuche*, 30.10.44, S. 1, Bl. 176.

[274] BArch, RH 11-1/54: Infanterieschule, Abteilung IIIa: *M.P.-Versuch*, 14. Sept. 44, S. 1, Bl. 109.

During the trials, platoons were also equipped with MP 38/40 and semi-automatic rifles[275] instead of the MP 44 for comparison. The disadvantages of semi-automatic rifles were that they were too often stoppages, 10 rounds per magazine were not enough, it was not possible to fire bursts and they were unhandy in close combat. The disadvantages of the MP 38/40 were the inaccuracy beyond a distance of 100 m, which was worsened by the limitation that semi-automatic fire was not possible.[276] It was also mentioned:

"Comparative firing in single shot proved the superiority of the M.Pi.44 in firing performance over the semi-automatic rifle and the M.Pi.38/40."[277]

The final organization of the assault platoon consisted of 2 assault squads, 1 fire squad and the platoon headquarters.

A previous organization as can be seen in Supplement 1: *Preliminary Pamphlet: The SMG-Platoon of the Grenadier-Company* of February 1, 1944, did not yet have a fire squad. The 3 SMG squads were equipped with the MP 43/1 and a rifle-grenade rifleman. This organization had some disadvantages and was therefore changed. The rifle-grenade riflemen were concentrated in the platoon headquarters, and a fire squad with light machine guns was added.

The *Interim Report on the SMG-Troop Trial* of 14, September 1944 mentions about this change:

"The organization of the platoon into fire and assault squads as well as the combination of the rifle-grenade launchers into platoon headquarters is considered appropriate. Even during the short test period, this organization has already proved itself practically and represents a simplification in terms of training and command."[278]

---

[275] Note that the literal translation of "Selbstlader" is "self loader".
[276] BArch, RH 11-1/54: Feld-Uffz.-Schule d.Inf: *Stellungnahme auf Grund der durch-geführten M.P.-Versuche*, 30.10.44, S. 1, Bl. 176.
[277] BArch, RH 11-1/54: Feld-Uffz.-Schule d.Inf: *Stellungnahme auf Grund der durch-geführten M.P.-Versuche*, 30.10.44, S. 1, Bl. 176.
[278] BArch, RH 11-1/54: Infanterieschule, Abteilung IIIa: *M.P.-Versuch*, 14. Sept. 44, S. 1, Bl. 109.

Ein Auszug aus der Stellungname der Feld-Unteroffiziersschule vom Oktober 1944 gibt eine guten Überblick:

„Die Gliederung des Zuges ist für alle Kampfarten, bis auf die Verteidigung, als günstig anzusehen. Sie bedingt jedoch eine taktische Schulung der Zugführer und verlangt taktische Verständnis von ihnen. Die Führung des Zuges ist nicht leichter geworden, während die Ausbildung des Zuges in der neuen Gliederung vereinfacht wird. Im Kampf muß der Zugführer besonders im Hinblick auf stoßtruppartige Führung des Kampfes anstreben, sich stets eine Reserve zurückhalten."[279]

Der ursprüngliche Name für den Sturmzug war MP-Zug wie aus der Ergänzung 1: *Vorläufiges Merkblatt: Der M.P.-Zug der Grenadier-Kompanie* vom 1. Februar 1944 klar hervorgeht.[280]

Es liegt nahe, dass der Name Sturmzug durch die Namensänderung von MP 44 auf Sturmgewehr 44 bedingt ist. Allerdings wurden bereits im *Zwischenbericht zum M.P.-Truppenversuch* vom 14. September 1944 der Infanterieschule Döberitz von Sturmgruppen gesprochen und der Name Sturmgewehr 44 wurde erst im Oktober 1944 von Hitler vorgeschlagen und befohlen.[281] Dementsprechend ist es auch möglich, dass der Name Sturmzug von den Gruppen Namen abgeleitet wurden, denn diese hießen ursprünglich auch MP-Gruppen.

Es sei noch angemerkt, dass es für die Panzergrenadiere auch einen Sturmzug gab, er war jedoch anders gegliedert.[282]

---

[279] BArch, RH 11-1/54: Feld-Uffz.-Schule d.Inf: *Stellungnahme auf Grund der durchgeführten M.P.-Versuche*, 30.10.44, S. 1, Bl. 176.
[280] Siehe auch: BArch, RH 11-1/54: *Gliederung des M.P.-Zuges der Gren.- und Füs.-Kp.*, 19.10.44, Bl. 165.
[281] BArch, RH 11-1/54: Infanterieschule, Abteilung IIIa: *M.P.-Versuch*, 14. Sept. 44, S. 1, Bl. 109.
[282] *Kriegsstärkenachweisung (Heer): Nr. 1114 a (fG): Panzergrenadierkompanie (fG)* vom 1. November 1944.

An excerpt from the statement of the Field NCO School of October 1944 gives a good overview:

"The organization of the platoon is to be regarded as favorable for all types of combat, except defense. However, it requires tactical training of the platoon leaders and demands tactical understanding from them. The command of the platoon has not become easier, while the training of the platoon is simplified in the new organization. In combat, the platoon leader must always strive to keep a reserve, especially with a view to leading the combat like a shock troop."[283]

The original name for the assault platoon was SMG[284]-platoon as clearly stated in Supplement 1: *Preliminary Pamphlet: The SMG-Platoon of the Grenadier-Company* from February 1, 1944.[285]

It is reasonable to assume that the name assault platoon is due to the change of name from MP 44 to Sturmgewehr 44. However, the *Interim Report on the SMG-Troop Trial* of September 14, 1944, of the Döberitz infantry school already mentioned assault squads, and the name Sturmgewehr 44 was not suggested and ordered by Hitler until October 1944.[286] Accordingly, it is also possible that the name assault platoon was derived from the squad names, since these were originally also called SMG-squads.

It should be noted that there was also an assault platoon for the Panzergrenadiers, but it was organized differently.[287]

---

[283] BArch, RH 11-1/54: Feld-Uffz.-Schule d.Inf: *Stellungnahme auf Grund der durch-geführten M.P.-Versuche*, 30.10.44, S. 1, Bl. 176.

[284] SMG means submachine gun. Technically, this was not a submachine gun, but the designation machine carbine was abolished, and the designation assault rifle was only introduced at the end of 1944. Regarding the naming and general development see Supplement 9.

[285] See also: BArch, RH 11-1/54: *Gliederung des M.P.-Zuges der Gren.- und Füs.-Kp.*, 19.10.44, Bl. 165.

[286] BArch, RH 11-1/54: Infanterieschule, Abteilung IIIa: *M.P.-Versuch*, 14. Sept. 44, S. 1, Bl. 109.

[287] *Kriegsstärkenachweisung (Heer): Nr. 1114 a (fG): Panzergrenadierkompanie (fG)* vom 1. November 1944.

Verbindungsgraben: Verbindungsgräben wurden auch Kampfgräben genannt. Sie verliefen generell parallel zur Front und wurden benutzt um Kampfanlagen, Widerstandsnester und Stützpunkte miteinander zu verbinden.[288]

Visierlinie: Die Visierlinie ist jene gedachte Linie die sich die vom Auge über die Kimme des Visiers, durch das Korn und bis zum Ziel geht: „Gedachte Linie: Auge – Kimme des Visiers – Korn – Ziel ist die Visierline."[289]

Vortröpfeln: „Drängt die Zeit nicht, so sind Strecken, die unter beobachtetem Feuer liegen oder die einzusehen sind, durch ‚Vortröpfeln', das heißt einzeln oder paarweise mit großen Abständen, zu überwinden."[290]

Zielkontrollspiegel: Der Zielkontrollspiegel ist ein Gerät, welches es einer weiteren Person ermöglicht zu sehen wohin der Schütze zielt, ohne ihn dabei zu stören. Üblicherweise wird dies von Schießausbildern verwendet.

Zug: Siehe Schützenzug, Sturmzug.

Zwischenfeld: Das Zwischenfeld wurde von Altrichter folgendermaßen beschrieben: „Das Gelände zwischen den Widerstandslinien [beim hinhaltenden Widerstand] heißt Zwischenfeld."[291] Ebenso heißt in *Truppenführung* in der Sektion zum hinhaltenden Widerstand: „Die Abwehr aus dem Gelände zwischen den Widerstandslinien (Zwischenfeld) soll das Folgen des Gegners verzögern und Zeit für das Einrichten in der nächsten Widerstandslinie gewinnen."[292]

---

[288] *Merkblatt 57/5: Bildheft Neuzeitlicher Stellungsbau.* OKH, General der Pioniere: 1. Juni 1944, siehe Vorbemerkungen Teil A.

[289] Zimmermann, Bodo: *Infanteriedienst. Für den Einzelschützen der aktiven Truppe, der Reserve und der Landwehr.* 18. Auflage (Kriegsausgabe) der „Soldatenfibel". Verlag „Offene Worte": Berlin, Germany, 1940, S. 28.

[290] BArch, RH 1/1217: *H.Dv. 130/20: Ausbildungsvorschrift für die Infanterie. Heft 20. Die Führung des Grenadier-Regiments.* Vom 21. 3. 1945. Verlage „Offene Worte": Berlin, Germany, 1945, S. 41.

[291] Altrichter, Friedrich: *Der Reserveoffizer. Ein Handbuch für den Offizier und Offizieranwärter des Beurlaubtenstandes aller Waffen.* Vierzehnte, durchgesehene Auflage. Verlag von E. S. Mittler & Sohn: Berlin, Germany, 1941, S. 265.

[292] *H.Dv. 300/1: Truppenführung (T.F.) I. Teil. Abschnitt I – XIII.* Verlag Mittler & Sohn: Berlin, 1936, S. 200.

Fire Trench (Verbindungsgraben[293]): Fire trenches were also called "Kampfgräben" [combat trenches]. They generally ran parallel to the front line and were used to connect combat installations, resistance nests and bases.[294]

Sight radius (Visierlinie): The sight radius is the imaginary line that runs from the eye over the rear sight, through the front sight and to the target: "Thought line: eye - rear sight - front sight - target is the sight radius."[295]

[Infiltrating/ No equivalent] (Vortröpfeln[296]): "If time is not pressing, then stretches, which lie under observed fire or which can be seen, are to be overcome by 'infiltrating', that is individually or in pairs with large distances."[297]

Aim-Checking Device[298] (Zielkontrollspiegel): The aim-checking device is a tool that allows another person to see where the rifleman is aiming without disturbing him. Usually this is used by marksmanship instructors.

Platoon (Zug): See Rifle Platoon (Schützenzug), Assault Platoon (Sturmzug).

Intermediate Area (Zwischenfeld): The intermediate area was described by Altrichter in the following way: "The area between the resistance lines [in the delaying action] is called the intermediate area."[299] Likewise, in the section for delaying action in *Unit Command* it is noted: "The defense from the terrain between the resistance lines [intermediate area] is to delay the enemy's follow-up and gain time for the setup in the next resistance line."[300]

---

[293] The literal translation of "Verbindungsgraben" would be "connection trench", but a "Verbindungsgraben" ran parallel to the frontline, such trenches were called "fire trenches" according to *FM 5-15: Engineer Field Manual – Field Fortifications*,1940. See also Merkblatt 57/5: Bildheft Neuzeitlicher Stellungsbau. OKH, General der Pioniere: 1944.

[294] *Merkblatt 57/5: Bildheft Neuzeitlicher Stellungsbau.* OKH, General der Pioniere: 1. Juni 1944, siehe Vorbemerkungen Teil A.

[295] Zimmermann, Bodo: *Infanteriedienst. Für den Einzelschützen der aktiven Truppe, der Reserve und der Landwehr.* 18. Auflage (Kriegsausgabe) der „Soldatenfibel". Verlag „Offene Worte": Berlin, Germany, 1940, S. 28.

[296] "Vortröpfeln" literally means "dripping forward". It means that movement should happen in pairs or alone. See Glossary: Infiltrating (Vortröpfeln).

[297] BArch, RH 1/1217: H.Dv. 130/20: Ausbildungsvorschrift für die Infanterie. Heft 20. Die Führung des Grenadier-Regiments. Vom 21. 3. 1945. Verlage „Offene Worte": Berlin, Germany, 1945, S. 41.

[298] The literal translation of "Zielkontrollspiegel" would be "target control mirror".

[299] Altrichter, Friedrich: *Der Reserveoffizier. Ein Handbuch für den Offizier und Offizieranwärter des Beurlaubtenstandes aller Waffen.* Vierzehnte, durchgesehene Auflage. Verlag von E. S. Mittler & Sohn: Berlin, Germany, 1941, S. 265.

[300] *H.Dv. 300/1: Truppenführung (T.F.) I. Teil. Abschnitt I – XIII.* Verlag Mittler & Sohn: Berlin, 1936, S. 200.

Ergänzung 9: Überblick über die „Vorläufer" des Sturmgewehrs 44

Da das Sturmgewehr 44 von zentraler Bedeutung für den Sturmzug war, empfiehlt es sich mit den „Vorläufer" einem kurzen Überblick vertraut zu machen. Dabei sind die Unterschiede teilweise gering, weshalb wir von „Vorläufer" im allgemeinen Sinn sprechen. Je nach Betrachtungsweise handelt es sich um verschiedene Waffen oder verschiedene Varianten einer Waffe. So schreibt Sturmgewehr-Experte Dieter Handrich: „[...] in der deutschen Waffengeschichte ist eine Waffe noch nie in einem so kurzen Zeitraum so oft unbenannt worden."[301]

Dies kommt auch im Entwurf der Bekanntgabe für das Heerestechnische Verordnungsblatt[302] zur Einführung des Sturmgewehrs 44, welches auf die meisten verschiedenen Bezeichnungen kurz eingeht, zur Geltung:

„Vorläufer dieser Waffe ist

a) der M Kb 42 (H)   (unterschiedliche Teile, geringe Stückzahl)

b) die M P 43/1[303]   (geringe Abweichungen)

c) die M P 44   (gleiche Ausführung, Stempel MP 43 und MP 44).

Magazine mit der Stempelung M Kb 42/H, MP 43/1, MP 43, MP 44 und St G 44 sind für alle Waffen verwendbar."[304]

Des Weiteren soll auch kurz auf das Sturmgewehr von Walther eingegangen werden, welches abgelehnt wurde.

---

[301] Handrich, Dieter: *Sturmgewehr 44. Vorgänger, Entwicklung und Fertigung der revolutionärsten Infanteriewaffen.* 2. überarbeitete und erweiterte Auflage. dwj Verlags-GmbH: Blaufelden, Germany, 2016, S. 121.

[302] Das Schreiben hatte die Angabe „Für Ht V Blatt". Der Text entspricht bis auf einem Doppelpunkt der publizierten Ausgabe vom 2. Januar 1945, siehe Abdruck in Handrich, Dieter: *Sturmgewehr 44*, S. 415.

[303] Anmerkung: bei „M P 43/1" und „M P 44" handelt es sich nicht um Tippfehler von uns.

[304] BArch, RH 11-I/54: In 2: *Einführung des Sturmgewehres 44.* Entwurf, November 1944, Bl. 195.

Supplement 9: Overview about the "Predecessors" of the Sturmgewehr 44

As the Sturmgewehr 44 is of central importance to the assault platoon, it would be prudent to familiarize oneself with the "predecessors" of this weapon. As the difference are relatively minor, we speak of "predecessors" in the more general sense. Depending on how you look at it, one is faced with different weapons or different variants of a weapon. As the assault rifle expert Dieter Handrich writes: "[...] never before in German gun history has a weapon been so often renamed in such a short time."[305]

This is also exemplified by the draft of the announcement for the Technical Army Regulation Sheet[306] for the introduction of the Sturmgewehr 44, which deals briefly with most of the different designations:

"Predecessor of this weapon is

    a) the M Kb 42 (H)   (different parts, small quantity)

    b) the M P 43/1[307]   (minor deviations)

    c) the M P 44   (same design, stamp MP 43 and MP 44).

Magazines with the stamps M Kb 42/H, MP 43/1, MP 43, MP 44 and St G 44 can be used in all weapons."[308]

In the following section we will also briefly address the assault rifle developed by Walther, which was rejected.

---

[305] Handrich, Dieter: *Sturmgewehr 44. Vorgänger, Entwicklung und Fertigung der revolutionärsten Infanteriewaffen*. 2. überarbeitete und erweiterte Auflage. dwj Verlags-GmbH: Blaufelden, Germany, 2016, S. 121.

[306] The letter had the instruction "Für Ht V Blatt" (For Ht V Sheet). Except for a colon, the text corresponds to the published edition of January 2, 1945, see reprint in Handrich, Dieter: *Sturmgewehr 44, S. 415*.

[307] Note: "M P 43/1" and "M P 44" are not typing errors by us.

[308] BArch, RH 11-I/54: In 2: *Einführung des Sturmgewehres 44*. Entwurf, November 1944, Bl. 195.

Vorgeschichte - Kurzpatrone

Die Vorgeschichte des Sturmgewehrs beginnt je nach Ansicht in der Zwischenkriegszeit oder bereits davor. Im Ersten Weltkrieg hatte sich gezeigt, dass die Maschinenpistolen zwar auf kurze Entfernungen sehr effektiv waren, allerdings hatten sie aufgrund der schwachen Ladung eine ziemlich kurze Reichweite und eine ungeeignete Flugbahn.[309] Dies stand im Gegensatz zur Gewehrmunition, die mit ihrer größeren Ladung eine längere Reichweite erzielte. Die Reichweite der Gewehre war dadurch höher als die effektive Schussweite, da mit freien Auge nur auf eine begrenzte Entfernung gezielt werden kann. Außerdem zeigte sich, dass die übliche Kampfentfernung nur ein paar hundert Meter war. Aus diesem Grund gab es mehrere Ansätze eine sogenannte Kurzpatrone zu entwickeln. Die Pulverladung sollte zwischen der Pistolen- und Gewehrmunition liegen. Die Vorteile wären ein geringeres Gewicht und ein geringerer Gasdruck. Dies würde außerdem eine einfachere Entwicklung von Selbstladegewehren ermöglichen. Es gab verschiedene Entwicklungen zu Kurzpatronen und entsprechenden Gewehren in der Zwischenkriegszeit.[310] Die Entwicklung, die sich schließlich durchsetzte war die Maschinenkarabiner-Patrone 7,92 x 33 mm der Firma Polte, die auf Vorgaben von WaPrüf 1[311] entwickelt wurde.[312] Im Vergleich dazu, die reguläre Gewehrmunition hatte die Dimensionen 7,92 x 57 mm und die Pistolenmunition 9 x 19 mm. Die Gewehrmunition mit 7,92 x 57 mm wurde verwendet in Waffen wie dem Karabiner 98k, Gewehr 41, Gewehr/Karabiner 43, MG 34, MG 42 und Fallschirmjägergewehr 42. Wohingegen die Pistolenmunition 9 x 19 mm in Waffen wie der MP 18, MP 38/40, Pistole 08 (Luger) und Walther P.38 benutzt wurde.

---

[309] Hahn, Fritz: *Waffen und Geheimwaffen des deutschen Heeres 1933-1945. Band 1.* Dörfler Verlag: Eggolsheim, o.J., S. 38.

[310] Hahn, Fritz: *Waffen und Geheimwaffen des deutschen Heeres 1933-1945. Band 1.* Dörfler Verlag: Eggolsheim, o.J., S. 38.

[311] Waffenamt Prüfwesen: Wa Prüf 1 war die Abteilung für Munition und Ballistik.

[312] Handrich, Dieter: *Sturmgewehr 44*, S. 97-98.

Historical Background – Kurzpatrone

Depending on how one looks at it, the historical background of the assault rifle begins in the interwar period or even before. World War I had shown that submachine guns were very effective at short distances, but due to the weak charge they had a rather short range and a poor trajectory.[313] This was in contrast to rifle ammunition which had a longer range with its greater charge. The range of the rifles was higher than the effective firing range, as a rifle can only be aimed at a limited distance with the naked eye. It also showed that the typical combat distance was only a few hundred meters. For this reason, there were several approaches to develop a so-called short cartridge. The powder charge was to be between the pistol and rifle ammunition. The advantages would be a lower weight and gas pressure. This would also allow semi-automatic rifles to be developed more easily. There were various developments for short cartridges and corresponding rifles in the interwar period.[314] The development that finally prevailed was the machine carbine cartridge 7.92 x 33 mm from the company Polte, which was developed according to the specifications of WaPrüf 1[315].[316] In comparison, the regular rifle ammunition had the dimensions 7.92 x 57 mm and the pistol ammunition 9 x 19 mm. The rifle ammunition with 7.92 x 57 mm was used in weapons like the Karabiner 98k, Gewehr 41, Gewehr/Karabiner 43, MG 34, MG 42 and Fallschirmjägergewehr 42, while the pistol ammunition 9 x 19 mm was used in weapons such as the MP 18, MP 38/40, Pistole 08 (Luger) and Walther P.38.

---

[313] Hahn, Fritz: *Waffen und Geheimwaffen des deutschen Heeres 1933-1945. Band 1.* Dörfler Verlag: Eggolsheim, o.J., S. 38.
[314] Hahn, Fritz: *Waffen und Geheimwaffen des deutschen Heeres 1933-1945. Band 1.* Dörfler Verlag: Eggolsheim, o.J., S. 38.
[315] Waffenamt Prüfwesen (Weapons Office Testing): Wa Prüf 1 was the department of ammunition and ballistics.
[316] Handrich, Dieter: *Sturmgewehr 44*, S. 97-98.

Maschinenkarabiner 42 (H)

Der Maschinenkarabiner 42 (H) ist der direkte Vorläufer des Sturmgewehrs 44. Das Wort „Maschinenkarabiner" setzt sich aus den Begriffen „Maschinen" und „Karabiner" zusammen, und beschreibt dadurch sowohl die Funktionalität wie auch den Waffentyp. „Maschinen" steht hier für die Fähigkeit, dass die Waffe vollautomatisch feuern kann, wobei „Karabiner" generell leichtere und kürzere Ausführungen von Gewehren waren.[317] Die Entwicklung des Maschinenkarabiner 42 (H) begann 1938 nach einem Auftrag bei der Firma Haenel. Aus dem Firmennamen bezog man das Suffix „(H)".[318] Maschinenkarabiner wurde abgekürzt mit „MKb", da die Abkürzung „MK" bereits für Maschinenkanonen verwendet wurde.[319] Aus dieser Konstellation ergab sich MKb 42 (H).

Erstmalig vorgeführt wurde diese Waffe in Döberitz im März 1942 gemeinsam mit einem Konkurrenzmodell der Firma Walther, dem Maschinenkarabiner 42 (W). Zu diesem Zeitpunkt fehlte am Maschinenkarabiner 42 (H) der Handschutz, Staubschutzdeckel und die Seitengewehrhalterung. Ebenso war der Kolben zu groß.[320] Bei Truppenversuchen der Infanterieschule Döberitz wurde die geringe Präzision im Einzelfeuer bemängelt, da es sich um eine zuschießende Waffe handelte.[321] Daher wurden Prototypen entwickelnd, die aufschießend waren.[322] Allerdings wurde parallel die Serienproduktion mit dem zuschießenden Typ gestartet.[323]

Im Dezember 1942 kam es schließlich zum Vergleichstest zwischen den Maschinenkarabinern 42 (H) und (W), wobei laut Handrich der aufschießende Typ des Maschinenkarabiner 42 (H) getestet wurde und als klarer Gewinner aus dem Test hervorging.[324]

---

[317] Lidschun, Reiner; Wollert, Günter: Infanteriewaffen. Illustrierte Enzyklopädie der Infanteriewaffen aus aller Welt bis 1945. Parragon: Bath, UK, o.J., S. 38.
[318] Handrich, Dieter: *Sturmgewehr 44*, S. 96.
[319] Handrich, Dieter: *Sturmgewehr 44*, S. 122.
[320] Handrich, Dieter: *Sturmgewehr 44*, S. 373.
[321] Handrich, Dieter: *Sturmgewehr 44*, S. 141 & 374.
[322] Handrich, Dieter: *Sturmgewehr 44*, S. 141.
[323] Handrich, Dieter: *Sturmgewehr 44*, S. 374.
[324] Handrich, Dieter: *Sturmgewehr 44*, S. 151-154.

Maschinenkarabiner 42 (H)

The Maschinenkarabiner 42 (H) is the direct predecessor of the Sturmgewehr 44. The word "machine carbine" is composed of the terms "machine" and "carbine" and thus describes both the functionality and type of weapon. "Machine" here stands for the ability of the weapon to fire fully automatically, while "carbines" were generally lighter and shorter versions of rifles.[325] The development of the Maschinenkarabiner 42 (H) began in 1938 after an order at the Haenel company. The suffix "(H)" is taken from this company.[326] Machine carbine was abbreviated with "MKb", because the abbreviation "MK" was already in use for machine cannons.[327] This constellation resulted in MKb 42 (H).

This weapon was first demonstrated in Döberitz in March 1942 together with a competitor's model from the Walther company, the Maschinenkarabiner 42 (W). At that time, the Maschinenkarabiner 42 (H) lacked hand guard, dust cover and the bayonet mount. Additionally, the butt was too large.[328] As an open-bolt weapon, the low precision in semi-automatic fire was criticized in the troop trials of the Döberitz infantry school.[329] As a consequence prototypes were developed which were closed-bolt.[330] At the same time, however, series production of the open-bolt type was started.[331]

In December 1942, the comparative test between the Maschinenkarabiner 42 (H) and (W) was finally carried out. According to Handrich, the newer closed-bolt type of the Maschinenkarabiner 42 (H) was used in this comparison and emerged as the clear winner from the test.[332]

---

[325] Lidschun, Reiner; Wollert, Günter: Infanteriewaffen. Illustrierte Enzyklopädie der Infanteriewaffen aus aller Welt bis 1945. Parragon: Bath, UK, o.J., S. 38.
[326] Handrich, Dieter: *Sturmgewehr 44*, S. 96.
[327] Handrich, Dieter: *Sturmgewehr 44*, S. 122.
[328] Handrich, Dieter: *Sturmgewehr 44*, S. 373.
[329] Handrich, Dieter: *Sturmgewehr 44*, S. 141 & 374.
[330] Handrich, Dieter: *Sturmgewehr 44*, S. 141.
[331] Handrich, Dieter: *Sturmgewehr 44*, S. 374.
[332] Handrich, Dieter: *Sturmgewehr 44*, S. 151-154.

Anfang 1943 wurden die Maschinenkarabiner generell in Maschinenpistole umbenannt. Der Hintergrund hierfür ist wahrscheinlich, dass man Hitler den Maschinenkarabiner als Ersatz für die Maschinenpistole empfehlen wollte.[333]

Vom Maschinenkarabiner 42 (H) wurden von November 1942 bis September 1943 etwas weniger als 12 000 Stück in Serie produziert.[334]

Maschinenkarabiner 42 (W)

Beim Maschinenkarabiner 42 (W) handelt es sich nicht um einen „Vorgänger" des Sturmgewehr 44. Allerdings sehen sich auch diese beide Waffen sehr ähnlich. Es handelte sich hierbei um eine Entwicklung der Firma Walther. Dies ist auch am Suffix „(W)" zu erkennen. Im Dezember 1942 kam es zum Vergleichstest was dazu führte das einige Nachteile, gerade zum Konkurrenzmodel der Firma Haenel, bemängelt wurden. Die Konstruktion des Model der Firma Walther war sowohl kompliziert wie auch empfindlich. Im Vergleich zum Maschinenkarabiner 42 (H) zeigte sich, dass dessen Konstruktion sowohl einfacher als auch widerstandsfähiger war.[335]

MP 43/1 & MP 43

Die aufschießende Variante des Maschinenkarabiners 42 (H) wurde Anfang 1943 als MP 43/1 bezeichnet. Im Sommer 1943 begann die Serienfertigung.[336]

Dass die Bezeichnung Maschinenpistole nicht wirklich passend war geht auch auf einen undatierten Entwurf der Organisationsabteilung hervor, worin es hieß: „Zur Beseitigung von Unklarheiten in der Bearbeitung der KStN[337] und KAN[338] wird gebeten, folgendes zu veranlassen:

Im Hauptband für KAN ist unter der Bezeichnung ‚MP' nur die MP 38/40 bezw. die anstelle der MP 38/40 gefertigte ital. MP ‚Beretta' aufzunehmen.

---

[333] Handrich, Dieter: *Sturmgewehr 44*, S. 374 & 165.
[334] Handrich, Dieter: *Sturmgewehr 44*, S. 399.
[335] Handrich, Dieter: *Sturmgewehr 44*, S. 151-154.
[336] Handrich, Dieter: *Sturmgewehr 44*, S. 374.
[337] Kriegsstärkenachweisung.
[338] Kriegsausrüstungsnachweisung.

In early 1943, the machine carbines were generally renamed submachine guns. The reason for this is probably the intention to recommend the machine carbine to Hitler as a replacement for the submachine gun.[339]

From November 1942 to September 1943, slightly less than 12 000 Maschinenkarabiner 42 (H) were produced in series.[340]

Maschinenkarabiner 42 (W)

The Maschinenkarabiner 42 (W) is not a "predecessor" of the Sturmgewehr 44, but both weapons look very similar. Instead, this was a development of the Walther company. This can also be identified by the suffix "(W)". In December 1942, a comparative test was conducted in which some disadvantages, especially in comparison to the competitor of the company Haenel, were cited. The construction of Walther's model was both complicated and sensitive. In comparison with the Maschinenkarabiner 42 (H), it turned out that its construction was both simpler and more resilient.[341]

MP 43/1 & MP 43

The closed-bolt variant of the Maschinenkarabiners 42 (H) was designated as MP 43/1 in early 1943. Series production began in the summer of 1943.[342]

The fact that the term submachine gun was not really appropriate for this weapon can also be seen from an undated draft of the organization department in which it was stated: "In order to eliminate ambiguities in the processing of the KStN[343] and KAN[344], the following is requested:

In the main volume for KAN, only the MP 38/40 or the Italian MP 'Beretta' manufactured instead of the MP 38/40 is to be included under the designation 'MP'.

---

[339] Handrich, Dieter: *Sturmgewehr 44*, S. 374 & 165.
[340] Handrich, Dieter: *Sturmgewehr 44*, S. 399.
[341] Handrich, Dieter: *Sturmgewehr 44*, S. 151-154.
[342] Handrich, Dieter: *Sturmgewehr 44*, S. 374.
[343] The literal translation of "Kriegsstärkenachweisung" is "war strength certificate", it is a table of organization and equipment.
[344] The literal translation of "Kriegsausrüstungsnachweisung" is "war equipment certificate", it was a detailed list of all the authorized equipment for a unit.

Die MP 44 ist dagegen unter der Bezeichnung ‚Gewehre, Selbstladegewehre, Zielfernrohrgewehre' mit aufzunehmen, mit dem ausdrücklichen Hinweis, daß die Ausstattung mit MP 44 nur innerhalb der Inf.-Kompanien und auch hier nur innerhalb von MP-Zügen erfolgt."[345]

Die Waffe wurde kontinuierlich weiterentwickelt. Insbesondere die Umgestaltung des Laufendes und Kornhalters für die Anbringung des Gewehrgranatgerätes wurden hierbei beachtet. Hierzu „[...] wurde das vordere Laufende stufenförmig verjüngt und der Kornhalter gekürzt. Weiterhin entfielen die am Visierfuß angebrachten Schienen, die zur Aufnahme der Montage des ZF[346] 41 bestimmt waren. Die so geänderte Waffe erhielt die Bezeichnung MP 43."[347]

Handrich führt weiters an, dass die offiziellen Fertigungsübersichten nicht zwischen MP 43/1 und MP 43 unterscheiden. Die Serienfertigung der MP 43/1 lief im Dezember 1943 aus.[348]

Ein wahrer Namenswirrwarr offenbart sich, wenn man die Erfahrungsberichte von der Front betrachtet. Dort kamen unter anderem folgende Bezeichnungen vor:

- M.Pi. 43[349]
- M.P. 43 a, M.P. 43 (a), M.P. 43, M.P.43, MP 43[350]
- Maschinen-Karabiner 43A[351]
- M.P. / A 43[352]
- M.K. 43[353]
- M.K.B.43A[354]

---

[345] BArch, RH 11-I/54: Org.-Abteilung: *Ausstattung mit MP 44, Entwurf*, ohne Datum, Bl. 102.
[346] Zielfernrohr.
[347] Handrich, Dieter: *Sturmgewehr 44*, S. 375.
[348] Handrich, Dieter: *Sturmgewehr 44*, S. 233-234 & 375.
[349] BArch, RH 12-2/138: Generalkommando XXVI. A.K, Bl. 101.
[350] BArch, RH 12-2/138: 1. Division, Bl. 102-106.
[351] BArch, RH 12-2/138: F.P.Nr. 02210 B, Bl. 113.
[352] BArch, RH 12-2/138: H. Müller, Bl. 118.
[353] BArch, RH 12-2/138: 7.G.R. 43, Bl. 119.
[354] BArch, RH 12-2/138: 4./G.R.44, Bl. 146.

The MP 44, on the other hand, is to be included under the designation 'rifles, semi-automatic rifles, telescopic sight rifles', with the explicit indication that the equipment with MP 44 is only to be used within the infantry-companies and here too only within SMG[355]-platoons."[356]

The weapon has been continuously improved. Particular attention was paid to the redesign of the barrel and the front sight for the attachment of the rifle-grenade launcher. For this "[...] the front end of the barrel was tapered in steps and the front sight holder was shortened. Furthermore, the rails attached to the sight base, which were intended to hold the mounting of the ZF[357] 41, were omitted. The weapon modified in this way was given the designation MP 43."[358]

Handrich further states that the official production overviews do not distinguish between MP 43/1 and MP 43. Serial production of the MP 43/1 ended in December 1943.[359]

A true confusion of names is revealed when one looks at the experience reports from the front. Among others, the following names were used there:

- M.Pi. 43[360]
- M.P. 43 a, M.P. 43 (a), M.P. 43, M.P.43, MP 43[361]
- Maschinen-Karabiner 43A[362]
- M.P. / A 43[363]
- M.K. 43[364]
- M.K.B.43A[365]

---

[355] SMG means submachine gun. Technically, this was not a submachine gun, but the designation machine carbine was abolished, and the designation assault rifle was only introduced at the end of 1944.

[356] BArch, RH 11-I/54: Org.-Abteilung: *Ausstattung mit MP 44, Entwurf*, ohne Datum, Bl. 102.

[357] "Zielfernrohr" is telescopic sight.

[358] Handrich, Dieter: *Sturmgewehr 44*, S. 375.

[359] Handrich, Dieter: *Sturmgewehr 44*, S. 233-234 & 375.

[360] BArch, RH 12-2/138: Generalkommando XXVI. A.K, Bl. 101.

[361] BArch, RH 12-2/138: 1. Division, Bl. 102-106.

[362] BArch, RH 12-2/138: F.P.Nr. 02210 B, Bl. 113.

[363] BArch, RH 12-2/138: H. Müller, Bl. 118.

[364] BArch, RH 12-2/138: 7.G.R. 43, Bl. 119.

[365] BArch, RH 12-2/138: 4./G.R.44, Bl. 146.

Der Hintergrund hierfür liegt auch daran, dass MKb 42 (H) für die zuschießende Variante und MP 43 für die aufschießende Variante verwendet werden sollte. Dieser Unterschied wurde wohl nicht immer klar verdeutlicht da die Waffe teilweise nur unter dem Namen MP 43 bekannt und umgangssprachlich auch so identifiziert wurde. Daher „[...] fügte man vor Beginn der Truppenversuche an der Front der Bezeichnung ‚MP 43' die Buchstaben ‚A' und ‚B' zu."[366] Dies fügte natürlich nochmal zwei neue Typendesignationen in das schon vorhandene Namenschaos hinzu.

MP 44

Im April 1944 wurde schließlich auf Befehl Hitlers das Gewehr 43 in Karabiner 43 und die Maschinenpistole 43 in Maschinenpistole 44 umbenannt. Dies wurde getan um eine klarere namentliche Unterscheidung der Waffen zu erreichen.[367]

Nachdem so eine Umbenennung mit einem nicht geringen Verwaltungsaufwand zusammenhängt, kam von mindestens einer Dienststelle im Mai 1944 die Bitte um die Aufhebung des Befehls. Diese Bitte inkludierte eine Auflistung der nun notwendigen Änderungen. Dazu kamen zum Beispiel: Änderung sämtlicher Stempel, der Beschriftungen sämtlicher Fertigungsunterlagen, etc.[368] Das Schreiben endet mit folgenden Absatz:

„Unter Hinweis auf die bereits mit Bezug 1.) erbetene Aufhebung des gegebenen Befehls wird aus den vorstehend aufgeführten Gründen nochmals dringendst diese Bitte wiederholt. Die Jnfanterieabteilung[369] ist der Ansicht, dass die geringen Vorteile für eine klare Unterscheidung der Waffen durch die der Fertigung und dem Nachschub erwachsenden Schwierigkeiten mehr als aufgehoben wird."[370]

---

[366] Handrich, Dieter: *Sturmgewehr 44*, S. 165-166.

[367] Handrich, Dieter: *Sturmgewehr 44*, S. 234-235.

[368] BArch, RH 11-/52 b: Chef H Rüst und B d E, AHA/Jn 2 (IIb): *Umbenennung G 43 und MP 43*, Bl. 461.

[369] Dies ist kein Tippfehler, das „J" als erster Buchstabes eines Wortes, welches mit einem „I" (großes „i") beginnt, wurde damals generell häufig genutzt: Dies hat zum Teil historische und zum Teil praktische Gründe, da es in gewissen Schriftarten zu Verwechslungen zwischen dem kleinen „L" und großen „i" kommen kann.

[370] BArch, RH 11-/52 b: Chef H Rüst und B d E, AHA/Jn 2 (IIb): *Umbenennung G 43 und MP 43*, Bl. 461.

The reason for this is that MKb 42 (H) was to be used for the open-bolt variant and MP 43 for the closed-bolt variant. It seems that this difference was not always made clear because the weapon was sometimes only known as the MP 43 and colloquially identified as such. Therefore "[...] the letters 'A' and 'B' were added to the designation 'MP 43' before the beginning of the troop trials at the front."[371] Of course, this also added two more designations into an already confusing mix.

MP 44

Finally, in April 1944, on Hitler's orders, the Gewehr 43 was renamed Karabiner 43 and the Maschinenpistole 43 was renamed Maschinenpistole 44. This was done to achieve a clearer differentiation of the weapons by name.[372]

Since such a renaming involved a considerable administrative effort, at least one office requested that the order be lifted in May 1944. This request included a list of all the necessary changes that now would have to be made. This included, for example: change of all the stamps, the inscriptions of all production documents, etc.[373] The letter ends with the following paragraph:

"With reference to the already with regard to 1.) requested cancellation of the given order, this request is urgently repeated for the reasons mentioned above. The infantry[374] department believes that the small advantages for a clear distinction of the weapons are more than offset by the difficulties involved in manufacturing and replenishing them."[375]

---

[371] Handrich, Dieter: *Sturmgewehr 44*, S. 165-166.

[372] Handrich, Dieter: *Sturmgewehr 44*, S. 234-235.

[373] BArch, RH 11-/52 b: Chef H Rüst und B d E, AHA/Jn 2 (IIb): *Umbenennung G 43 und MP 43*, Bl. 461.

[374] The "Jnfanterie" was not a typo, the "J" as the first letter of a word, which starts with an "I" (capital "I"), was generally used frequently at that time: This has partly historical and partly practical reasons, because in certain fonts there can be confusion between the small "L" and the capital "i".

[375] BArch, RH 11-/52 b: Chef H Rüst und B d E, AHA/Jn 2 (IIb): *Umbenennung G 43 und MP 43*, Bl. 461.

StG 44

Im Oktober 1944 wurde schließlich von offizieller Seite angeordnet, dass die MP 44 den Karabiner 98k ersetzen soll. Diese Anordnung resultierte auch in der letzten Namensänderung dieser Waffe. Der Wortlaut einer Abschrift war wie folgt:

„Die M.P. 44 wird in Zukunft den Karabiner 98 k in der Bewaffnung der deutschen Infanterie ersetzen. Damit erhält der Grenadier eine Waffe, die den gezielten Einzelschuß mit zuverlässiger Treffgenauigkeit ebenso ermöglicht wie die Abgabe von Feuerstößen.

Die Bezeichnung ‚M.P.' entspricht nicht der Waffe und ihrer Verwendungsmöglichkeit.

Die‘M.P. 44' [sic!] erhält deshalb die Bezeichnung:

‚Sturmgewehr 44'

Bleistiftnotiz: Vom Führer genehmigt. Die M.P. 44 erhält die Bezeichnung ‚Sturmgewehr 44'."[376]

Laut Handrichs Aufstellung wurden von Juli 1943 bis März 1945 insgesamt etwas weniger als 426 000 MP 43/1, MP 43, MP 44 und StG 44 abgenommen.[377] Die Summe bei Hahn von 1943 bis 1945 weicht nur um 33 Stück mehr für das Jahr 1945 ab.[378]

---

[376] BArch, RH 11-I/54: *Abschrift Einführung Sturmgewehr 44*, Bl. 169.
[377] Handrich, Dieter: *Sturmgewehr 44*, S. 399-401.
[378] Hahn, Fritz: *Waffen und Geheimwaffen des deutschen Heeres 1933-1945. Band 1.* Dörfler Verlag: Eggolsheim, o.J., S. 40.

StG 44

Finally, in October 1944 it was officially ordered that the MP 44 should replace the Karabiner 98k. This order also resulted in the last designation change of the weapon. The wording of a transcription was as follows:

"In the future, the M.P. 44 will replace the Karabiner 98 k in the armament of the German infantry. This will give the grenadier a weapon that enables him to fire single shots with reliable accuracy as well as to deliver bursts of fire.

The designation 'M.P.' does not fit this weapon and its possible uses.

The'M.P. 44' [sic!] is therefore given the designation:

'Sturmgewehr 44'

Pencil note: Approved by the Führer. The M.P. 44 is given the designation 'Sturmgewehr 44'."[379]

According to Handrich's listing, from July 1943 to March 1945, a total of slightly less than 426 000 MP 43/1, MP 43, MP 44 and StG 44 were accepted.[380] The total amount by Hahn from 1943 to 1945 differs only by 33 more for 1945.[381]

---

[379] BArch, RH 11-I/54: *Abschrift Einführung Sturmgewehr 44*, Bl. 169.
[380] Handrich, Dieter: *Sturmgewehr 44*, S. 399-401.
[381] Hahn, Fritz: *Waffen und Geheimwaffen des deutschen Heeres 1933-1945. Band 1.* Dörfler Verlag: Eggolsheim, o.J., S. 40.

Hitlers Ablehnungen und Namensgebung

Hitler lehnte die Einführung des Sturmgewehrs, ursprünglich als Maschinenkarabiners bezeichnet, mehrfach ab.[382] Es ist daher nicht ohne Ironie, dass er schließlich den Namen Sturmgewehr anordnete und damit dieser neuen Gewehrart ihren Namen gab.[383]

Hitler wurden im April 1942 die Maschinenkarabiner 42 von Haenel (H) und Walther (W) vorgeführt. Dabei lehnte er die Waffe jedoch ab. Als Gründe wurden angeführt, dass die Waffe nicht genug Reichweite für den Wüstenkrieg hätte, dass 4 Millionen Stück für die komplette Ausstattung der Truppe nötig wären, dass der Maschinenkarabiner 42 eine andere Munition benötigte und dass Maschinengewehre sowie Zielfernrohre nötiger wären. Des Weiteren soll Hitler als Hauptnachteil angeführt haben, dass die neue Munition für Probleme bei der Produktion und Nachschub sorgen würde. Allerdings wurde die Entwicklung vom Oberkommando des Heeres (OKH) trotz Hitlers Ablehnung fortgeführt.[384]

Es folgte eine weitere Ablehnung im November 1942, wo angeführt wurde, dass ein Selbstladegewehr und eine verbesserte Maschinenpistole für die Infanterie nötig sei. Er lehnte die Schaffung einer „Einheitswaffe" wie auch einer neuen Munition ab.[385] Eine weitere Ablehnung erfolgte im Februar 1943.[386] Dennoch begann die Serienfertigung des Maschinenkarabiners 42 (H) und die Vorbereitung der MP 43/1. Dies wurde von Hitler bemerkt und er gab sein Einverständnis für eine beschränkte Serienfertigung.[387] Schließlich folgte im Oktober 1943 der Befehl für die Massenfertigung, um dabei die MP 40 durch die MP 43 zu ersetzen.[388] Im Januar 1944 wurde schließlich der Großversuch für die MP 43 angeordnet, wo überprüft werden sollte, ob es möglich wäre die damaligen Gewehre vollständig mit dieser neuen Waffe ersetzen zu können.[389] Der Großversuch musste allerdings wegen Munitionsmangel vorerst verschoben werden.[390]

---

[382] Handrich, Dieter: *Sturmgewehr 44*, S. 118-119, 149-150 & 166-169.
[383] BArch, RH 11-I/54: Bl. 167, 169 & 193.
[384] Handrich, Dieter: *Sturmgewehr 44*, S. 118-119.
[385] Handrich, Dieter: *Sturmgewehr 44*, S. 149-150.
[386] Handrich, Dieter: *Sturmgewehr 44*, S. 167-169.
[387] Handrich, Dieter: *Sturmgewehr 44*, S. 169.
[388] Handrich, Dieter: *Sturmgewehr 44*, S. 198.
[389] Handrich, Dieter: *Sturmgewehr 44*, S. 222.
[390] Handrich, Dieter: *Sturmgewehr 44*, S. 227.

Hitler's Rejections und Choice of Name

Hitler rejected the introduction of the assault rifle, originally called machine carbine, on several occasions.[391] It is therefore not without irony that he finally ordered the name assault rifle and thus gave this new type of rifle its name.[392]

Hitler was shown the Maschinenkarabiner 42 by Haenel (H) and Walther (W) in April 1942, which he rejected. The reasons given were that the weapon would not have enough range for the desert warfare, that 4 million units would be needed to fully equip the troops, that the Maschinenkarabiner 42 needed a different ammunition and that machine guns and telescopic sights would be more necessary. Furthermore, Hitler is said to have cited as the main disadvantage that the new ammunition would cause problems in production and supply. However, the Army High Command (OKH) continued the development despite Hitler's rejection.[393]

This was followed by a further rejection in November 1942, where it was argued that a semi-automatic rifle and an improved submachine gun were needed for the infantry. He rejected the creation of a "standard weapon" as well as the production of a new ammunition type.[394] A further rejection took place in February 1943.[395] Nevertheless the series production of the Maschinenkarabiner 42 (H) and the preparation of the MP 43/1 began. This was noticed by Hitler and he gave his consent for a limited series production. Finally, in October 1943, the order for mass production followed to replace the MP 40 with the MP 43.[396] In January 1944, the large-scale test for the MP 43 was finally ordered, where it was to be examined whether it would be possible to completely replace the rifles currently in use with this new weapon type.[397] However, the large-scale test had to be postponed due to a lack of ammunition.[398]

---

[391] Handrich, Dieter: *Sturmgewehr 44*, S. 118-119, 149-150 & 166-169.
[392] BArch, RH 11-I/54: Bl. 167, 169 & 193.
[393] Handrich, Dieter: *Sturmgewehr 44*, S. 118-119.
[394] Handrich, Dieter: *Sturmgewehr 44*, S. 149-150.
[395] Handrich, Dieter: *Sturmgewehr 44*, S. 167-169.
[396] Handrich, Dieter: *Sturmgewehr 44*, S. 198.
[397] Handrich, Dieter: *Sturmgewehr 44*, S. 222.
[398] Handrich, Dieter: *Sturmgewehr 44*, S. 227.

„Bei der Munitionsversorgung sollte sich Hitlers Furcht zum Teil bewahrheiten: Für die anfänglich geplanten 200 Millionen Schuß pro Monat waren 86 000 zusätzliche Arbeitskräfte notwendig, die gab sie aber nicht. Die ab Februar 1944 geplanten 400 Millionen Schuß pro Monat waren völlig utopisch, ab Februar 1945 wurde die Zahl dann auf realistische 110 Millionen reduziert."[399]

Hier lohnt sich ein Vergleich zur regulären Gewehrpatrone 7,92 x 57 mm. Diese wurde in 1943 2200 und in 1944 3862 Millionen mal produziert, was einen Monatsschnitt von 183 und 322 Millionen ergibt.[400] Allerdings ist hier zu beachten, dass in 1943 der Bestand an Munition kontinuierlich absankt und Reserven aufgebracht wurden. Des Weiteren sei angemerkt, dass die Abnahmezahlen geringer als die Produktionszahlen waren.[401]

Der Großversuch wurde schließlich erst im Sommer 1944 durchgeführt.[402] Dafür wurden aufgrund der Munitionslage nur 5000 MP 44 freigegeben.[403] Der Großversuch wurde von der 1. Infanterie-Division durchgeführt, deren Erfahrungsbericht vom 14. September 1944 positiv ausfiel.[404] Hier ein kurzer Ausschnitt zum Thema Kampfkraft:

„1.) Wie wird die Verstärkung der Kampfkraft der Jnfanterie[405] durch Einführung der M.P. 44 beurteilt ?

Kampfkraft und Beweglichkeit der Jnfanterie hat sich durch Umbewaffnung auf M.P. 44 wesentlich verstärkt. Bei Ausfall einzelner M.P. leidet die Kampfkraft einer M.P. Gruppe nicht so, wie bei entsprechendem Gewehrausfall in der alten Schtz.[406] Gruppe.

---

[399] Hahn, Fritz: *Waffen und Geheimwaffen des deutschen Heeres 1933-1945. Band 1.* Dörfler Verlag: Eggolsheim, o.J., S. 40.

[400] Hahn, Fritz: *Waffen und Geheimwaffen*, S. 33.

[401] Hahn, Fritz: *Waffen und Geheimwaffen*, S. 34-37.

[402] Handrich, Dieter: *Sturmgewehr 44*, S. 242.

[403] BArch, RH 11-I/54: General der Infanterie: *Großversuch mit MP 44*, 1. Juni 1944, Bl. 20.

[404] BArch, RH 12-2/139: 1.Inf.Div: *Erfahrungsberichte über Grossversuch mit M.Pi. 44*, Bl. 29-35.

[405] Dies ist kein Tippfehler, das „J" als erster Buchstabes eines Wortes, welches mit einem „I" (i) beginnt, wurde damals generell häufig genutzt: Dies hat zum Teil historische und zum Teil praktische Gründe, da es in gewissen Schriftarten zu Verwechslungen zwischen dem kleinen „L" und großen „I" kommen kann.

[406] Schützen.

"With the supply of ammunition, Hitler's fears were to come true in part: For the initially planned 200 million rounds per month, 86,000 additional workers were necessary, but they were not available. The 400 million rounds per month planned from February 1944 onward were completely utopian; from February 1945 onward, the number was reduced to a realistic 110 million."[407]

A comparison to the regular 7.92 x 57 mm rifle cartridge is helpful in this instance. The production of this ammunition amounted to 2200 cartridges in 1943 and 3862 million in 1944, giving a monthly average of 183 and 322 million.[408] However, it should be noted here that in 1943 the stock of ammunition continuously decreased, and reserves were used to cover the demand. Furthermore, it should be noted that the accepted numbers were lower than the production numbers.[409]

The large-scale test was finally carried out only in the summer of 1944.[410] Due to the ammunition situation, only 5000 MP 44s were released for it.[411] The large-scale test was carried out by the 1st Infantry Division, whose report of experience of September 14, 1944, was positive. [412] Here is a short excerpt on the subject of combat effectiveness[413]:

"1.) How is the increase of the combat effectiveness of the infantry[414] with the introduction of the M.P. 44 evaluated ?

The combat effectiveness and mobility of the infantry was considerably increased by rearmament with the M.P. 44. In case of failure of individual M.P.s the combat effectiveness of a SMG[415] squad does not suffer as much as in the old rifleman squad.

---

[407] Hahn, Fritz: *Waffen und Geheimwaffen des deutschen Heeres 1933-1945. Band 1.* Dörfler Verlag: Eggolsheim, o.J., S. 40.

[408] Hahn, Fritz: *Waffen und Geheimwaffen*, S. 33.

[409] Hahn, Fritz: *Waffen und Geheimwaffen*, S. 34-37.

[410] Handrich, Dieter: *Sturmgewehr 44*, S. 242.

[411] BArch, RH 11-I/54: General der Infanterie: *Großversuch mit MP 44*, 1. Juni 1944, Bl. 20.

[412] BArch, RH 12-2/139: 1.Inf.Div: *Erfahrungsberichte über Grossversuch mit M.Pi. 44*, Bl. 29-35.

[413] The literal translation of "Kampfkraft" is "combat strength".

[414] The "Jnfanterie" was not a typo, the "J" as the first letter of a word, which starts with an "I" (capital "i"), was generally used frequently at that time, because in certain fonts there can be confusion between the small "L" and the capital "i".

[415] SMG means submachine gun. Technically, this was not a submachine gun.

In der Abwehr gewährleistet die M.P. gezielten Einzelschuss bis 600 m und einen dichten Feuervorhang auf nahe Entfernung. Dem Gegenstoss verleiht die M.P. selbst bei mitll. [sic!] Mun.-Einsatz durch die ausserordentliche moralische Wirkung des Dauerfeuers besonderen Schwung. Dasselbe gilt für den Angriff einer M.P. K[om]p[anie]."[416]

Generell, stand die Truppe der Sturmgewehr 44 bzw. seiner „Vorläufer" positiv gegenüber.

Ergänzung 10: Abbildung Sturmgewehr 44 mit Beschriftung aller Teile

Auf der nächsten Seite folgt ein Foto eines Sturmgewehr 44, welches zum Reinigen auseinandergenommen ist. Dabei handelt es sich um eine nachgestelltes Foto aus der Vorschrift *D 1854/4: Sturmgewehr 44 Gebrauchsanleitung* vom Dezember 1944. Wir haben nur wenige Punkte ergänzt um die Beschriftung zu vollenden.

---

[416] BArch, RH 12-2/139: 1.Inf.Div: *Erfahrungsberichte über Grossversuch mit M.Pi. 44*, Bl. 30.

In the defense, the M.P. guarantees targeted single shots up to 600 m and a dense curtain of fire at close range. The M.P. gives special momentum to the hasty counterattack[417], even with medium use of ammunition, through the extraordinary morale effect of continuous fire. The same applies to the attack of an SMG company."[418]

In general, the troops had a positive attitude towards the Sturmgewehr 44 and its "predecessors".

Supplement 10: Illustration of the Sturmgewehr 44 and its Parts

On the next page there is a photo of an Sturmgewehr 44, which has been taken apart for cleaning. This is a recreated photo from the regulation *D 1854/4: Sturmgewehr 44 Instruction Manual* from December 1944. We have only added a few points to complete the descriptions.

---

[417] The Germans distinguished between a hasty counterattack ("Gegenstoß") and regular counterattack ("Gegenangriff"). See Glossary: Hasty Counterattack and Counterattack.

[418] BArch, RH 12-2/139: 1.Inf.Div: *Erfahrungsberichte über Grossversuch mit M.Pi. 44*, Bl. 30.

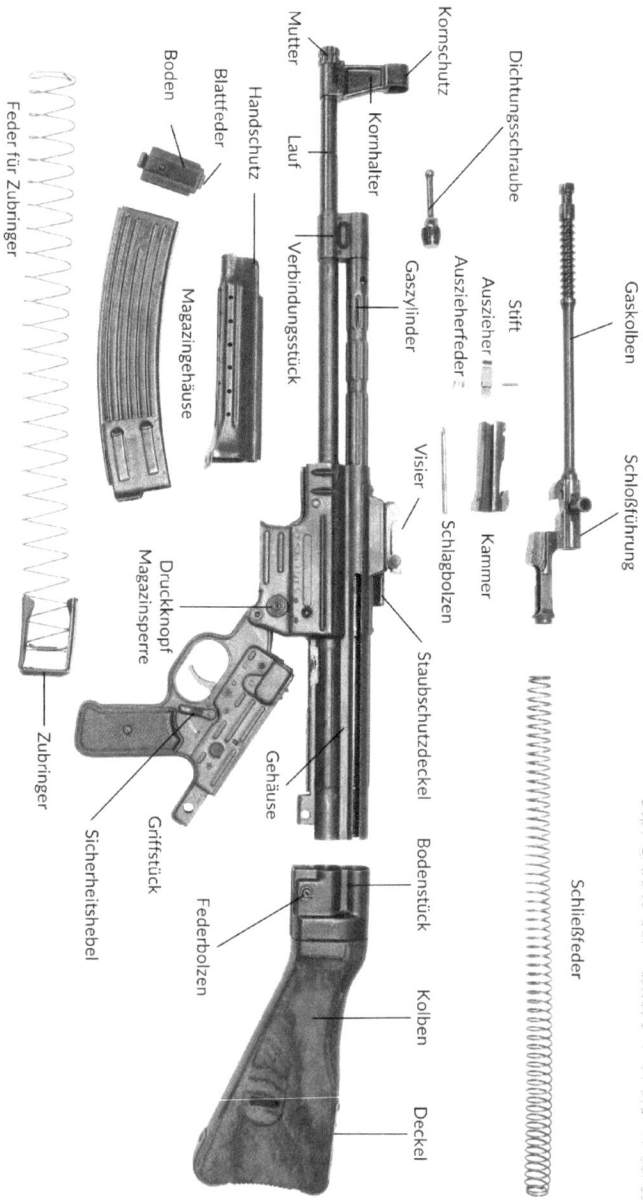

Kornschutz
Mutter
Boden
Blattfeder
Handschutz
Lauf
Kornhalter
Feder für Zubringer
Magazingehäuse
Verbindungsstück
Gaszylinder
Dichtungsschraube
Stift
Auszieher
Auszieherfeder
Kammer
Schlagbolzen
Visier
Gaskolben
Schloßführung
Zubringer
Druckknopf
Magazinsperre
Staubschutzdeckel
Sicherheitshebel
Griffstück
Gehäuse
Federbolzen
Bodenstück
Kolben
Deckel
Schließfeder

DE-133

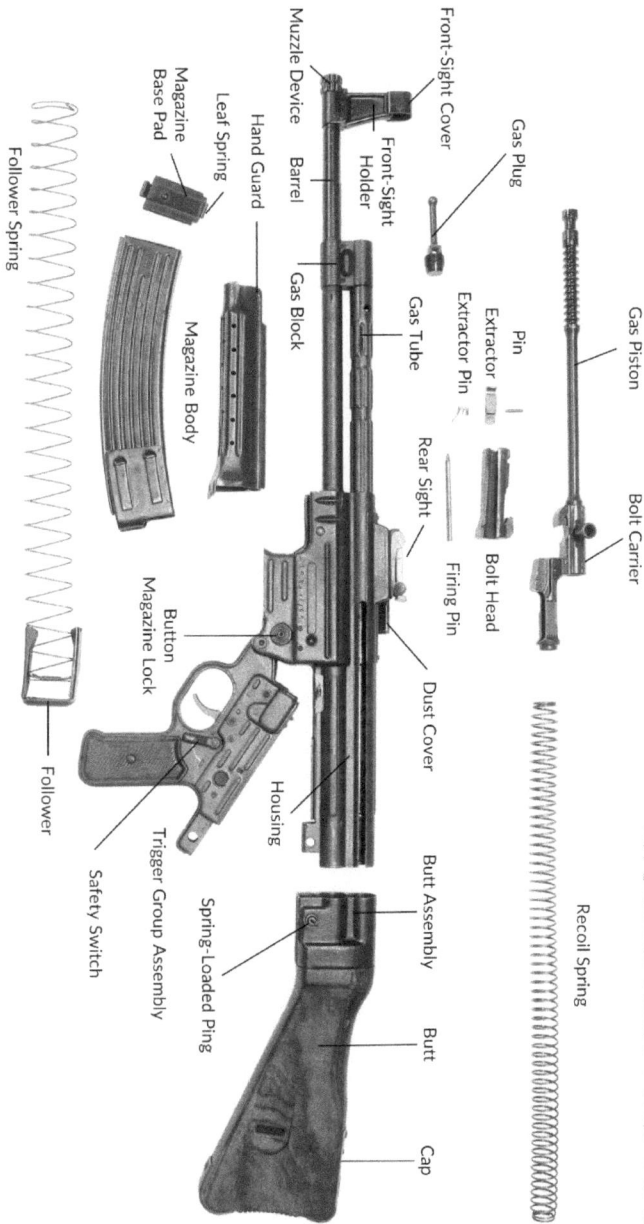

Front-Sight Cover
Muzzle Device
Front-Sight Holder
Barrel
Hand Guard
Leaf Spring
Magazine Base Pad
Follower Spring
Gas Plug
Gas Block
Gas Tube
Magazine Body
Follower
Pin
Extractor
Extractor Pin
Gas Piston
Rear Sight
Bolt Head
Firing Pin
Bolt Carrier
Button Magazine Lock
Dust Cover
Housing
Recoil Spring
Safety Switch
Trigger Group Assembly
Spring-Loaded Ping
Butt Assembly
Butt
Cap

EN-133

Bibliographie / Bibliography

Quellen Archive / Primary Sources Archives

BArch, RH 1/1217: *H.Dv. 130/20: Ausbildungsvorschrift für die Infanterie. Heft 20. Die Führung des Grenadier-Regiments.* Vom 21. 3. 1945. Verlage „Offene Worte": Berlin, Germany, 1945.

BArch, RH 1/1463: *H.Dv. 240/2 Entwurf: Kriegsnahe Schießausbildung des Einzelschützen mit Gewehr, Sturmgewehr 44, leichtem Maschinengewehr und Pistole.* 2. November 1944.

BArch, RH 1/2063: *H.Dv. 271: Bildliche Darstellung der Kartenzeichen in den amtlichen deutschen Karten (KARTENFIBEL).* Januar 1941.

BArch, RH 2/3684: *Merkblatt 25/3: Anleitung für den Nahkampf und die Handgranatenausbildung, 15.4.1944.*

BArch, RH 11-I/14: *Entwurf zur Heeresdienstvorschrift [sic!]*[1] *240/2.* Dezember 1944.

BArch, RH 11-I/52 b: General der Infanterie im OKH: *Waffen und Gerät. Die neue Maschinenpistole und ihre Verwendung.*

BArch, RH 11-I/54: General der Infanterie im OKH: *Waffen und Gerät. Entwicklung, Erprobung sowie Erfahrungsberichte: Bd. 3: Sturmgewehr.* Juni 1944 – Februar 1945.

---

[1] This actually should be "Heeresdruckvorschrift", since "H.Dv." in the Wehrmacht meant "Heeresdruckvorschrift" only for the post-war Bundeswehr it would "Heeresdienstvorschrift".

BArch, RH 11-I/83: *Merkblatt 25a/16: Vorläufiges Merkblatt „Der M.P.-Zug der Grenadier-Kompanie", 1.2.1944.*

BArch, RH 11-I/84: *Merkblatt 25a/15: Der Sturmzug der Grenadier-Kompanie, 15.11.1944.*

BArch, RH 12-2/139: Inspektion der Infanterie (In 2): *Erprobung der Waffen, Verwendung von Zubehör.* 1943-1945.

BArch, RH 17/809: Schule VII für Fahnenjunker der Infanterie: *Taktische Grundbegriffe und Ausdrücke.* August 1944.

TsAMO, F 500, Op. 12480, D 137: *Nachrichtenblatt der Panzertruppen. Nr. 1,* 15. Juli 1943. (https://wwii.germandocsinrussia.org/)

Generelle Quellen / General Primary Sources

ADP 3-90: *Offense and Defense.* Headquarters, Department of the Army: Washington DC, 31st July 2019.

Allgemeine Heeresmitteilungen. 9. Jahrgang, 17. Ausgabe. 21. Juli 1942. Berlin, Germany, 1942.

Allgemeine Heeresmitteilungen. 9. Jahrgang, 25. Ausgabe. 7. November 1942. Berlin, Germany, 1942.

Allgemeine Heeresmitteilungen. 11. Jahrgang, 27. Ausgabe. 7. Dezember 1944. Berlin, Germany, 1944.

Altrichter, Friedrich: *Der Reserveoffizer. Ein Handbuch für den Offizier und Offizieranwärter des Beurlaubtenstandes aller Waffen.* Vierzehnte, durchgesehene Auflage. Verlag von E. S. Mittler & Sohn: Berlin, Germany, 1941.

Bieringer, Ludwig: *Nachschubfibel. Zweite verbesserte Auflage.* Verlag „Offene Worte", Berlin, Germany, 1938.

Bundesministerium der Verteidigung: *Katalog der Druckvorschriften der ehemaligen deutschen Wehrmacht – Teil 1 Heer.* Bonn, Germany, 1960.

D 1854/4: Sturmgewehr 44 Gebrauchsanleitung. Vom 3. 6. 44. Veränderter Nachdruck Dez. 1944. (Reprint)

FM 5-15: Engineer Field Manual – Field Fortifications. War Department: Washington, 1940.

FM 5-15: Field Fortifications. Corps of Engineers. War Department: Washington, February 1944.

FM 17-10: Armored Force Field Manual: Tactics and Technique. War Department: Washington, USA, March, 1942.

FM 17-32: Armored Force Field Manual: The Tank Company, Light and Medium. War Department: Washington, USA, August, 1942.

FM 22-5: Basic Field Manual & Infantry Drill Regulations. War Department: Washington, 1941. Annotated Edition by Timothy O'Neill. Available at: http://www.29thdivision.com/Library/FM22-5-InfantryDrillRegulations.pdf

Gesterding, Schwatlo; Feyerabend, Hans-Joachim: *Unteroffizierthemen. Ein Handbuch für den Unteroffizierunterricht.Fünfte, neubearbeite Auflage.* E. S. Mittler & Sohn: Berlin, Germany, 1938.

Gesterding, Schwatlo; Feyerabend, Hans-Joachim: *Unteroffizierthemen. Ein Handbuch für den Unteroffizierunterricht. Siebente, neubearbeite Auflage.* E. S. Mittler & Sohn: Berlin, Germany, 1943.

H.Dv. 30: Schrift- und Geschäftsverkehr der Wehrmacht. Vom 1. November 1939. Verlag von E. S. Mittler & Sohn: Berlin, Germany, 1939.

H.Dv. 130/2a: Ausbildungsvorschrift für die Infanterie. Heft 2a. Die Schützenkompanie. Entwurf. Vom 16. März 1941. Verlag „Offene Worte": Berlin, Germany, 1941.

H.Dv. 130/2b: Ausbildungsvorschrift für die Infanterie. Heft 2. Die Schützenkompanie. Teil b. Der Schützenzug und die Schützenkompanie. Vom 24. März 1936. Verlag „Offene Worte": Berlin, Germany, 1936.

H.Dv. 272: Muster für taktische Zeichen des Heeres. Vom 23. Mai 1943. Unveränderter Nachdruck 1944. OKH: 1943.

H.Dv. 300/1: Truppenführung (T.F.) I. Teil. E. S. Mittler & Sohn: Berlin, Germany, 1936 (17. Oktober 1933).

H.Dv. 316: Pionierdienst aller Waffen. Nachdruck 1936. Vom 11. 2. 1935. Verlag E.S. Mittler & Sohn: Berlin, 1936 (11. 2. 1935).

H.Dv. 470/7: Ausbildungsvorschrift für die Panzertruppe. Heft 7: Die mittlere Panzerkompanie. Reichsdruckerei, Berlin, Germany, 1. Mai 1941.

Haas, Walter: *Soldatenlexikon. Ein Merkbuch für den Infanteriedienst.* Franckh'sche Verlagshandlung: Stuttgart, Germany, o.J.

Kriegsstärkenachweisung (Heer): Nr. 130 n: Stabskompanie eines Infanterieregiments(n.A.) vom 1. Mai 1944.

Kriegsstärkenachweisung (Heer): 131 n Schützenkompanie (n.A.) vom 1. Oktober 1943.

Kriegsstärkenachweisung (Heer): Nr. 131 n: Schützenkompanie (n.A.) vom 1. Mai 1944.

Kriegsstärkenachweisung (Heer): Nr. 1114 a (fG): Panzergrenadierkompanie (fG) vom 1. November 1944.

Kühlwein, Fritz: *Die Gruppe im Gefecht. (Die neue Gruppe).* E. S. Mittler & Sohn: Berlin, Germany, 1940.

Merkblatt 41/23: Merkblatt über Handhabung, Mitführung und Verwendung der Gewehrgranate. Vom 20. 10. 42, OKH: Berlin, 1942. (Reprint)

Merkblatt 57/5: Bildheft Neuzeitlicher Stellungsbau. OKH, General der Pioniere: 1. Juni 1944.

Merkblatt für Gliederung und Kampfweise der Schützenkompanie zu 12 Gruppen. Zum Einlegen in die H.Dv. 130/2b. Verlage „Offene Worte", Berlin, Germany, 1939.

Military Intelligence Service: *The German Squad in Combat. Special Series, No. 9. MIS 461.* War Department, January 25, 1943.

Reibert, Wilhelm: *Der Dienstunterricht im Heere. Ausgabe für den Schützen der Schützenkompanie. Zwölfte, völlig neubearbeitete Auflage.* Jahrgang 1940. Verlag von E. S. Mittler & Sohn: Berlin, Germany, 1940. Reprint by The Naval & Military Press Ltd.

Schramm, Percy E. (Hrsg.): *Kriegstagebuch des OKW. Eine Dokumentation: 1942. Band 4. Teilband 2.* Bechtermünz: Augsburg, Germany, 2005.

Siwinna, Carl (Hrsg.); von Heygendorff, ohne Vorname: *Das Kommandobuch. Band 1: Die Schützenkompanie.* 16. Auflage. Neubearbeitet. Mars-Verlag: Berlin, Germany, 1936.

TM 30-506: German Military Dictionary, War Department: Washington, USA, May, 1944.

Zimmermann, Bodo: *Infanteriedienst. Für den Einzelschützen der aktiven Truppe, der Reserve und der Landwehr.* 18. Auflage (Kriegsausgabe) der „Soldatenfibel". Verlag „Offene Worte": Berlin, 1940.

Literatur / Secondary Sources

Buchner, Alex: *Das Handbuch der deutschen Infanterie 1939-1945*. Podzun-Pallas: Friedberg, 1987.

Condell, Bruce (ed.); Zabecki, David T. (ed.): *On the German Art of War. Truppenführung*. Stackpole Books: Mechanicsburg, PA, USA, 2009 (2001).

DiNardo, R.L.: *Mechanized Juggernaut or Military Anachronism. Horses and the German Army of WWII*. Stackpole Books: Mechanicsburg, USA, 2009.

Donat, Gerhard: *Beispiele für den Munitionsverbrauch der deutschen Wehrmacht im zweiten Weltkrieg*. In: Allgemeine schweizerische Militärzeitschrift, Band 129, Jahr 1963, Heft 2, S. 76. (Online Version). Letzter Zugriff: 4. November 2020: http://doi.org/10.5169/seals-40628

Duffy, Christopher: *The Army of Frederick the Great. Second Edition*. Helion & Company: Warwick, UK, 2020 (1996).

Elser, Gerhard: *Von der „Einheitsgruppe" zum „Sturmzug". Zur Entwicklung der deutschen Infanterie 1922 – 1945*, in: Der Infanterist, Heft 1, 2003, S. 84-91.

Filips, Katherina: *Typical Russian Words in German War-Memoir Literature*. In: The Slavic and East European Journal, vol. 8, no. 4, 1964, p. 407–414. JSTOR, www.jstor.org/stable/304421, last access: 31st October 2020.

Fleischer, Wolfgang: *Deutsche Infanteriekarren, Heeresfeldwagen und Heeresschlitten 1900-1945*. Waffen-Arsenal Band 153. Podzun-Pallas-Verlag: Wölfersheim, Germany, 1995.

Fleischer, Wolfgang: *Deutsche Nahkampfmittel. Munition, Granaten und Kampfmittel bis 1945.* Motorbuch Verlag: Stuttgart, Germany, 2018.

Fleischer, Wolfgang: *Militärtechnik des Zweiten Weltkriegs. Entwicklung, Einsatz, Konsequenzen.* Motorbuch Verlag: Stuttgart, Germany, 2020.

Grassi, Ernesto (Ed.): von Clausewitz, Carl: *Vom Kriege.* Rowohlt: Hamburg, Germany, 2005.

Groß, Gerhard P.: *Mythos und Wirklichkeit: Die Geschichte des operativen Denkens im deutschen Heer von Moltke d. Ä. bis Heusinger.* Zeitalter der Weltkriege, Band 9. Ferdinand Schönigh: Paderborn, Germany, 2012.

Hahn, Fritz: *Waffen und Geheimwaffen des deutschen Heeres 1933-1945. Band 1.* Dörfler Verlag: Eggolsheim, o.J.

Hahn, Fritz: *Waffen und Geheimwaffen des deutschen Heeres 1933-1945. Band 2.* Dörfler Verlag: Eggolsheim, o.J.

Handrich, Dieter: *Sturmgewehr 44. Vorgänger, Entwicklung und Fertigung der revolutionärsten Infanteriewaffen.* 2. überarbeitete und erweiterte Auflage. dwj Verlags-GmbH: Blaufelden, Germany, 2016.[2]

Keilig, Wolf: *Das Deutsche Heer 1939–1945. Gliederung – Einsatz – Stellenbesetzung.* Verlag Hans-Henning Podzun: Bad Nauheim, 1956ff.

---

[2] It is important to note that Handrich's book is probably the best and most detailed book on the Sturmgewehr 44. Yet, he expresses various interpretations on history that are backed up by little to no evidence, e.g., the preemptive war thesis. Additionally, he claims that the Commissar Order was rarely executed. Furthermore, he seems to uncritically cite Speer's memoirs, which are known to be a rather problematic source. His book is available in English, but we only know and used the German version.

141

Lidschun, Reiner; Wollert, Günter: *Infanteriewaffen. Illustrierte Enzyklopädie der Infanteriewaffen aus aller Welt bis 1945.* Parragon: Bath, UK, o.J.

Mueller-Hillebrand, Burkhart: *Das Deutsche Heer 1933-1945. Band I. Das Heer bis zum Kriegsbeginn.* E. S. Mittler & Sohn: Frankfurt am Main, Germany, 1954.

Mueller-Hillebrand, Burkhart: *Das Deutsche Heer 1933-1945. Band II. Die Blitzfeldzüge 1939-1941. Das Heer im Kriege bis zum Beginn des Feldzuges gegen die Sowjetunion im Juni 1941.* E. S. Mittler & Sohn: Frankfurt am Main, Germany, 1956.

Mueller-Hillebrand, Burkhart: *Das Deutsche Heer 1933-1945. Band III. Der Zweifrontenkrieg. Das Heer vom Beginn des Feldzuges gegen die Sowjetunion bis zum Kriegsende.* E. S. Mittler & Sohn: Frankfurt am Main, Germany, 1969.

Niehorster, Leo W.G.: *German World War II Organizational Series. Volume 1/I: Mechanized Army Divisions and Waffen-SS Units (1.09.1939).* The Military Press: Buckinghamshire, UK, 2007 (2004).

Niehorster, Leo W.G.: *German World War II Organizational Series. Volume 1/II-1: 1st and 2nd Welle Army Infantry Divisions (1 September 1939).* The Military Press: Buckinghamshire, UK, 2007 (2006).

Raths, Ralf: Vom Massensturm zur Stoßtrupptaktik. Die deutsche Landkriegstaktik im Spiegel von Dienstvorschriften und Publizistik 1906 bis 1918. Zentrum für Militärgeschichte und Sozialwissenschaften der Bundeswehr: Potsdam, Germany, 2019.

Schlicht, Adolf; Angolia, John R.: *Die deutsche Wehrmacht. Uniformierung und Ausrüstung 1933-1945. Band 1: Das Heer.* Motorbuch Verlag: Stuttgart, Germany, 2000.

Vego, Milan: *Clausewitz's Schwerpunkt. Mistranslated from German – Misunderstood in English*. In: Military Review, January-February 2007, p. 101-109.

Webseiten / Web Sites

Corff, Oliver (Ed.): von Clausewitz, Carl: *Vom Kriege*. Erstausgabe von 1832-1834. A4 Version basierend auf Textdaten bibliotheca Augustana. Clausewitz-Gesellschaft e.V.: Berlin, Germany, 2010. https://www.clausewitz-gesellschaft.de/wp-content/uploads/2014/12/VomKriege-a4.pdf, last access: 07th November 2020.

Kennedy, Gary John: *Organization of the German Infantry Battalion 1938 to 1945*. Battalion Organization during the Second World War. http://www.bayonetstrength.uk/GermanArmy/GerInfBn/OrgGerInfBn-headerpg.htm, last access: 31st October 2020.

Steps and Marching. Army Study Guide. https://www.armystudyguide.com/content/Prep_For_Basic_Training/prep_for_basic_drill_and_ceremony/steps-and-marching.shtml, last access: 5th November 2020.

Widmann-Awender, Christoph: *Kriegsetat: Schützenkompanie (n.A.) KStN 131n (1.10.1943)*. https://www.wwiidaybyday.com/kstn/kstn131n1okt43.htm, last access: 31st October 2020.